Salvation Is from the Jews
(John 4:22)

Saving Grace in Judaism and
Messianic Hope in Christianity

Aaron Milavec

A Michael Glazier Book

LITURGICAL PRESS
Collegeville, Minnesota

www.litpress.org

A Michael Glazier Book published by Liturgical Press

Cover design by David Manahan, O.S.B. Photo courtesy of iStockphoto, © Jon Horton.

1	2	3	4	5	6	7	8	9

Library of Congress Cataloging-in-Publication Data

Milavec, Aaron, 1938–
    Salvation is from the Jews (John 4:22) : saving grace in Judaism and messianic hope in Christianity / Aaron Milavec.
        p. cm.
    "A Michael Glazier book."
    Includes bibliographical references.
    ISBN-13: 978-0-8146-5989-2
    1. Salvation—Christianity—History of doctrines.   2. Judaism—Influence.   3. Christianity—Origin.   4. Christianity and other religions—Judaism.   5. Judaism—Relations—Christianity.   I. Title.
    BT752.M49 2007
    261.2'6—dc22   2007003228

This book is dedicated to Mr. Martin. He was the first living Jew I encountered as a teenager growing up in Euclid, Ohio. He was the first Jew I came to love. His justice and his generosity first turned my heart toward the spiritual plight of Jews. In so doing, he forced me to boldly confront the poison of anti-Judaism that infected my Catholic upbringing. For this I am eternally grateful. I am proud to acknowledge that my salvation came from a Jew.

Contents

Abbreviations   vii

Preface   xi

Chapter One: Saving Mr. Martin from Hellfire   1

Chapter Two: Law and Grace among Jews and Christians   23

Chapter Three: The Story of Salvation:
                The Return to Humility and Truth   57

Chapter Four: Parting of the Ways:
                The Emergence of the Church out of Judaism   84

Chapter Five: Jesus as Messiah:
                Christian Humility in the Face of Jewish
                Objections   116

Chapter Six: The Unsavory Odor of Christian Evangelization   152

Chapter Seven: Reflections on Covenant and Mission   173

Bibliography   183

Index   196

Abbreviations

Note: French and German citations within this volume have been translated by the author. Abbreviations within citations have been standardized. Archaic English spellings have been revised in accordance with standard English usage. Official church documents are referenced by paragraph numbers rather than page numbers.

1. Ancient Jewish texts

ARN	*Abot de Rabbi Nathan* (4th c.). This rabbinic treatise is an expansion of *m. ᵓAbot*.
b.	*Bavli* or *Babylonian Talmud* (600). In this volume, English translations are taken from Jacob Neusner (1988) unless otherwise noted.
Gen. Rab.	*Genesis Rabbah*
Lev. Rab.	*Leviticus Rabbah*
m.	*Mishnah* literally means "teaching" and represents the first written collection of oral traditions attributed to the rabbinic sages of the first two centuries. The *Mishnah* was compiled (ca. 200) by R. Judah the Prince at Yavneh (in Palestine).
Num. Rab.	*Numbers Rabbah*
Sib. Or.	*Sibylline Oracles* (ca. 100 B.C.E.–150 C.E.)
T. 12 Patr.	*Testaments of the Twelve Patriarchs*
t.	*Tosephta* (ca. 250 C.E.). *Tosephta* literally means "additions" and consists of an expansion of and commentary on the *Mishnah*.
Tg. Lev.	*Targum Leviticus*

Works of Philo of Alexandria (20 B.C.E.–50 C.E.)

Decal.	*De Decalogo*

Gaius	*De Legatione ad Gaium*
Vit. Mos.	*De Vita Mosis*
Spec. Leg.	*Special Laws (De Specialibus Legibus)*

Works of Flavius Josephus (35–100 C.E.)

Ant.	*Antiquities of the Jews*
Bell.	*Jewish War*
C. Ap.	*Contra Apionem*

2. Early Christian Writings

Adv. haer.	Irenaeus, *Adversus Omnes Haereses*
Barn.	*Letter of Barnabas*
Eccl. Hs.	Eusebius, *Ecclesiastical History*
Gos. Thom.	*Gospel of Thomas* (1st c.). This listing of 108 sayings of Jesus was found in the Nag Hammadi Library. The term "gospel" is never used in the original text and was assigned on the basis of the first line: "These are the secret sayings which the living Jesus spoke and which Didymus Judas Thomas wrote down."
Herm.	*Hermas* or *Shepherd of Hermas*

Works of Justin the Martyr (100–165 C.E.)

1. Apol.	*First Apology*
2. Apol.	*Second Apology*
Dial.	*Dialogue with Trypho*

Strom.	Clement of Alexandria, *Stromateis*

3. Church Documents

Guidelines	Commission for Religious Relations with the Jews, *Guidelines and Suggestions for Implementing the Conciliar Declaration Nostra Aetate (n. 4)*, December 1, 1974.
Jewish People	Pontifical Biblical Commission, *The Jewish People and Their Sacred Scriptures in the Christian Bible*, May 24, 2001.
Notes	Commission of the Holy See for Religious Relations with the Jews, *Notes on the Correct Way to Present the Jews and Judaism in Preaching and Catechesis in the Roman Catholic Church*. June 24, 1985.

Reflections	Consultation of the National Council of Synagogues and the Bishops' Committee for Ecumenical and Interreligious Affairs, USCCB, *Reflections on Covenant and Mission*, August 12, 2002.
Rites	*The Rites of the Catholic Church as Revised by Decree of the Second Vatican Ecumenical Council.* New York: Pueblo Publishing Co., 1976.
We Remember	Commission for Religious Relations with the Jews, *We Remember: A Reflection on the Shoah*, January 25, 1998.

4. General Abbreviations

AB	Anchor Bible
ABD	*The Anchor Bible Dictionary*, ed. David Noel Freedman. 6 vols. New York: Doubleday, 1992.
ABRL	Anchor Bible Reference Library
BRev	*Bible Review*
BTB	*Biblical Theology Bulletin*
CahRB	Cahiers de la Revue Biblique
CBQ	*Catholic Biblical Quarterly*
HUCA	*Hebrew Union College Annual*
JBL	*Journal of Biblical Literature*
JES	*Journal of Ecumenical Studies*
JSJ	*Journal for the Study of Judaism in the Persian, Hellenistic, and Roman Periods*
JTS	*Journal of Theological Studies*
LXX	*Septuagint*
NT	New Testament (the Christian Scriptures)
OT	Old Testament (Hebrew Scriptures or *Tanakh*)
par.	parallel(s)
S.T.	Thomas Aquinas, *Summa Theologica*. Translated by the Dominican Fathers. 2 vols. London: Burns & Oates, 1947.
TDNT	Gerhard Kittel and Gerhard Friedrich, eds., *Theological Dictionary of the New Testament*. Trans. Geoffrey W. Bromiley. 10 vols. Grand Rapids: Eerdmans, 1964–76.
TS	*Theological Studies*

Preface

The truth that I have come to realize is that my early Catholic formation tragically prepared me to pity, to blame, and to despise Jews. My conversion began in 1955 at the hands of a single Jew. Thanks to this graced encounter, I have undertaken a journey that brought me face to face with the psychological pain and the theological vendetta that the Catholic Church has used to denigrate Jews and Judaism for nearly eighteen hundred years. This book is a testament to my journey.

In the aftermath of Vatican II, I was both puzzled and pleased that my church had "come clean" and had identified the tragic poison of anti-Judaism at the heart of my Catholic upbringing. I was only too ready to embrace the bishops' fresh perspective that Jesus of Nazareth was born a Jew, lived as a Jew, and died as a Jew. This perspective, in itself, opened up a brave, new world in which I, as a Catholic, was for the first time officially encouraged to esteem Jews and Judaism in the very act of venerating Jesus of Nazareth as my Lord and my Redeemer. By honoring one Jew, I was accordingly urged to honor all Jews.

During the 80s, I became comfortable with the idea that the mainline churches, for the most part, had been healed of the poison of anti-Judaism. The explorations narrated in this book, however, prove just the contrary. In my own case, my initial contact with a single Jew in 1955 set me on a path to experience Judaism, not only as it is described in books, but as it is felt by living Jews. These contacts over a period of fifty years enabled me to detect the poison at the heart of my Catholic upbringing so deeply, so tenderly, and so honestly as to address even the pain and the distrust that Jews experience when they remember the smoke of the burning children in the camps. For Christian believers (including pastors, teachers, and theologians), my pioneering explorations will reveal how deeply anti-Judaism has gone underground—disfiguring not only the role of Israel in God's plan of salvation but also horribly twisting the faith, the forgiveness, and the salvation that Christians celebrate as coming to them through Jesus Christ. These revelations will be distressing and painful for some. Others will discover that this is the necessary first step for our mutual healing. And still others will come forward praising God "for salvation is from the Jews" (John 4:22).

How We Got to Where We Are Now

Three boundaries are very clear. The first is that Jesus was personally committed to Judaism; he trained his disciples to interpret the law of Moses (Torah) in anticipation of the kingdom of God that was ready to break into history. At no point did Jesus or his first disciples renounce their Judaism in favor of establishing a new religion. If the Jesus movement had consistently retained this legacy of Jesus it would undoubtedly have remained a subgroup within Judaism to this very day. But it did not.

This brings us to the second clear boundary. By the mid-second century, Gentile-dominated segments of the Jesus movement retained their self-definition as "the true Israel" while, at the same time, rejecting all forms of Judaism that were not absorbed into their own movement. History after this, Jacob Neusner reminds us, was marked by the intimacy and bitterness characteristic of a "family quarrel":

> We have ample evidence for characterizing as a family quarrel the relationship between the two great religious traditions of the West. Only brothers can hate so deeply, yet accept and tolerate so impassively, as have Judaic and Christian brethren both hated, and yet taken for granted the presence of, one another.[1]

The third boundary is also very clear. In the early 1960s the antagonisms fueled by this family quarrel were, for the first time, being rigorously reexamined because the smoke of burning children at Auschwitz was in our nostrils. Since then a small measure of mutual understanding and healing has been achieved. Official and unofficial dialogues between Jews and Christians have emerged nearly everywhere. After nineteen hundred years, Christians and Jews are again listening attentively to each other with respect. The painful topics that had been brushed under the rug for centuries can now be publicly aired.

1. Jacob Neusner, "The Jewish-Christian Argument in the First Century: Different People Talking About Different Things to Different People," *Religious Studies and Theology* 6 (1986) 9.

Yet much remains to be done, and the time is short. For, as the geo-political realism of John Paul II reminds us, "in order to be a blessing for the world, Jews and Christians need first to be a blessing for each other." May this volume move us toward this end!

Progress and Decline

Catholics officially abandoned the inflammatory rhetoric defining Jews as "Christ-killers" during the last session of the Vatican Council in 1965. Expanding on that prophetic impulse, the Vatican's 1985 *Notes on the Correct Way to Present Judaism* told Catholics point-blank that "Jesus was and always remained a Jew" (*Notes* 12), thereby putting an end to the imagined claim that Jesus himself rejected Judaism as a defective religion. In this same document Catholics were also made familiar with the ways in which Jesus shared common ground with the Pharisees of his day and were warned that "an exclusively negative picture of the Pharisees is likely to be inaccurate and unjust" (*Notes* 19). In 1998 Catholics were instructed: "No one can remain indifferent [to the *Shoah* / Holocaust], least of all the Church, by reason of her very close bonds of spiritual kinship with the Jewish people" (*We Remember* 1). Finally, in 2002, by virtue of "Reflections on Covenant and Mission," Catholics were asked to consider whether Judaism—"the faithful response of the Jewish people to God's irrevocable covenant"—ought to be regarded as "salvific" for Jews quite apart from any relationship with Jesus.

Each of these steps forward was the triumph of grace. Each such step forward, however, was hindered by the troubling tension Christians felt between their own fierce embrace of the crucified Christ and the over-whelming Jewish rejection of Jesus as the Messiah. Catholic preachers, consequently, routinely exalted the wisdom and grace that have come to them through Jesus and Mary; seldom, if ever, did these same preachers draw any significant attention to the wisdom and grace that came to them through the children of Abraham and Sarah. Even the Vatican's 1985 *Notes on the Correct Way to Present Judaism* said many wonderful things about Jews and Judaism but then turned around and starkly de-clared that the "Church and Judaism cannot then be seen as two parallel ways of salvation" (*Notes* 7). Even Jews, therefore, who "remain very dear to God" (*Nostra Aetate* 4), appear to be, like the followers of other world religions, "objectively speaking . . . in a gravely deficient situa-tion in comparison with those who, in the Church, have the fullness of the means of salvation" (*Dominus Jesus* 22). Those who reject Christ, meanwhile, are frequently harassed by evangelical Christians bent upon converting them before the end times begin.

How This Book Began Fifty Years Ago

The reflections of this book began as I myself was torn by the love-hate relationship between Catholics and Jews in an ethnic suburb of Cleveland. My early religious training within Catholic schools and my early cultural training at the outbreak of World War II made it quite natural for me to pity, blame, and despise Jews. Had I been bombarded by Hitler's speeches blaming and shaming Jews, I would undoubtedly have cheered him on. The greater number of my family and neighbors would have done the same. In point of fact, however, I never had contact with a single living Jew. "Let them stay where they belong" was my Dad's favorite line. But then, in an unexpected moment, a real flesh and blood Jew, Mr. Martin, made his way into my life.

I was an impressionable boy of sixteen in 1955. Mr. Martin agreed to employ me part-time as a stock boy in his dry goods store on East 185th Street. I desperately needed a larger income than my *Cleveland Plain Dealer* route had been able to afford me; hence I felt lucky to have landed this new job. But I was also anxious since Mr. Martin was a Jew, and I was a committed Christian. Would he want to exploit me? Would he treat me fairly? Would he want me to work on Sundays or other religious holidays?

Over the months I was testing Mr. Martin and, unbeknownst to me, he was testing me as well. One evening after closing I was sweeping the floor when I found a crumpled twenty-dollar bill under the counter. My starting salary was fifty cents per hour, and twenty dollars represented a lot of money for a teenager in 1955. Yet I did not think twice; my Christian instincts prompted me to turn the money over to Mr. Martin "lest someone come asking for it." It didn't even occur to me that the money would be mine if no one claimed it or that I might receive a handsome reward if someone did.

As for my tests, Mr. Martin passed with flying colors. He was genuinely sensitive to my religious convictions and school obligations when it came to scheduling my work hours. He treated me fairly, at times even generously, and this disarmed all my reservations in working for a Jew. In fact, I came to admire Mr. Martin, and this admiration presented me with a new problem, a theological problem. I knew that God had slated all Jews for eternal damnation because of what they did to Jesus. I also knew that Jews couldn't go to confession to obtain pardon for such a grievous sin. On the other hand, it seemed unfair, somehow, that God should hold Mr. Martin guilty for such a crime. If he did not harm me, even in little ways, how could he ever have consented to handing an innocent man over to Roman torturers two thousand years ago? Thus began my soul-searching journey to try and find a way to rescue just one Jew from the fires of hell.

As it happened, the righteousness of one Jew, Mr. Martin, ignited a fire in my brain that refused to go out. This book, accordingly, is dedicated to the man who set me on the road to discover a world of Judaism I would never have imagined existed. I was sixteen then. Now I am sixty-eight. It took me fifty years to gain the wisdom and experience to write this book that fulfills the tacit promise I made to Mr. Martin—namely, that I would free him from the fires of hell to which my childhood religion wanted to consign him.[2]

Details of What One Will Find in This Volume

This book is not for the fainthearted. Most readers will come to this topic with the perspective that the poison of anti-Judaism is found only in a few isolated doctrines and biblical passages (wrongly interpreted). The thesis of this volume is that the poison of anti-Judaism has not only misrepresented and disfigured the centrality of Israel in God's plan of salvation, but that it has horribly twisted the faith, the forgiveness, and the salvation brought to us through Jesus Christ as well. Accordingly, this book will systematically unravel how the major aspects of Christian theology and spirituality have secretly been shaped by eighteen hundred years of systematic propaganda that has carefully concealed the primacy of Israel and engineered an image of Jesus Christ that promotes an understanding of salvation designed to portray Judaism as totally bankrupt and entirely superceded by Christianity.

2. On further reflection, I don't precisely know why I was chosen to write such a book. Was it the isolation and pain that I felt for Mr. Martin? Maybe so. Maybe, still more, it was the havoc wreaked upon the Jewish community age after age in the name of Jesus Christ. Maybe it was the grim experience of hearing Holocaust survivors describe life in the camps or hearing the fear of college-age Jews reporting how "friends" dropped them at a moment's notice as soon as they discovered their Jewishness. Maybe it was American Jews confiding to me that they never felt "truly and entirely safe" before they visited the land of Israel. In any case, I honestly don't know any book quite like this and, believe me, I have been looking for a book like this all my life. My disappointment, in the end, may be the real reason why I was chosen while others pursued less arduous and less dangerous paths.

The reader of this volume should prepare to be distressed and afflicted by the depths of the distortion that has secretly shaped the Christian soul. This pain, however, is the first step toward coming clean and acknowledging how our ancestors have distorted both Jesus and his Judaism. The healing, then, will follow as day follows night. At each step of the way this book will endeavor to build bridges of mutual understanding that will aid both Christians and Jews to cross the chasm of distrust that has infected both church and synagogue over the centuries. In the end, both Judaism and Christianity will be understood and admired as sister religions with a common bond that intimately unites one to the other in God's drama of salvation.

In what follows, the following issues will be explored:

- How law and grace function within Judaism as well as within Christianity. How Jews familiarly experience God as Father independent of Jesus.
- How the history of salvation formulated within traditional Christianity overlooks and distorts the decisive Jewish contribution to God's plan of redemption. How Jews find divine forgiveness independent of Jesus. How the theology of the atoning death of Jesus puts Jews and Judaism at risk.
- When and why the church broke its ties with Judaism. How to challenge and replace superficial myths regarding the origins of the church. How the Christian Scriptures retain a firm attachment to the priority of Israel in God's plan.
- Why Jews object to the messianic character of Jesus and how Christians, in response, are groping toward a more honest assessment of Jesus as Messiah. How the Jewish "no" to Jesus was providentially necessary in order that Gentiles might find their way to the Father.
- How programs of Christian evangelization have terrified and continue to terrify Jews. Reflections on why such programs are not what Jesus and the early church intended. Examination of the mission God continues to assign to Israel.

"Israel" Not to be Confused with the "State of Israel"

In the Hebrew Scriptures and in the rabbinic texts, the term "Israel" designates those religious peoples who accept Abraham and Sarah as their ancestors (whether by biological generation or by religious conversion) and who live by the covenants that God made with his people. The term "Israel" as used in this volume is not to be confused with the "State of Israel."[3] As such, the theological and biblical foundations for Israel presented in this volume cannot be applied indiscriminatingly to the State of Israel.

Among religious Jews, one finds varied responses to the policies of the State of Israel. Needless to say, however, the secular government of Israel does not presuppose that it can or should define how Torah is to be interpreted or practiced by Jews throughout the world. While most Jews support the existence of the State of Israel as a "Jewish homeland," this does not mean that they imagine that they must take up residence therein as a religious obligation or that they must approve of every policy undertaken as a mark of their loyalty. It should be recognized that, even among Orthodox Jews, there are some who call into question the religious legitimacy of the State of Israel.[4] Overall, therefore, just as Catholics have no single-minded perception of the politics within the Vatican State, Jews likewise have no uniform judgment regarding the policies of the State of Israel.

Dialogue between Jews and Christians invariably reaches the point where events of the Middle East enter into the discussion. At this point, it is all the more urgent to recognize that the state of Israel is not to be equated with the "Israel" of the Jewish sources and that the deeds of a few cannot be allowed to characterize the whole. Here, more especially, great care must be taken to safeguard the freedom of expression and legitimate concerns of all parties. The Jewish New Testament scholar, Amy-Jill Levine, offers the following helpful cautions for these circumstances:

3. For details, see p. 59 n. 5. Many Christians have greeted the formation of the State of Israel in 1948 as the fulfillment of biblical prophesy relative to signs preceding Jesus' second coming. According to the Pew Research Center, 63 percent of white Evangelicals in the United States hold this view. Only 16 percent of religiously committed Catholics, meanwhile, hold this view. On the other hand, 30 percent of nominal Catholics agree with this view. The hierarchy of the Catholic Church has withheld assigning any religious significance to the State of Israel. See http://people-press.org/reports/display .php3?PageID=725 for further details.

4. According to *Neturei Karta* ("Jews United Against Zionism"), for example, the following principles apply: (a) The Jewish people are forbidden to oppress another people; (b) The State of "Israel" does not speak in the name of Jews, they have stolen the name "Israel" from the Jewish people; and (c) The government of the illegitimate State of "Israel" continually attempts to uproot the Torah and its statutes. For details, see Neturei Karta, "Orthodox Jews Demand End to Zionist Atrocities in the Middle East" (18 July 2006) http://www.nkusa.org/activities/Statements/2006July18.cfm.

Be particularly careful when engaging in conversation about the Middle East. Prepare for conversation by exploring the history of the conflict, and do so by looking at a variety of sources. Do not equate Israel's relationship to the Palestinians with the Nazi treatment of the Jews . . . ; do not state that all Palestinians left their homes in 1948 "voluntarily"; do not equate all Palestinians with the violent few, and do not dismiss the suffering they face.[5]

5. Amy-Jill Levine, *The Misunderstood Jew: The Church and the Scandal of the Jewish Jesus* (San Francisco: HarperSanFrancisco, 2006) 224–25. To better understand why Christians and Jews find it difficult to openly discuss the policies of the State of Israel in the United States, see Mark H. Ellis, "At the End of an Era: A Meditation on Ecumenism, Exile and Gratitude" *Cross Currents* 53/1 (Spring 2003), http://www.crosscurrents.org/Ellisspring2003.htm.

One

Saving Mr. Martin from Hellfire

> If Mr. Martin did not harm me, even in little ways,
> how could he ever have consented to handing an innocent man
> over to Roman torturers two thousand years ago?
>
> —Aaron Milavec at age 16

Beginning at Vatican II, the church overturned its theological vilification of Jews and put forward in its place a positive image of Judaism in which God's eternal covenant with Israel was upheld and honored. Despite this monumental progress, the Vatican continues to affirm that the church is the "universal sacrament of salvation" and to deny that Jews can be said "to come to the Father" or "to find salvation" solely within the covenant God made with Israel. This opening chapter will endeavor to examine some of the complexities surrounding this issue and to resolve them in a way that would allow Christians to affirm that the covenant God made with Israel will always remain the divinely authorized "sacrament of salvation" for Jews.

How I Tried to Save One Jew

Confronted with the conundrum I have described in the Preface, what was I to do about Mr. Martin's salvation? I never took my theological problem to any of my teachers or pastors. Given my upbringing, I felt secretly ashamed that I had developed an emotional attachment to a Jew. I suspected that I might be ridiculed for what I was attempting to do. Thus I was left to work out a private solution to my problem. For starters, I already knew that for someone to commit a mortal sin, three things were necessary:

1

> First, the thought, desire, word, action, or omission must be seri-
> ously wrong or considered seriously wrong; second, the sinner
> must be mindful of the serious wrong; third, the sinner must fully
> consent to it. (*Baltimore Catechism* #69)[1]

Thus, when it came to the death of Jesus I had to believe that God could only condemn those Jews who knowingly and willingly recognized the enormity of the sin and then went ahead and wanted to do it anyway. It was hardly imaginable to me that Mr. Martin was that kind of Jew. With a certain boyish simplicity, therefore, I felt that I had succeeded in finding a theological loophole that made Mr. Martin safe from the fires of hell.

A week later, another problem popped up. Mr. Martin may not have committed a mortal sin, but he still had that original sin that every human being inherited from our first parents, Adam and Eve. I had to admit that Mr. Martin was not a Catholic and he did not have access to the sacrament of baptism that would remove that original sin. I knew original sin could be a serious obstacle since, without baptism, even Catholic babies were prevented from ever going to heaven.[2] At best, they could expect to go to a place of natural happiness called limbo. Thus I felt sorry for Mr. Martin. While he was safe from eternal hellfire, I was forced to see him relegated, for all eternity, to some minor place in the world to come.

Never, never, never in my wildest imagination, could I, in 1955, have perceived that the "blood guilt" of the Jews was a poison distilled in the third century and systematically passed down as part of Catholic iden-tity to all future generations. After all, I was assured that Jesus had sent

---

1. A note on catechisms: Following the Council of Trent, the *Roman Catechism* was cre-ated in order to provide priests with a comprehensive outline of Catholic doctrine, which they were expected to communicate to their parishioners. The *Baltimore Catechism* pro-duced in the United States in 1858 was a brief version of the *Roman Catechism* that served for the religious formation of American Catholics for four generations prior to Vatican II. The post-Vatican II *Catechism of the Catholic Church* represents the updated *Roman Cate-chism*. It corrects the deficiencies of both earlier catechisms by incorporating the teachings and spirit of Vatican II.

2. The International Theological Commission is currently preparing a document in which they propose setting aside appeals to speculations regarding limbo in favor of re-lying on the mercy of God in those instances when infants die prior to baptism. See Cindy Wooden, "Catholic theology moves from limbo—Vatican commission sees unbaptized babies welcomed by God in heaven," Catholic News Service (06 October 2006), http:// www.catholic.org/international/international_story.php?id=21542.

the Holy Spirit to guide the teachers of my church and to preserve them from all error until the end of time. It seemed unthinkable to me that my parents, my teachers, my pastors—people I knew and loved—could be the mindless purveyors of such a demonic distortion. I mention these things not by way of casting blame on my Catholic forebears, but to indicate how blind even sympathetic and thoughtful persons can be when their hearts and minds are taken over by dark tendencies that claim to have God's endorsement.

Faced with this realization, I find little comfort in Dr. Eugene Fisher's reminder to Jews that the popes and councils of the church never actually defined blood guilt as part of the deposit of faith.[3] The shocking truth is that the popes and people alike so routinely accepted the notion of blood guilt that no concerted attack ever arose from any quarter within the church such that a council or a pope would have had occasion to resolve the disputed question. Nor was it only ill-informed and venial prelates who preached a gospel of contempt for Jews. Rather, as the Jewish scholar Emil Fackenheim reminded his audience during the Sixth National Workshop on Christian-Jewish relations, "it was also the saints and the bishops who preached contempt for Jews."

The Shocking Solution of Vatican II

Against the backdrop of my religious upbringing, one can imagine the existential shock I felt in 1965 when the bishops of Vatican II completely abandoned the eighteen-hundred-year-old tradition of blood guilt. Their exact words were:

> True, authorities of the Jews and those who followed their lead pressed for the death of Jesus; still, what happened in his Passion cannot be blamed upon all the Jews then living, without distinction, nor upon the Jews of today. (*Nostra Aetate* 4)

---

3. Dr. Eugene Fisher was appointed to his present post as Executive Secretary of the Secretariat for Catholic-Jewish Relations of the National Conference of Catholic Bishops (NCCB) in May of 1977. He succeeded Father Edward H. Flannery, who had held the post since its establishment in 1968 as part of the NCCB Secretariat for Ecumenical and Interreligious Affairs. In 1981 he was named Consulter to the Vatican Commission for Religious Relations With the Jews. He is one of nine consulters to the Vatican commission worldwide, and one of two Americans. He is also a member of the International Catholic-Jewish Liaison Committee, representing the Holy See. His attempt to calm the fear of Jews by explaining to them that no pope or council ever dogmatically defined "blood guilt" was aptly responded to by Fackenheim.

The genius of this solution is that it carefully acknowledges that there was some Jewish guilt without deciding just whose and how much. What continues to stun me, however, is that the bishops completely bypassed my boyhood insight that excused some Jews because they lacked the "full and deliberate consent" required for a mortal sin. Nor did the bishops choose to speak of forgiving the Jews on the basis of Jesus' own anguished prayer on the cross, "Father, forgive them, for they do not know what they are doing" (Luke 23:34). Nor did the bishops try to convince us that Jesus died for all our sins and, as a result, "all our sins" and not just "Jewish sins" had to be accounted for as bringing about the horrible death of Jesus.[4]

The Unfinished Agenda:
Whether Jews Find Salvation within Judaism

While the defective theology branding Jews as "Christ-killers" has been officially abandoned, it still remains deeply lodged within Catholicism's historical instincts. Thus, even while *Nostra Aetate* (§ 4) reaffirmed that "Jews remain very dear to God," this did not prevent official documents after the council from continuing to affirm (a) that "the definitive meaning of the election of Israel does not become clear except in light of the complete fulfillment (Rom 9–11)" (*Guidelines* II.1) and (b) that the "Church and Judaism cannot then be seen as two parallel ways of salvation" (*Notes* 7). Thus, while offensive language has been weakened, the church has not, within its theology and its spirituality, resolved the historical tension between its own firm affirmation of Jesus as the Christ and the Jewish rejection of this affirmation. Furthermore, while the church today boldly affirms the eternal covenant between God and God's people, Judaism is still not seen or spoken of as a legitimate path of salvation *for Jews*. This is the point where my troubling reflections must now begin.

At first glance one can easily understand how, during the long period when Jesus was understood as having rejected Judaism in favor

---

4. Eugene Fisher reinforced this point during his 1999 John Courtney Murray Lecture when he explained that "if a Christian could blame 'the Jews' for the death of Jesus, then one would not have to take responsibility for the real culprit, one's own sins." Fisher here sets up a false dichotomy, and nothing is served by drawing attention to the *Catechism of the Council of Trent* and some editions of the *Baltimore Catechism* proposing such dubious speculation. When the question is correctly examined, neither Jews nor Christians living today can be held responsible for the death of Jesus.

of founding the true religion of Christianity, it was natural to suppose that only the participants in that religion were destined for salvation. At the present time, however, all official documents (including the liturgy and children's textbooks) have been rewritten to correct this mistaken notion. In the 1985 Vatican *Notes on the Correct Way to Present Jews and Judaism*, accordingly, one finds the Jewishness of Jesus and his followers boldly affirmed:

> Jesus was and always remained a Jew; his ministry was deliberately limited "to the lost sheep of the house of Israel" (Matt 15:24). Jesus is fully a man of his time and his environment—the Jewish Palestinian one of the first century. . . . There is no doubt that he wished to submit himself to the law [Torah] (cf. Gal 4:4), that he was circumcised and presented in the temple like any Jew of his time (cf. Luke 2:21, 22-24), that he was trained in the law's [Torah's] observance. He extolled respect for it (cf. Matt 5:17-20) and invited obedience to it (cf. Matt 8:4). . . . It should be noted that Jesus often taught in the synagogues (cf. Matt 4:23; 9:35; Luke 4:15-18; John 18:20, etc.) and in the temple (cf. John 18:20, etc.) that he frequented, as did the disciples even after the resurrection (cf., e.g., Acts 2:46; 3:1; 21:26, etc.). (*Notes* 20)

While the Jesus movement did eventually break its ties with Judaism, this break could not and would not take place until Gentile converts swelled the ranks of Christian assemblies and the Jewish identity of the movement was considerably diluted. How and when this break took place will be explored in chapter 4. For our purposes here it suffices to note that the reluctance of the Vatican to acknowledge Judaism as a divinely endorsed path of salvation for Jews today stands in contradiction to the fact that Jesus and his disciples embraced their Judaism as the path of their salvation.

A second glance reveals another inconsistency. As long as Jews were routinely perceived as cursed by God due to their crime of killing Jesus,[5]

5. The notion of "divine retribution" became the standard story line Christians used in analyzing the fate of the Jewish people. Eusebius, the father of church history, established this pattern in the early fourth century when he took it upon himself to trace the progress of the Christians from the time of Jesus to that of Constantine. Again and again Eusebius drives home the point that every famine, every siege, every disorder plaguing the Jewish people was to be interpreted according to the following refrain: "Thus then the divine justice overtook the Jews in this way for their crimes against Christ" (*Eccl. Hs.* 2.5, 2.6, 2.7). In this way the Christian imagination became so distorted that it habitually discovered in every bad thing happening to Jews a confirmation of the divine displeasure that followed upon their implication in Jesus' crucifixion.

it was easy to imagine that Jews had to abandon the synagogue and enter the church to obtain God's grace and salvation. The moment, however, that Catholics acknowledge that "the Jews remain most dear to God" (*Nostra Aetate* 4), then it would seem to follow that God's election of Israel stands firm independent of Israel's stance regarding Jesus. For Jews, therefore, it would follow that their election, their divinely approved way of life, and their promise of salvation is found precisely within Judaism. How then can the Vatican refuse to allow that Jews find both grace and salvation *within their Judaism* both before and after the appearance of Jesus of Nazareth? Thus, here too, a certain embarrassed inconsistency remains.

Old habits die hard. In 1987, Joseph Cardinal Ratzinger (elected Pope Benedict XVI in 2005) was quoted in the popular press as urging Catholic-Jewish dialogue on the grounds of "our union with the faith of Abraham, but also the reality of Jesus Christ, in whom the faith of Abraham finds its fulfillment."[6] Ratzinger then immediately used Edith Stein, a Carmelite nun who had converted from Judaism, as an example of a Jew who, "on finding faith in Christ, entered into the full inheritance of Abraham." Both Jewish and Christian voices raised an immediate alarm. Ratzinger appeared to be promoting conversion as the fruit of Catholic-Jewish dialogue and falling into the traditional trap of exalting Christianity by denigrating Judaism. Whatever happened to the declaration of Vatican II to the effect that "the Jews remain most dear to God" (*Nostra Aetate* 4) due to their participation in the faith of Abraham (without any reference to Jesus Christ)? Faced with this seeming inconsistency and with the Jewish fear that Catholics might be using dialogue to promote conversion, Dr. Eugene Fisher, after consulting with Cardinal Ratzinger, drafted a statement meant to calm the waters. Fisher wrote that the Cardinal's intent was to say that dialogue "implies our union with the faith of Abraham, but also the reality of Jesus Christ, in whom, *for us*, the faith of Abraham finds its fulfillment."[7] The addition of two additional words reaffirmed Catholic participation in the faith of Abraham through Christ without implying that Jews must somehow find "the fulfillment" of their faith by converting to Jesus Christ.

---

6. Ratzinger's original statement was published in *Il Sabato* (October 24, 1987). It, and the clarification, were reported in the *New York Times* (November 19, 1987).

7. See n. 4 above.

Dominus Jesus

Ratzinger's release of *Dominus Jesus* on September 9, 2000, again appeared to undercut the declaration that "the Jews remain most dear to God." *Dominus Jesus* reaffirms the traditional understanding that Christ brings to Catholics the fullness of truth and salvation. The church[8] is "the universal sacrament of salvation" (*Notes* 20). Here again I am going to do what Eugene Fisher did and correct Ratzinger's statement by adding the two critical words "for us." Thus Christ does bring Catholics the fullness of truth and of salvation; hence, *for us,* the church is the universal sacrament of salvation.

Having said this, Ratzinger then immediately moves on to consider how it is that "God our Savior . . . desires everyone to be saved" (1 Tim 2:4). Prior to Vatican II, Catholics were led to believe that God "desires everyone to be saved" by joining the Catholic Church. Ratzinger, needless to say, solidly embraces Vatican II on this point. He goes further, then, and tries to examine how the grace of salvation is experienced outside the visible boundaries of the church:

> For those who are not formally and visibly members of the Church, salvation in Christ is accessible by virtue of a grace which, while having a mysterious relationship to the Church, does not make them formally part of the Church, but enlightens them in a way which is accommodated to their spiritual and material situation. This grace comes from Christ; it is the result of his sacrifice and is communicated by the Holy Spirit. (*Dominus Jesus* 21)

The foundational assumption built into *Dominus Jesus* is that the forgiveness of sins depends, at all times and in all places, on the merits of Jesus' crucifixion. This was the framework I was trapped in as a teenager when I was trying to save Mr. Martin from eternal hellfire. Once one enters completely into this horizon of understanding, it follows as night follows day that every person, no matter what his or her religious

---

8. In a lengthy interview with the German newspaper *Frankfurter Allgemeine Zeitung,* Cardinal Ratzinger explained that *Dominus Jesus* did not use the expression of Pius XII, according to which "The Roman Catholic Church is the only Church of Jesus Christ," even though this was the constant dogmatic teaching of the Catholic Church until Vatican II. Instead, he showed how the document preferred the Vatican II expression: "The Church of Christ subsists in the Catholic Church." In so doing Ratzinger wanted to reaffirm "that the being of the Church as such is a larger identity than the Roman Catholic Church." For details on the significance of this change see http://www.sedos.org/english/McBrien.htm.

identity, finds the grace of forgiveness because of Jesus (even if they have no knowledge of Jesus), "for there is no other name under heaven given among mortals by which we must be saved" (Acts 4:12). Beyond this, the grace of enlightenment is also seen as coming from the sacrifice of Christ, which releases the Holy Spirit into the world.

Does Cardinal Ratzinger, accordingly, want us to imagine that Jews receive the forgiveness of their sins and their spiritual enlightenment through the sacrifice of Christ on the cross? The instruction *Dominus Jesus* is unclear on this point, and the next three chapters will examine this proposition in detail.

When it comes to the world religions other than Judaism, however, *Dominus Jesus* is very clear. Given the assumption, as noted above, that Jesus' death on the cross is the universal means of salvation, Cardinal Ratzinger cannot imagine that any of the world religions offers any means for salvation "complementary to" or "equivalent to" the sacrifice of Christ:

> It would be contrary to the faith to consider the Church as *one way* of salvation alongside those constituted by the other religions, [whether] seen as complementary to the Church or substantially equivalent to her. (21)

Here again he should have said that "for us, the Church is the one way."[9] But even aside from this, Cardinal Ratzinger does stand on firm ground when he implies that none of the world religions (Judaism included) can be seen by Catholics as "complementary" or "equivalent" to the church. This helps explain how the Vatican's 1985 *Notes on the Correct Way to Present Judaism* can say such wonderful things about Jews and Judaism but then turn around and affirm that the "Church and Judaism cannot then be seen as two parallel ways of salvation" (*Notes* 7). Even Jews who "remain very dear to God," it would appear, might be classified with the followers of the other world religions as being

---

9. Ratzinger's assertion that the grace of Christ exists outside the visible boundaries of the church precludes the possibility that salvation is limited exclusively to those who are Christians. For those who find the grace of Christ and the enlightenment of the Holy Spirit outside the church, accordingly, the church is not the "one way." Therefore, while Catholics can regard the sacrifice of Christ as the universal means of salvation, the church must be seen as the "one way *for us*" because it enables us to find the salvation of Jesus Christ. Thus, as things stand, even Ratzinger's characterization of the church as "the one way of salvation" is open to misinterpretation.

"objectively speaking . . . in a gravely deficient situation[10] in comparison with those who, in the Church, have the fullness of the means of salvation" (*Dominus Jesus* 22).

The responses to *Dominus Jesus* varied. Many sought to correct the strident tones sounded throughout. Bishop Joseph A. Fiorenza, President of the National Council of Catholic Bishops, issued a public statement in which he thanked the Congregation for the Doctrine of the Faith for its "valuable service in summarizing and clarifying the teaching of the Church," but then he went on to add:

> The salvation offered through Jesus Christ and his Church is a gift to all humanity. We believe that Christ invites every human being to find in him "the way, the truth, and the life." Having been blessed with faith in Christ through no merit of our own, the members of the Church humbly seek to give as a gift the faith we received as a gift.
>
> Our belief in this regard in no way diminishes the sincere respect we have for the religions of the human family or our conviction that their followers can receive divine grace.
>
> This respect—and love—goes in a special way to the Jewish community to which Christians are closely related through Christ himself and the revealed word of God in the Old Testament.[11]

Cardinal Ratzinger must have read this and received many other personal challenges as well. It appears that he might have taken some of them to heart, since, in a front-page article in the Vatican's newspaper four months after the publication of *Dominus Jesus*, the cardinal was quoted as saying that dialogue with Jews belonged to a unique category because the Jewish faith "for us is not another religion, but the foundation of our faith."[12] It is for this reason that, when Ratzinger affirmed in *Dominus Jesus* that "with the coming of the Savior Jesus Christ, God has willed that the Church founded by him be the instrument for the

---

10. Among those Protestant churches that have been seeking to set aside strident language and to look for ways toward mutual affirmation, the language and tone of *Dominus Jesus* were a setback in ecumenical relations. Interested persons might examine the Church of Ireland's response at http://www.ireland.anglican.org/issues/domiesus. html and http://www.catholiccommunications.ie/pressrel/18-jan-2001.html.

11. Statement of Bishop Joseph A. Fiorenza, President of the NCCB, on the issuance of *Dominus Jesus: On the Unicity and Salvific Universality of Jesus Christ and the Church*, September 5, 2000, http://www.bc.edu/research/cjl/meta-elements/texts/cjrelations/news/News_Sep2000.htm#Fiorenza.

12. *Osservatore Romano* (December 29, 2000) 1.

salvation of all humanity," (22) he may not have wanted this to apply to Jews.[13]

Reexamining the Pauline Theology of Judaism

One might think that Paul echoes Ratzinger's position. After all, Paul did say, quite categorically, that "if you confess with your lips that Jesus is Lord and believe in your heart that God raised him from the dead, you will be saved" (Rom 10:9). Upon examination of his letter to the Romans,[14] however, one finds Paul nuancing his position relative to Judaism in such a way that he, like Cardinal Ratzinger, might not want us to believe that Jews need to be saved by believing in Jesus.

In Romans 4, to begin with, Paul presents a fascinating argument whereby Abraham is honored as exemplifying saving faith both as a Jew

13. In Ratzinger's book *God and the World*, released shortly after the appearance of *Dominus Jesus*, the cardinal again affirmed that "Christianity, as compared with the religion of Israel, is not a different religion; it is simply the Old Testament read anew with Christ." Ratzinger allows that the church has no agenda to convert the Jews, yet, in the end, the Jews will have to recognize that Christ is the Messiah of Israel—"It is in God's hands, of course, just in what way, when, and how the reuniting of Jews and Gentiles, the reunification of God's people, will be achieved" (citations taken from http://www.carl-olson.com/book%20reviews/god_world_ratzinger.html). By the end of this volume we will find that the Roman Catholic Church in 2006 is preparing itself to officially and irrevocably affirm that "the Church believes that Judaism, i.e., the faithful response of the Jewish people to God's irrevocable covenant, is salvific for them, because God is faithful to his promises" (Walter Cardinal Kasper, "Dominus Iesus." Address delivered at the 17th meeting of the International Catholic-Jewish Liaison Committee, New York, May 1, 2001).

14. Scholars are generally agreed that Paul drafted his letter to the Romans for the purpose of addressing the Christians at Rome in preparation for a visit there. In this letter he gives considerable space to setting out his position relative to the relationship of the people of Israel and the Gentile mission. In Paul's letter to the Galatians, on the other hand, he sets his hand to the refutation of troublemakers within a community he had founded. In this letter Paul writes that "all who rely upon works of the law [Torah] are under a curse" (Gal 3:10) and "Christ redeemed us from the curse of the law [Torah]" (Gal 3:13). Such strong words, however, are not addressed to Jews in general but to those Jewish Christians who would like to require circumcision and training in Torah for male Gentile adherents in the church. Paul never presupposes that Jewish Christians ought to abandon Torah in order to become Gentile believers. With even greater force, Paul denies that he or any other Jew ought to abandon the Torah (see especially Rom 3:31; 7:1, 7, 12, and Gal 3:21). For a brief summary of recent transitions in Pauline theology regarding this topic see John G. Gager, "Paul's Contradictions—Can They Be Resolved?" *BRev* 14 (2000) 32–39. For a superb pastoral and scholarly discussion prepared in an ecumenical setting see *Re-Reading Paul: A Fresh Look at his Attitude to Torah and to Judaism* (1995), prepared by the Council of Christians and Jews (Victoria) and made available at http://www.jcrelations.net/en/?id=789.

and as a Gentile. When Abraham trusted God (before his circumcision and without Torah), Paul says that "it was reckoned to him as righteousness" (Rom 4:3). This is the situation of the believing Gentile. Later, after Abraham was circumcised, Paul again asserts that Abraham maintained "the righteousness of faith" (4:13). This, then, is the case of the believing Jew. In sum, Paul argues that God's providential plan was to make Abraham "the ancestor of all who believe without being circumcised . . . and likewise the ancestor of the circumcised" (4:11-12). If this theology were to be renewed in the church today, it would mean effectively that Christians could and would claim Abraham as "their spiritual father" and Sarah as "their spiritual mother" along with the Jews.

To do so, however, would have consequences. Paul, it must be remembered, deliberately used the case of Abraham because he was well aware that Jews honored this patriarch as "their father." If Abraham was justified in God's eyes prior to his circumcision (and before the giving of Torah), Paul was effectively prompting his Jewish opponents to allow that Gentiles trusting in God (without circumcision and without Torah) might be justified in God's eyes as was Abraham. Today, however, this argument has to be turned around. The churches have no difficulty accepting the salvation of the righteous Gentiles; they are hesitating to extend that salvation to the Jews. When Paul is reread correctly, the case of Abraham stands forth as a witness of how justification comes *by faith* both before and after circumcision. In this case, however, the efficacious faith of Abraham was surely not the acceptance of the creed of the Catholic Church but, following upon the root meaning of "faith" *(pistis),* a profound trust in God (Rom 4:16-25). Jews today, therefore, who practice the Torah and trust in God to secure their future might be seen by us (as also by Paul) as joining themselves with the saving faith of Abraham.

If Judaism is not a path of salvation, then, to be consistent, Catholics must negate Romans 4 and insist that Abraham could not be justified by God either before or after his circumcision because he did not "confess with [his] lips that Jesus is Lord" (Rom 10:9). Paul, however, never imagines such a counterargument. Therefore one must seriously examine the possibility that Paul believed that "faith in God" without confessing Jesus Christ served to justify Abraham. To affirm Paul's argument today, consequently, would mean reaffirming the salvation of the children of Abraham (without any reference to Jesus). Romans 11 pushes this agenda even further. Paul openly speaks of Jewish transgressions and unfaithfulness, yet staunchly maintains that, despite failures, God has not "rejected his people" (11:1). This is the very character of God: faithfulness even when we are not faithful. As a consequence, numerous theologians have gone on record to affirm that the new covenant does not abrogate the old; quite the contrary: the new covenant serves to reconcile both Jew and Gentile within the same posture of finding grace and forgiveness through a total reliance on God.[15] In affirmation of Romans 11, therefore, the Catholic bishops were able to specify that "according to the Apostle [Paul], the Jews still remain most dear to God because of their fathers, for he does not repent of the gifts he makes nor of the calls he issues" (*Nostra Aetate* 4). If the covenant God made with "their fathers" stands today, even Christians must acknowledge that Jews can expect to find grace and salvation within this covenant (quite apart from Jesus and the church). If God continues to affirm his calling to Jews to be faithful to the covenant he made with their ancestors, then it follows that Jews, even today, are sanctified and saved precisely because of their Judaism and not because of some mysterious connection with Jesus and his church.

But then what are we to do with Paul's notion that God deliberately hardened the hearts of Israel so that "they stumbled" (Rom 11:11-12), thereby making it possible that "through their stumbling salvation has come to the Gentiles" (Rom 11:11; see also Acts 13:46-47)? Paul clarifies his point here by using the image of the cultivated olive tree being pruned of "natural branches" in order that "a wild olive shoot" (the Gentiles) might be grafted in their place. Through this metaphor Paul makes clear that salvation comes to Gentiles only if and when they are grafted onto the "rich root of the olive tree" (Rom 11:17). This olive tree that the Lord has planted and nurtured is clearly Israel. The natural branches that have been pruned are not, as some have wrongly expected,

---

15. Modern scholars are not in agreement about whether God has two covenants or only one covenant with two modalities. Scholars such as James Parkes, Rosemary R. Ruether, and J. Coert Rylaarsdam prefer to speak of two covenants that are different but complementary. The covenant with the Gentile church comes about by an act of grace through Jesus Christ whereby "outsiders" become "adoptive children" (Rom 8:14-17). The people of Israel, meanwhile, attain this status through the covenant and promises made to their ancestors. Scholars such as Paul Van Buren, Roy Eckardt, and Monika Hellwig prefer to speak of one covenant with two modalities. The children of Israel are the native sons and daughters with whom God established his covenant. Gentiles, in the course of time, became adoptive sons and daughters of Abraham through Jesus. The Christian church separates itself from the synagogue in order to reach out to the Gentiles and make the God of Israel known, loved, and served among them. In reality, however, church and synagogue share the same spiritual heritage and are bound together under the same covenant.

thrown into the fire. Rather, Paul boldly foresees the "mystery" (the hidden plan of God) whereby, in the end times, "these natural branches [will] be grafted back into their own olive tree" (Rom 11:24) so that "all Israel will be saved" (Rom 11:26).

"All Israel Will Be Saved"

Paul's assurance that "all Israel will be saved" (Rom 11:26) has attracted much attention in fundamentalist circles. According to their reading of the text, the conversion of the Jews is one of the divinely promised signs that will characterize the end times prior to the return of the Lord. Since the end times have begun, as signaled by the return of the Jews to their homeland, fundamentalist churches have sent missionaries and Bibles to the state of Israel, anticipating that, sometime soon now, they can expect (following Romans 11) a wholesale conversion of the people of Israel. When this happens, the churches expect to be swamped with Jewish converts who, on confessing their sins and acknowledging Jesus Christ as their personal savior, will anticipate being raptured into the clouds when the Lord comes.

The Vatican, for its part, has specifically kept itself free of any indication that the countdown for the last days has begun. Moreover, the Vatican has refrained from setting up programs in Israel directed toward the conversion of the Jews.[16] Nonetheless, *Dominus Jesus* does advocate interfaith dialogue as part of the church's "evangelizing mission":

> Because she believes in God's universal plan of salvation, the Church must be missionary. Inter-religious dialogue, therefore, as part of her evangelizing mission, is just one of the actions of the Church in her mission *ad gentes*. . . . Indeed, the Church, guided by charity and respect for freedom, must be primarily committed to proclaiming to all people the truth definitively revealed by the Lord, and to announcing the necessity of conversion to Jesus Christ and of adherence to the Church through Baptism and the other sacraments, in order to participate fully in communion with God, the Father, Son and Holy Spirit. (22)

16. See the excellent review article by Eugene J. Fisher, "Historical Developments in the Theology of Christian Mission," in *Christian Mission—Jewish Mission*, eds. Martin A. Cohen and Helga Croner (New York: Paulist Press, 1982).

The first sentence is dangerously close to affirming that God's universal plan of salvation is accomplished solely through the missionary activity of the church. The second is likewise problematic, since it suggests that interreligious dialogue is a disguised form of missionizing. If we leave these problematic areas aside for the moment, we may observe that the subsequent lines would appear to require that conversion and baptism must be seen as the divinely sanctioned means whereby even Jews "participate fully in communion with God." Upon closer examination, however, since the document specifically speaks here of the mission *ad gentes* ("to the Gentiles"), one can safely say that the Vatican document wanted expressly to exclude Jews from "her evangelizing mission." One might legitimately ask whether Jews are excluded from evangelization because it is understood that Jews find their graced intimacy with God within their Judaism.

Returning to Paul, we must more closely examine his assurance that, in the end times, "all Israel will be saved" (Rom 11:26). François Refoulé has prepared a book-length examination[17] of this text and has endeavored to recover Paul's original intention. For our purposes here it suffices to note how Refoulé dismisses three misrepresentations frequently read into this text:

(a) Paul never hints that he is offering a divine revelation to the effect that some future generation of Jews will accept the Gospel and become Christians. The very notion that Jews who are disobedient now will, in the end-times, "be grafted back *into their own* olive tree" (Rom 11:24) would even preclude the notion that Jews somehow will cease being Jews and be grafted onto a new root—that of the Gentile church.

(b) Paul never hints that the Gentile church displaces Israel as the sole recipient of divine election. Paul's metaphors demonstrate that salvation comes to the Gentiles because they are cut off from their wild stock (paganism) in order to be grafted onto the root of Israel. "Remember that it is not you that support the root, but the root that supports you" (Rom 11:18). According to Paul's theology, therefore, Israel is the "universal sacrament of salvation." The church, consequently, can only lay claim to participate in this function if and when it acknowledges having been grafted onto the root God planted, namely Israel.

(c) Finally, Paul never hints that only the remnant of faithful Jews serves God's purposes while the unfaithful majority hinders it;

17. Francois Refoulé, *"Et ainsi tout Israël sera sauvé"* (Paris: Cerf, 1984).

quite the opposite. Just as Paul in Romans 4 argued that Abraham is father of both the circumcised and the uncircumcised, in Romans 11 he argues that God deliberately needed the disobedience of the many in order to make possible the harvesting of the Gentiles.

Pinchas Lapide, an Orthodox rabbi and Israeli scholar, has developed a way of understanding the overwhelming Jewish "no" to Jesus in a way that strikes me as quite harmonious with what one finds in Paul. In his public dialogue with the Lutheran scholar Jürgen Moltmann, Lapide explained his position as follows:

> Three things were necessary for the founding of the Gentile church to which you belong. . . . First, a Jewish people in its biblical homeland in order to bring Jesus and the apostles into this world. Secondly, there was needed a small Jewish yes to Jesus—that is the primitive community, together with Paul and his helpers. Finally, however, there was needed a large Jewish no. For if there had been no Jewish no . . . the entire church would have remained intra Jewish—and to be honest, we did not need it. Since Sinai we have known the way to the Father. You on the other hand were very much in need of it. Therefore, your becoming Christian is for me a portion of God's plan of salvation, and I do not find it difficult to accept the church as an instrument of salvation. But please, you do not need to sprinkle sugar on top of honey, as you do when you wish to baptize us. The sugar on top of honey is simply superfluous. We are already "with the Father" and we know the way. . . .[18]

Thus Lapide joins his voice to that of Paul in assigning a providential and necessary role to the small "yes" and the large "no" of the Jewish people. If our churches would find their way to adopt such a formulation for themselves, it would mean that the massive Jewish rejection of Jesus as the Messiah would constitute the *felix culpa* (happy fault) that was historically necessary for there to be a Gentile mission. And just as the medieval church rejoiced at the sin of Adam as "the *felix culpa*, the necessary sin by which we gained so great a redeemer" (as the Exultet sung during the Easter Vigil would have it), so too Christians today might be taught to bless Jews *precisely because their ancestors rejected Jesus.*

As things now stand, fundamentalist Christians and the Vatican are naturally hesitant to allow the synagogue any role in God's plan of

18. Pinchas Lapide and Jürgen Moltmann, *Jewish Monotheism and Christian Trinitarian Doctrine* (Philadelphia: Fortress Press, 1981) 69–70.

redemption precisely because the synagogue finds faith and holiness apart from Jesus. If, however, the continued rejection of Jesus by the synagogue were honored as the *felix culpa*, it would be possible for Catholics and fundamentalists to join with Paul in welcoming the massive Jewish rejection of Jesus as the Messiah as the providential plan whereby we, as Gentiles, were included in the divine plan of salvation for Israel.

One final point: according to Acts, Paul identifies Israel as having the divinely mandated mission to be "light for the Gentiles" (Acts 13:47, citing Isa 49:6). If so, it follows that when this mission was advanced by Jesus (Matt 4:13), his disciples (Matt 28:19), and Paul, they acted by virtue of their Jewish identity. Consequently, the Gentile church must be understood as at best a derivative participation in Israel's mission to be "light to the Gentiles." Just as the historic church formerly exalted its "new" covenant while claiming that God had abrogated his "old" covenant with the Jews, so now the distinct possibility arises that Vatican efforts to exalt the universal mission of the church while overlooking God's expressed *mission* assigned to Israel is a remnant of its own former pattern of anti-Judaism. Time and space do not allow a detailed treatment of this issue at this point. It will be taken up in subsequent chapters.

"No One Comes to the Father Except Through Me"

In John's gospel Jesus expressly affirms: "No one comes to the Father except through me" (John 14:6; see 1 John 2:22-23; 4:3; 5:12; 2 John 9). These words appear to support the position that Jews can find no access to the Father without acknowledging Jesus. How could Jesus possibly say to the Samaritan woman, "Salvation is from the Jews" (John 4:22) and then turn around later in the gospel and tell his disciples, "No one comes to the Father except through me" (John 14:6). This needs to be examined.

John the Evangelist does not presume to have received word-for-word dictation of the words of Jesus. Rather, the inspired writer offers theological reflections on the life of Jesus that are presented to the faithful in the form of long discourses placed on the lips of Jesus.[19] Thus, since the

19. John 20:30-31 makes it clear that John the Evangelist was intent on producing a document based on faith and not on history. Nonetheless, John's gospel does contain historical memories that have been carefully expanded and reworked to fit the organizing schema of the author. To a lesser degree one could say the same of each of the Synoptics. Raymond Brown makes this point: "Although we think that the Fourth Gospel reflects historical memories of Jesus, the greater extent of the theological reshaping of those

Gospel of John was prepared for reading aloud in the church, it is the faithful baptized who hear and say "no one comes to the Father except through Jesus." This is objectively true relative to their experience. As for those in the synagogue across the street, on the other hand, they come and will continue to come to the Father through Moses and the prophets.[20] It would be blasphemy to imagine that the Scriptures lied when they affirmed that "the Lord used to speak to Moses face to face, as one speaks to a friend" (Exod 33:11; Num 2:8; Deut 34:10; Sir 45:5). It would be blasphemy to imagine that Abraham and Sarah did not, in faith, serve the living God. Similarly, it would be blasphemy to suggest that Jesus could not have said to the Samaritan woman, "We [Jews] worship what we know, for salvation is from the Jews" (John 4:22). Raymond Brown reflects on this as follows:

> [Rudolph] Bultmann would reduce this [saying] to a gloss [a later addition] since it does not fit with Johannine hostility to "the Jews." However, the Jews against whom Jesus elsewhere speaks harshly really refer to that section of the Jewish people that is hostile to Jesus, and especially to their rulers. Here, speaking to a foreigner, Jesus gives to the Jews a different significance, and the term refers to the whole Jewish people. This line is a clear indication that the Johannine attitude to the Jews cloaks neither an anti-Semitism of the modern variety nor a view that rejects the spiritual heritage of Judaism.[21]

---

memories makes Johannine material much harder to use in the quest of the historical Jesus than most Synoptic material" (Raymond E. Brown, *The Gospel According to John*. AB 29, 29A [Garden City, NY: Doubleday, 1970] 1:xlix).

20. This same observation could be made relative to *Dominus Jesus*. Quite clearly this encyclical is addressed to "bishops, theologians, and all the Catholic faithful" (sec. 3). Insiders speaking to insiders, consequently, can rightly affirm that the "full revelation of divine truth" comes through Jesus Christ and his church. In this context it is right for Roman Catholics to deny that the Catholic Church is "complementary" to other religions or "one way" among many. On the other hand, it is normal to imagine that Buddhists, when speaking to each other, affirm for themselves a non-relativistic adherence to the Buddha, the Dharma, and the Sangha. Likewise for Muslims, insiders addressing insiders can be expected to leave no doubt that Allah's revelation to Mohammed is complete and irreversible. Each of us, consequently, is absolutely rooted by virtue of our belonging. Relative to the outsider, however, *Dominus Jesus* affirms that "inter-religious dialogue, which is part of the church's evangelizing mission, requires an attitude of understanding and a relationship of mutual knowledge and reciprocal enrichment, in obedience to the truth and with respect for freedom" (2). In dialogue, consequently, my absolutely rooted faith reaches out to encounter your absolutely rooted faith.

21. Ibid., 1:172.

This does not mean that Moses is greater than Jesus or that Jesus is just another Moses. For the reader of John's gospel, Jesus is identified as the eschatological prophet anticipated by Moses:

> For John, Jesus *is* the supreme and final fulfillment of the eschatological prophet-like-Moses (Deut 18:15, 16-19; see John 4:25; 8:28; 12:49-50). For John the kingship of Jesus is real, but he is not a *Davidic* king. He is a Mosaic king. In early Judaism and in Samaritan theology people talked about "King Moses." For John, Jesus is the royal prophet like Moses (cf. John 3:14 with Greek Num 21:8-9).[22]

It is for this reason that John never uses the title "Son of David" for Jesus. This is also why the Samaritan woman has the expectation that the Messiah who is coming will settle all the issues regarding where and how God is to be worshiped (John 4:25). In this context John has no hesitation in allowing Jesus to declare: "I am he [i.e., the awaited Messiah]" (John 4:26). Here again, however, this declaration on Jesus' lips gives voice to the faith of John's community. In contrast, the Synoptics, remaining closer to the historical Jesus, take care to present Jesus as distancing himself from preempting God's election by proclaiming himself as Messiah (Mark 8:29-30 par.). Details of this issue will be taken up in chapter 5.

All in all, the result of this whole discussion is the recognition that the wonderful things said about Jesus in John's gospel are to be received as confessional statements on the part of the Johannine church. In speaking to the baptized it would be foolhardy to exalt Abraham and Moses, since the baptized in this community found grace and intimacy with God through the one who was sent to them to be "the way, the truth, and the life" (John 14:6). Hence those assembled inside the church must witness to what they have experienced, namely, "no one [here] comes to the Father except through me" (John 14:6). Such a bold statement of faith, however, does not preclude the necessity of allowing that, in the synagogue, no one there came to the Father except through Abraham and Moses. In the end, therefore, Jesus' words to the Samaritan woman, namely, "We [Jews] worship what we know, for salvation is from the Jews" (John 4:22), need not be nullified.

---

22. Edward Schillebeeckx, *Christ: The Experience of Jesus as Lord* (New York: Seabury Press, 1980) 317, 321.

Witness of the Holy Week Liturgy

The thesis of this opening chapter can be understood from the vantage point of changes in the Good Friday liturgy. For centuries Christians believed that they had triumphed over Judaism and received the divine election with which Jews were favored until the time when they crucified Jesus. The liturgy, consequently, prayed that God would bring these "faithless Jews" to their senses:

> Let us also pray for the faithless Jews: that our God and Lord would withdraw the veil [of ignorance?] from their hearts that they also may acknowledge our Lord Jesus Christ. (*Roman Missal* 1952)

When the liturgical renewal was in full swing after Vatican II the offensive judgmental language ("faithless Jews") was dropped, but the milder language that replaced it remained equally troublesome:

> Let us also pray that Our God and Lord will look kindly on the Jews, so that they too may acknowledge the Redeemer of all, Jesus Christ. (*Roman Missal* 1969)

Thus, as late as 1969, the positive appraisal of Judaism found in *Nostra Aetate* had not yet entered into the church's prayer. Moreover, the prayer continued to imply that until Jews acknowledge Jesus as the "Redeemer of all" they would have no part in the world to come. One had to wait until 1985 for the praying church to catch up with the (official) believing church:

> Let us pray for the Jewish people, the first to hear the word of God, that they may continue to grow in the love of his name and in faithfulness to his covenant. (*Roman Missal* 1985)[23]

Here one now hears the first entirely positive assessment of the Jewish people. In fact, this prayer allows that the Jewish people have a certain

---

23. The Church of England has also had to deal with the vexing issue of Jewish conversion that was called for in the Good Friday liturgy. In fact, in the 1662 version of the revised liturgy not only was the conversion of the Jews being prayed for, but "Turks (= Muslims), Infidels (= atheists), and Hereticks (= Catholics)" as well. The General Synod of 1980 revised this to focus on Jews alone. Only in 1984 did the Good Friday prayers develop a positive esteem for Israel:

> Let us pray for God's ancient people, the Jews, the first to hear his word— for greater understanding between Christian and Jew, for the removal of our blindness of heart, that God will grant us grace to be faithful to his covenant and grow in the love of his name.

priority insofar as they were "first to hear [and respond to] the word of God." This aligns itself well with the theology of Paul in his letter to the Romans and with the sentiments voiced by Pope John Paul II when he broke a long prohibition in 1986 by joining in a prayer service in the principal synagogue in Rome. During this visit he addressed his Jewish audience with these words:

> The Jewish religion is not "extrinsic" to us but, in a certain way, is "intrinsic" to our own religion. With Judaism, therefore, we have a relationship that we do not have with any other religion. You are our dearly beloved brothers, and in a certain way, it could be said that you are our elder brothers.[24]

With a startling clarity of expression, John Paul II acknowledges that the validity of Christianity rests on the prior validity of Judaism. The Good Friday service, consequently, also reaffirms the priority of the Jewish people in hearing and responding to the word of God. In view of this, the petition asks that the Jewish people may "*continue* to grow in the love of his name and in faithfulness to his covenant," namely, the Mosaic covenant. In the end, therefore, Jews are honored for being as God called them to be and their future with God is spoken of as marked by a continued "faithfulness." Thus *the praying church has turned full circle.* Before 1969 the Jews were "faithless" and God was being petitioned to bring them to acknowledge Jesus. Since 1985 they are seen as "faithful" and the church's petition is directed toward continued growth in their Jewishness.

Conclusion

One can only lament the fact that the *Notes* published in 1985 did not include a firm statement allowing that the Catholic Church is "the all-embracing means of salvation" for Catholics while, for Jews, the faith

---

This prayer uses many of the phrases found in the Roman Catholic revision of 1985. The entire Anglican prayer, however, after the first line, turns toward petitions on behalf of Christians and thereby defeats this prayer as being on behalf of the Jews. The collect that follows prays for "the coming of your kingdom, when Israel shall be saved, the Gentiles gathered in, and we shall dwell together in mutual love and peace." This segment clearly focuses on the hope of Israel. See Albert Radcliffe, "How Dialogue with Jews Has Transformed the [Anglican] Holy Week Liturgy," *Jewish-Christian Relations*, http://www.jcrelations.net/en/?item=952. The Episcopal Church (USA) in its *Book of Common Prayer* omits this collect altogether, retaining a single prayer for all "who have not received the Gospel of Christ."

24. Pope John Paul II, cited in the *New York Times*, April 14, 1986.

of Abraham and the Torah of Moses rightly guide them to know, love, and serve their Lord and Father. One must likewise lament the fact that *Dominus Jesus,* published in 2001, did not specify that the Lord himself declared "salvation is from the Jews" (John 4:22), and that consequently the church's saving grace and efficacious mission to the Gentiles finds its roots and sanction within the Judaism practiced by Jesus and his disciples. Only when the church acknowledges the priority of Judaism within its faith and practice will it attain "the fundamental condition of dialogue: respect for the other as [s/]he is" (*Notes* 4). In this regard one can pray that the *lex orandi* ("the rule of praying") found in the Good Friday liturgy may quickly become the *lex credendi* ("the rule of believing") for all those who follow Jesus.

Prayers alone are not enough. The poison of anti-Judaism needs the antidote of a careful examination of those doctrines and practices that have enabled Christians to boast of their faith in Jesus at the expense of downgrading Jewish faith and practice. We are living in the first generation that has undertaken to examine the poison of hatred that has affected our Christian identity. To date we have taken a few bold steps toward eliminating long-established theological and cultural habits of denigration. We have also been able to present, in their place, a positive assessment of Judaism. Ambiguities, however, remain. Some of these have surfaced in this chapter. They will be examined more thoroughly in what follows.

1. *Tension surrounding the Jewish rejection of Jesus*—The church has not, within its theology and spirituality, resolved the historical tension between its own firm affirmation of Christ and the persistent Jewish rejection of Jesus as the Messiah. Yet, just as the medieval church rejoiced at the sin of Adam as the *"felix culpa, the necessary sin by which we gained so great a redeemer,"* so too Christians today might be taught to bless Jews precisely because their ancestors rejected Jesus (Romans 11) and thereby prompted the Jewish disciples of Jesus to turn more attention toward the Gentiles.

2. *Tension surrounding the persistence of Judaism*—As long as Jews were routinely perceived as cursed by God due to their crime of killing Jesus, it was easy to imagine that Jews had to abandon the synagogue and enter the church in order to obtain God's grace and salvation. The moment, however, that Catholics acknowledged that "the Jews remain most dear to God" (*Nostra Aetate* 4), it became problematic to recognize Jews as "most dear to God" while at the same time refusing to acknowledge that

their religious identity and spiritual practices are also "dear to God."

3. *Tension surrounding whether Judaism is a divinely approved path of salvation for Jews*—The reluctance of the Vatican to acknowledge Judaism as a divinely endorsed path of salvation for Jews stands in contradiction to the fact that Jesus and his disciples embraced their Judaism as their path of salvation. Paul understood Abraham to be the father of both the circumcised and the uncircumcised (Romans 4) without, at the same time, imposing the judgment that the latter is superior to or the fulfillment of the former. Should we not be invited to embrace Paul and do the same?

Two

Law and Grace among Jews and Christians

Christians must strive to learn by what essential traits
the Jews define themselves in the light of their own religious experience.

—Commission of the Holy See for Religious Relations with Jews

When I, as a youth, tried to save Mr. Martin from eternal hellfire, I did so by finding a message of mercy within the Christian system of salvation. It never occurred to me that grace and salvation might already be present within Judaism. In fact, since I understood Jews as bound to the Law of Moses, I felt sad that Mr. Martin would never know the intimacy with the Father that I had known, that he would never know the forgiveness of his sins, that he would never experience the joy of going to heaven. The sympathy I felt for the plight of Mr. Martin, however, was the first step in my own conversion. Mr. Martin's acts of justice and generosity forced me to boldly confront the poison of anti-Judaism that infected my Catholic upbringing. For this I am eternally grateful.

How Far We Have Come

In the textbooks, the homilies, and in the chance conversations of my youth, Jews were routinely maligned. It seemed unthinkable to me in 1955 that those I loved and respected—my parents, my teachers, my pastors—were the vehicles of a horrendous indoctrination that was bent on denigrating Jews along these lines:

1. Jews were collectively responsible for crucifying Jesus.
2. The tribulations of the Jewish people throughout history constitute God's punishment for their role in killing Jesus.

23

3. The children of Israel were God's original chosen people by virtue of an ancient covenant. By rejecting Jesus, Jews forfeited their chosenness. Accordingly, God chose Christians—the new Israel—to replace the Jews as God's covenanted people.

Then, in June of 1960, Pope John XXIII met with Jules Isaak to discuss Catholic-Jewish relations. Soon thereafter, when he announced his decision to convoke the Second Vatican Council, he simultaneously decided to submit to the Council a revised vision of Judaism. He specifically asked the well-respected German Old Testament scholar Augustin Cardinal Bea to prepare the first draft. Debates both inside and outside the Council in 1963 served to expand the scope of the projected declaration to address not only a revised vision of Judaism, but a new view of Islam, Buddhism, and Hinduism as well. After vigorous debates and a multitude of revisions, the assembled bishops overwhelmingly voted on October 28, 1965, with 2221 votes in favor and 88 against, to promulgate the *Declaration on the Relation of the Church to Non-Christian Religions*. This declaration, known from its first Latin words as *Nostra Aetate* ("In this age of ours"), directly addresses and overturns each of the three propositions named above:

1. Even though the Jewish authorities and those who followed their lead pressed for the death of Christ, neither all Jews indiscriminately at the time nor Jews today can be charged with the crimes committed during his Passion.
2. The Jews should not be spoken of as rejected or cursed as if this follows from Holy Scripture.
3. Jews for the most part did not accept the Gospel. . . . Even so, the apostle Paul maintains that the Jews remain very dear to God, for the sake of the patriarchs, since God does not take back the gifts he bestowed or the choice he made. (*Nostra Aetate* 4)

After Vatican II all the standard textbooks, liturgical manuals, and homilies had to be revised to reflect these altered ways of understanding Jews and Judaism. In other areas, however, few, if any, changes were being made. This is especially true where the superiority of Christianity was contrasted with the deficiencies of Judaism:

1. Jesus and his followers (the church) emphasized the mercy, grace, and love of God. The Jews, meanwhile, adhered to the Law of Moses and accordingly emphasized the justice, judgment, and wrath of God.

2. Jesus was unique in presenting God as a warm, loving Father caring for his children. Judaism, on the other hand, presented God as a distant, inaccessible Lawgiver bent on punishing sinners.

3. The Pharisees represented the religious legalism rampant in Jesus' day. Jesus was on the mark when he characterized their teachings as oppressive and their conduct as hypocritical.

4. Jews try to earn their salvation by a slavish adherence to the Mosaic Law. Christians, in contrast, are freed from the Law because their salvation comes to them as a gift (a grace) uniquely merited for them by Jesus' death on the cross.

Each of these statements represents a caricature of Jews and Judaism. Since Vatican II did not directly address these issues, their influence continued, at least at first, largely undetected and unchallenged.

In the present chapter the erroneous character of these statements will come to light. The way will then be open for a much more nuanced and accurate depiction of Judaism. The bishops of Vatican II pointed the direction toward this mutual understanding in the following terms:

> Since Christians and Jews have a common spiritual heritage, this sacred Council wishes to encourage and further mutual understanding and appreciation. This can be obtained, especially, by way of biblical and theological enquiry and through friendly discussions. (*Nostra Aetate* 4)

For twenty-five years I have been pursuing this path of study and dialogue with Jews. Here are some of the foundational ways in which I gradually learned to embrace a more accurate appreciation of Jews and Judaism.

Experiencing God as "Father" within Judaism

Contrary to what many Christians have been taught, modern Jews do sometimes think of God as their "Father" and, accordingly, regard themselves as "God's children." Should one take the time to join them in their prayers, one quickly discovers that God is sometimes even addressed as "Father." More importantly, if one listens empathetically between the lines one discovers an implied intimacy that surprised and astonished me when I first heard it. Consider, for example, the following prayer used by Reform Jews at the beginning of their Sabbath service:

Heart's Delight, Source of Mercy, draw your servant into your arms:
I leap like a deer to stand in awe before you.
Your love is sweeter to me than the taste of honey.
World's Light, Shining Glory, my heart is faint for love of you:
Heal it, *Lord,* help my heart, show me your radiant splendor.
Let me return to strength and have joy forever.
Have compassion, *O Faithful One,* pity for your loved child:
How long have I hoped to see your glorious might.
O God, my heart's desire, have pity, hold back no more.
Show yourself, *Beloved,* and cover me with the shelter of your
    peace.
Light up the world with your presence that we may exult and
    rejoice in you.
Hurry, *Loved One,* the holy day [of our deliverance] has come:
    show us grace as [you did] long ago.[1]

Maybe one might think that such a prayer represents a development in modern Judaism that was absent in the period of formative Judaism. But such is not the case. When one examines the Hebrew Scriptures one finds no fewer than fifteen occasions when God's conduct is compared to that of a human father (see, e.g., Deut 1:31; 8:5; Ps 103:13; Prov 3:12). Moses, for example, taught the people of Israel a hymn after writing down the words delivered to him on Mount Sinai. It contains these lines:

I will proclaim the name of the Lord; ascribe greatness to our God! The Rock, his work is perfect, and all his ways are just. A faithful God, without deceit, just and upright is he. . . . Is not he *your father,* who created you, who made you and established you [as his people]? (Deut 32:3-4, 6; emphasis added)

Here the term "father" refers to the historical action of God in creating and electing Israel to become his beloved children (see also Isa 63:16; 64:8; Jer 31:9, 20; Hos 11:8; Mal 1:6; 8:5). One can conclude from this that even the ancient people of Israel felt the freedom to address God as "my Father" (See Jer 3:4, 19).

---

1. *Gates of Prayer: The New Union Prayerbook* (New York: Central Conference of American Rabbis, 1975) 159. *Gates of Prayer* is the standard prayerbook used in Reform synagogues in the United States. The various titles for God are italicized. I can note, in passing, that the various versions of the Roman Catholic Eucharist used every Sunday neither have the poetry nor evoke the implied intimacy of these Jewish prayers. Private prayer books are quite another thing. The Roman liturgy prefers to evoke a sober and thoughtful mood. Paradoxically, it is the Eucharist designed for use with children that I find to contain the most evocative official prayers for Sunday worship.

At other times the term "Father" shows up in the Hebrew Scriptures to designate God's special relationship to the king (2 Sam 7:14; 1 Chr 17:13; 22:10; 28:6; Ps 89:26). Psalm 89 celebrates the "steadfast love" (Ps 89:1, 24, 28) the Lord has for his people Israel and for his servant David. Relative to David, the psalmist reveals what might have been the king's habitual prayer, "You are *my Father, my God,* and *the Rock* of my salvation!" (Ps 89:26). Taken at face value this would indicate that, long before the time of Jesus, the people of Israel in general and those who prayed or sang the psalms in particular relished the experience of appealing to God as Father.

Aseneth's Experience of God as Father and Mother

The book of *Joseph and Aseneth*[2] relates a conversion story that takes place a hundred years before the time of Jesus. This Jewish source narrates how Aseneth, the beautiful and virtuous daughter of an Egyptian priest, converts to Judaism and so becomes the fitting bride for Joseph, who has gained great favor with Pharaoh in Egypt. This source is important, for it demonstrates how a recent convert to Judaism might have been expected to address the God of Israel in the midst of the terror accompanying her conversion.

The narrative opens within the household of the Egyptian priest Pentephres. The narrator anticipates the drama about to unfold when he introduces Pentephres' eighteen-year-old daughter "as tall as Sarah, and as beautiful as Rebecca, and as fair as Rachel" (1:8). As such, she was much sought after by men, yet the narrator tells us that "Aseneth despised all men and regarded them with contempt" (2:1). In Joseph, however, Aseneth encounters a truly exceptional man, and upon first hearing his virtuous words "her eyes were filled with tears" (8:8). When Joseph blesses her, invoking "the God of my father Israel" (8:10), Aseneth abruptly leaves Joseph.

When Aseneth was alone in her chambers, "she wept bitterly, and she repented of her gods she used to worship" (9:2). The next morning Aseneth "took all her innumerable gold and silver gods and broke them up into little pieces and threw them out of the window for the poor and

2. In what follows, version *d* (the "shorter recension") of *Joseph and Aseneth* will be used because it provides an "unquestionably Jewish" document written in Egypt around 100 B.C.E. The translation is Marc Philonenko's, appearing in H. F. D. Sparks, ed., *The Apocryphal Old Testament* (Oxford: Clarendon Press, 1984) 468–70.

needy" (10:13). Later, she took her royal dinner "and all the sacrifices for her gods and the wine-vessels for their libations; and she threw them all out of the window as food for the dogs" (10:14). Aseneth then put on mourning clothes and covered herself with ashes. For seven nights and days she remained alone, without food or drink, weeping bitterly and groaning.

On the eighth day "she stretched her hands out toward the east, and her eyes looked up to the heaven" (12:1) and she expressed for the first time her prayer of repentance and conversion, imploring God "like a child [speaking] to her father and her mother" (12:7).

> To you, O Lord . . . will I cry:
> Deliver me from my persecutors, for to you I have fled,
> *Like a child to her father and her mother.*
> *O Lord, stretch forth your hands over me,*
> *As a father who loves his children and is tenderly affectionate,*
> Snatch me from the hands of the enemy . . . .
> The gods of the Egyptians whom I have abandoned and
>   destroyed
> And their father the Devil is trying to destroy me . . . .
> Save me, O Lord, deserted as I am,
> For my father and mother denied me,
> Because I destroyed and shattered their gods;
> And now I am an orphan and deserted,
> And I have no other hope save in you, O Lord. (12:8-9, 11, alt.;
>   emphasis added)

What appeals to me in this prayer of Aseneth is that Aseneth is keenly aware that her father and mother have denied and deserted her "because I destroyed and shattered their gods." She is thus "an orphan" and expects the Lord acknowledged by Joseph to become her new "father and mother"—one who is "tenderly affectionate" and, at the same time, sufficiently powerful to "snatch me from the hands of the enemy."

Jesus, in his day, referred to God's protection as like that of "a hen [who] gathers her brood under her wings" (Matt 23:37; Luke 13:34; see also 2 *Esdr.* 1:30). Since his hearers did not bristle at this metaphor one can surmise that they were not fixated on experiencing God only as "Father." To the best of our knowledge, however, none of the official prayers of the ancient synagogue or church ever actually addressed God as "Mother." The reason for this is not, as some suppose, that God wants to be exclusively thought of as male—even though God is, properly speaking, without gender.[3] Nor is the reason for this that Jesus never experienced God as a "mother"—something that cannot be known with any certainty. Rather, the reason is found elsewhere, as will be revealed momentarily.

Some may object that Aseneth does not actually address God as "Father" (or as "Mother," for that matter). This objection does not stand up to close scrutiny. Does the intimacy in the psalms lose all merit just because, in most cases, God is not addressed as "Father"? Or, again, how about Tevye in the musical *Fiddler on the Roof*? Does Tevye's whimsical and familiar relationship with the Lord disappear simply because he never says "Father"? And what of Etty Hillesum, whose diaries from 1941 to 1943 are filled with intimate and direct conversations with God? When everyone in her Jewish circles in Amsterdam was obsessed with the daily prospect of being deported to a labor camp, Etty paradoxically found safety "in God's arms":

> I feel safe in God's arms . . . and no matter whether I am sitting at this beloved old desk now, or in a bare room in the Jewish district, or perhaps in a labor camp under SS guards in a month's time—I shall always feel safe in God's arms. They may well succeed in breaking me physically, but no more than that. I may face cruelty and deprivation the like of which I cannot imagine in even my wildest fantasies. Yet all this is as nothing to the immeasurable expanse of my faith in God. . . .[4]

Etty later died at Auschwitz at the age of twenty-nine. This did not mean that at any time she did not consider herself safely in God's arms for, as she said, "One thing is becoming increasingly clear to me: that you [God] cannot help us, that we must help you to help ourselves."[5] We will return to this point. For the moment it suffices to note that intimacy and safety with God must not be measured solely on the basis of titles used to address God. Alternately, many Christians routinely pray

3. God, according to the Jewish tradition, has no body (or any material form). On the other hand, Genesis relates that "God created humankind in his image . . . male and female he created them" (1:27). Thus the female and male equally bear the "image" of God. Going further, the rabbis did not hesitate to speak of God as "exhibiting emotions like those of human beings" and "doing deeds that women and men do" (Jacob Neusner, *The Incarnation of God: The Character of Divinity in Formative Judaism* [Philadelphia: Fortress Press, 1988] ix).

4. Etty Hillesum, *An Interrupted Life: The Diaries 1941–1943* (New York: Henry Holt, 1996) 176.

5. Ibid., 178.

"Our Father" without ever experiencing any intimacy or protective care from God. One must be careful, consequently, to look beyond the words themselves.

Soft Spots in Joachim Jeremias' Interpretation of Jesus' Use of "Father"

In the late 1960s, Joachim Jeremias popularized the notion that Jesus' use of "Father" was the "unique and special"[6] feature of his piety that set him apart from Judaism and exhibited his divine sonship. Jeremias interpreted the Greek term *pater* ("father") as reflecting the Aramaic *abba*, the familiar word used by Jewish children to address their fathers, much as "daddy" functions in modern English today. I remember vividly the first time I heard this term being used when I visited Israel. On a typical hot and dry day in a crowded bus station a boy cried out, "Abba! Abba!" as he spotted his father descending from a dusty bus. He quickly wedged his way through the crowd and his father immediately took him up into his arms. The child's eyes were filled with sheer delight. The use of such a familiar term to address God stood, in the mind of Jeremias, as a reflection of the unique and intimate relationship Jesus had with his Father. For Protestants as well as Catholics,[7] therefore, Jesus addressing God as "Father" came to be understood as expressing his spontaneous intimacy with God that formed the foundation of later dogmatic formulations of his unique sonship.

While some scholars have expressed reservations regarding Jeremias' conclusions,[8] Mary Rose D'Angelo has sifted the evidence to uncover soft spots in Jeremias' scholarship. In part, she concludes:

> Attempts to attribute "abba! father!" to Jesus have overemphasized . . . that Jesus' usage must be [uniquely] his because it

---

6. Joachim Jeremias, *Abba. Studien zur neutestamentlichen Theologie und Zeitgeschichte* (Göttingen: Vandenhoeck & Ruprecht, 1966); translated in *The Prayers of Jesus* (London: SCM, 1967) 11–65.

7. The uniqueness of Jesus' *abba*-experience has become widely accepted in both Protestant and Catholic circles. See, for example, James D. G. Dunn, *Jesus and the Spirit* (London: SCM, 1975) 21–37, and idem, *The Partings of the Ways* (London: SCM, 1991) 170, 181. As an illustration of uncritical Catholic use of Jeremias see Edward Schillebeeckx, *Jesus: An Experiment in Christology* (New York: Seabury, 1979) 256–71. For a Jewish-Catholic discussion of this issue see John T. Pawlikowski and Eugene B. Borowitz, *1987 Lecture Series: Proceedings of the Center for Jewish-Christian Learning* (St. Paul: College of St. Thomas, 1987).

8. John P. Meier, *A Marginal Jew* (New York: Doubleday, 1994) 358–59, n. 20.

would be unheard of or even impossible in early Judaism. This claim was built on a problematic use of evidence that was limited not only by the constraints of history but also by an unsympathetic reading of the Jewish materials. Much of this lack of sympathy can be attributed to the desire to establish the uniqueness of Jesus and especially of Jesus' teaching.[9]

Once the Jewish evidence is more expansively and sympathetically handled, Jesus' use of "father" is seen as within rather than against the stream of Jewish piety.[10] Furthermore, when the Christian sources are more rigorously examined even "Jeremias's claim that Jesus always addressed God as father cannot be supported."[11]

After examining approximately fifty instances in which "Father" is used to address God within Jewish prayers, D'Angelo summarizes:

> Three functions of "father" seem to have been particularly impor-
> tant in early Jewish literature. First, "father" functions to designate
> God as the refuge of the afflicted and persecuted. . . . Second,
> "father" frequently accompanies a petition for or an assurance of
> forgiveness. These two functions are grounded by a third: "father"
> evokes the power and providence that governs the world.[12]

In none of these three functions is there any sentimentality. In the ancient world the father was the undisputed head of the family. A good father was one who used his power for the welfare and protection of those entrusted to his care (wife, children, slaves).

---

9. Mary Rose D'Angelo, "*Abba* and 'Father': Imperial Theology and the Jewish Tradition," *JBL* 111 (1992) 611–30.

10. Joseph A. Fitzmyer, *The Gospel According to Luke* (Garden City, NY: Doubleday, 1983) 902–903, and idem, "Abba and Jesus' Relation to God," in *À Cause de L'Évangile: études sur les synoptiques et les Actes offertes au P. Jacques Dupont, O.S.B., à l'occasion de son 70e anniversaire*. LD 123 (Paris: Cerf, 1987). Alon Goshen-Gottstein, in his study, "God the Father in Rabbinic Judaism and Christianity," *JES* 38/4 (2001) 470–504, finds over a hundred instances wherein formative Judaism portrays God as Father. In many instances, the phrase, "Father in Heaven," is also used. R. Aqiba (d. 70 C.E.) laced his prayers with "Our Father, our King" (b. Tannit 25b). Furthermore, the rabbis favored parables wherein God and Israel show up under the thinly veiled images of Father and Son. All in all, Goshen-Gottstein concludes that, if one brackets the dogmatic issue as to whether Jesus was driven by his personal sense of a metaphysical sonship, then the array of parallels shows that "Jesus was not offering a new understanding [of God as Father] as much as calling for the deeper realization of an existing shared understanding" (n. 84).

11. D'Angelo, "*Abba* and 'Father,'" 617.

12. Ibid., 621.

As a case in point, consider the Lord's Prayer. "Father" in this prayer has none of the sentimentality with which Jeremias invested the term. "Father" combines power with benevolence (as in the prayer of Aseneth seen earlier). Thus the one addressed as "Father" is first and foremost the one coming in power to bring his kingdom "on earth as in heaven." Even in the book of Revelation the warm image of God taking his throne in order to "wipe every tear from their [his children's] eyes" (Rev 21:4) stands up as credible only because, in earlier chapters, this same God had previously commanded his seven angels to "pour out on the earth the seven bowls of the wrath of God" (Rev 16:1). Fuzzy hugs without power to subdue evil are useless. Raw power immune to fuzzy hugs is diabolical.

Reflections on the Gift Christians Received from the Jews

Once, in a public forum, someone disturbed about what I had been presenting asked me a very searching question: "What difference does it make if some Christians want to continue to cherish the romantic notion that Jesus was *unique* in approaching God as a warm, loving Father? Doesn't this notion enlarge the sense of gratitude that Christians have for Jesus?"

"Assuredly," I responded, "no one should think, for a single moment, that I would want to downplay the enormous gift we Christians have received from Jesus. Every time you and I go to prayer with a sense of confidence in our heavenly Father, we ought to say, 'Thank you, Jesus! Thank you for making this possible.' But here's the rub: I want to retrain myself to praise Jesus without, at the same time, distorting or demeaning Judaism in the process."

Rosemary Radford Ruether, in her book *Faith and Fratricide*, challenged Christians to take note of how our habit of putting down Jews and Judaism in order to elevate Jesus and Christianity exists as "the left hand of christology."[13] This phrase fits. With our right hand we multiply the titles, functions, and benefits of Jesus while, with our left hand, we deny these very things as having ever existed within Judaism. It is what the left hand is doing that needs to stop. Why? It is not honest. It is not charitable. And it has gone a long way toward constructing a world in which it is not safe to be a Jew.

---

13. Rosemary Radford Ruether, *Faith and Fratricide—The Theological Roots of Anti-Semitism* (New York: Seabury Press, 1974).

Let's go deeper. Let us assume, for a moment, that Jesus was absolutely unique in his experience of a warm, loving Father who cherished him as a beloved Son. If this were so, it might be expected that Jesus would occasionally brag about his intimacy with God (as sometimes comes across in John's gospel). Since he was the eternal Son of God he would not be prone to imagine that his disciples could or would have any intimacy with God that remotely approached his own. If they had aspired toward it, one can imagine that he would politely have discouraged them, saying, "Sorry, lads, I'm the unique Son of God; you're not. Hence you can't expect to have the intimacy with God that I have."

So far, so good. But someone might object that Jesus was not one to pull rank or to boast about his honors and privileges (except in John's gospel). In fact, he routinely presumed that his disciples would become like him. The Synoptic Gospels, accordingly, show no surprise when they present the disciples of Jesus as being sent out two by two to perform the very feats done by Jesus—namely, heralding the kingdom, healing the sick, exorcizing the possessed (Matt 10:1-5 par.). The Jesus of John's gospel even goes so far as to have Jesus say, "The one who believes in me will also do the works that I do and, in fact, will do greater works than these" (14:12). At one point the disciples failed to cast out a demon (Matt 17:15-21 par.). To our surprise, Jesus doesn't chide them, saying "only I, as the Son of God, can do this!" Rather, the entire narrative presupposes that the disciples should have succeeded. Jesus, if the truth be told, displays some huffy impatience that they did not succeed (Matt 17:17). The disciples, embarrassed and confused at their failure, privately ask Jesus, "Why could we not cast it out?" This question is revealing. It presupposes that they had attempted this exorcism because they had succeeded in such cases in the past (Mark 6:13 par.).[14]

This same pattern shows up when it comes time to pray. Jesus doesn't say to his disciples, "I talk to my Father because I know him intimately. You do not know him, so you need to tell me what matters you want me to take up with him, and I, as his only beloved Son, will present it to him in a way that I know will be well received." Not only this, but Jesus does not presume to lead prayers in any synagogue or, for that matter, even to lead prayers with his disciples when they are on the road with him. The truth behind this is that Jesus and his disciples were already living in a milieu in which every Jew took it for granted that God invited him or

---

14. For a fuller development of this failure on the part of the disciples see Aaron Milavec, *To Empower As Jesus Did* (New York: Edwin Mellen, 1982) 18–24.

her to pray regularly and familiarly, directly to God.[15] No intermediaries were required or desired. Thus when the disciples come to Jesus asking him to teach them how to pray "as John taught his disciples" (Luke 11:1), Jesus trains them to pray "Our Father." Here again we must marvel that Jesus does not train them to say "Dear Father of Jesus." No. The Jewish milieu in which the disciples had grown up (especially as promoted by the Pharisees) made it clear to them that they were all sons or daughters of God. Thus the disciples of Jesus did not express any surprise that Jesus invited them to address God familiarly as "Father."

The disciples would have recognized that the "Lord's prayer" was really a prayer template they would improvise on each day. That is why Matthew and Luke do not have any word-for-word agreement as to what was given to the disciples as the "Lord's prayer." Within the Judaism of the day, improvisation in prayer was expected.[16] Christians later got the notion that the words of Jesus were meant to be memorized and recited verbatim. They even got into fights as to what the authentic words of Jesus were. But for the Jewish disciples of Jesus this would have seemed pure silliness and an obstacle to true prayer. After all, no son or daughter addressed his or her human parents using memorized lines. No Jew, consequently, not even Jesus himself, would have imagined that rote prayers were somehow safer or better suited to address our Father in heaven. That was all to come later.

---

15. For details, see the Appendix at the end of chapter 4.

16 .While the later rabbis tried to introduce some standardization into the prayer life of those who followed their lead, Jakob Petuchowski notes that "spontaneous expression of our deepest concerns" was always encouraged, following the mandate of Rabbi Eliezer: "He who makes his prayers a fixed task—his prayers are not [valid] supplications" (*m. Berakhot* 4:4) (*Understanding Jewish Prayer* [New York: Ktav, 1972] 3, 9). By "fixed task" the Babylonian Talmud understood either prayers recited "as a burden" or said by rote, "in which one cannot say something new" (*b. Berakhot* 29b). The *Mishnah* also cites in the name of Rabbi Akiva: "If one's prayer is fluent, he prays the [full] Eighteen [Benedictions]. But if not, [he should pray] an abstract of the Eighteen" (*m. Berakhot* 4:3). Most probably this means that someone capable of spontaneously expanding on each of the fixed themes should do so (see *m. Berakhot* 5:5). Someone unable to improvise, however, should recite an "abstract"—which, quite possibly, is a memorized synopsis. Finally, in the name of Rabbi Joshua, the *Mishnah* refers to the Eighteen Benedictions, saying: "One who walks in a place of danger prays a short prayer" (*m. Berakhot* 4:4)—meaning that, in cases of necessity one can shorten one's prayer. Each of these directives would make little sense if the Eighteen Benedictions were memorized word for word and deviations were not allowed. Within this setting one can surmise that the Lord's Prayer was an "abstract" of six key themes, inviting spontaneous expansion by gifted prayer leaders. It might also have served as a summary prayer for those who lacked the gift of improvisation.

As Christians, we have received from Jesus not only a knowledge of the true God but also a freedom to address God as a loving Father in our own words. That we receive this from Jesus, it does not mean that Jesus pioneered this mode of prayer or that Jesus regarded the Jews of his day as having failed to do this. Jesus is remembered as having criticized those fellow Jews who made a public show of praying (Matt 6:5-6) or who advanced their cause before God by maligning their neighbor (Luke 18:11). At no point, however, does Jesus say, "Your Jewish style of praying is bankrupt. Let me show you how it is to be done." Nor does he say, "I am the first one to approach God as Father." Reading between the lines, one can even surmise that Jesus was quite satisfied with the Jewish style of prayer used by his disciples. It is they, consequently, who decide to take up the issue with Jesus because they want to improve their already satisfactory skills in this area.

When Jesus is permitted to take his place as a Jew in the company of Jews, it even becomes possible for Christians to recognize that their debt of gratitude is owed not only to Jesus, but also to all the Jews before Jesus who made possible his familiarity with the Father. Jesus comes to us, at least in this respect, not as the exception but as an example of the grace and richness already present in Judaism. Every time you and I go to prayer with a sense of confidence in our heavenly Father, consequently, we ought to say, "Thank you, Jesus, for bringing us to embrace what thousands of Jews before and after you experienced as the fatherhood of God."

Gratitude is not such a bad thing. It can serve as an antidote to the thousands of putdowns that have routinely surfaced within Christian circles. In fact, the bishops of Vatican II wanted to press forward the possibility that Christians would rediscover a sense of gratitude toward Jews. They put it this way:

> The Church of Christ acknowledges that in God's plan of salvation the beginning of her faith and her election is to be found in the patriarchs, Moses, and the prophets. She professes that all Christ's faithful, who as men [and women] of faith are sons [and daughters] of Abraham, are included in the same patriarch's call. . . . The Church cannot forget that she received the revelation of the Old Testament by way of that people with whom God in his inexpressible mercy established the ancient covenant. Nor can she forget that she draws nourishment from the good olive tree onto which the wild olive branches of the Gentiles have been grafted. (*Nostra Aetate* 4)

The incarnation, as understood by most Christians, made possible God's spectacular familiarity with just one Jew. The covenant, on the other hand, made possible God's ordinary familiarity with every Jew. The incarnation of God without the covenant would have meant that one divine superstar blazed like a comet in the heavens and quickly burned out. The incarnation of God understood within the covenant with Israel, on the other hand, insures us that the divine superstar would be one with us in creating a fire of love that would renew the face of the earth. It was with this understanding that the Church Fathers loved to repeat: "We become by grace what Christ is by nature." Our Sunday liturgy still captures this in the ancient rite of adding a small amount of water to the cup of wine as the priest quietly says: "By the mingling of this water and wine may we come to share in the divinity of him who humbled himself to share in our humanity." In this spirit, consequently, our contemporary bishops are right on target when they invite us to remember that we draw nourishment from the good olive tree (Israel), and for this we need to be supremely grateful.

Meaning of "Torah"

Within the Jewish tradition *torah* refers to the practical wisdom and know-how that a loving parent passes on to his/her child. Being created by God is a condition enjoyed by everyone. Being "fathered" by God, being trained in his Torah, is quite another thing. This latter experience allowed Israel to realize that, collectively speaking, they were God's "beloved son" whom he had called out of Egypt and trained in the desert. Thus the inspired author explains:

> Remember how YHWH your God led you for forty years in the wilderness. . . . He humbled you, he made you feel hunger, he fed you with manna . . . to make you understand that man does not live on bread alone but man lives on everything that comes from the mouth of YHWH . . . Learn from this that YHWH your God was training you as a man trains his child . . . and so follow his ways [i.e., Torah] and reverence him. (Deut 8:2-6 JB)

In order to begin to address the issue of Jewish Law one has to first address the problem created by translations. When the Hebrew Scriptures were translated into Greek, *nomos* was used as a Greek equivalent for *torah*. In the Hellenistic world *nomos* was the familiar word used to designate what is proper according to Zeus. When the Scriptures were translated into Latin by Jerome and then into English at the beginning of the seventeenth century, both the Hebrew word *torah* and the Greek word *nomos* were rendered into Latin as *lex* and into English as "law" (always in the singular). The term "law" in English was then associated with the rules promulgated by the English kings to govern their peoples. Since the English kings were fondly regarded as "divinely chosen" to father the people, something of the ancient Jewish tradition of *torah* remained.

Today, however, laws are enacted by elected representatives. Legislators do not normally think of themselves as "divinely chosen" or as "fathering" their constituents. Civil laws serve to adjudicate the conflictual rights of citizens. Juridical bodies hear evidence, arrive at verdicts, and impose punishments. Within this modern climate, the term "law," used 430 times in the Jewish texts and 191 times in the Christian texts (72 times in Romans alone), easily takes on a legalistic and juridical flavor. God can easily be imagined as an autocratic master who imposes laws on his subjects and punishes them for violations. There is nothing to suggest a father imparting his wisdom for living to his beloved children.

For myself, every time I hear or read the word "law" in the Bible, I silently think *Torah* and imagine my beloved adopted father training me in the art of living. My own biological father had the habit of ordering me around and had little sense of how to relate to me as a son; hence, I have to think of my "adopted father," who was an expert in these things.

Torah within a Living Tradition of Interpretation

Given the success of the Pharisaic revolution, which had its origins just before the time of Jesus, all Jews today habitually think of Torah as a living tradition that began with Moses on Mount Sinai but renews itself in every generation down to the present day. It will come as a surprise to some Christians, therefore, that religiously educated Jews do not study the Bible when they want to discover what God wants of them. Rather, they study the rabbinic discussions collected in the *Mishnah, Tosephta,* and *Talmud.* The reason for this is that the practical matters of how to be Jewish (e.g., when to pray, how to pray, where to pray) are frequently not even discussed in the Five Books of Moses. Moreover, those things that are discussed (e.g., the rule of an eye for an eye and a tooth for a tooth) may have served to regulate the quick justice appropriate to desert nomads, but it failed to serve the settled town existence that came later.

The Pharisees and their successors, the rabbis, accordingly ignored rules that had become outmoded and adapted old rules to new circumstances. This became known as the "oral Torah," which the rabbis taught to their disciples and used to train the people in God's ways.

With the success of the Pharisaic revolution it became both necessary and helpful to record in a systematic fashion the interpretations of the Torah passed down by the rabbis. Judah the Prince, in 200 C.E., made the first systematic, written directory of the "oral Torah," which is commonly called the *Mishnah* (the Aramaic term for "oral tradition"). Formerly the Pharisees had, for various reasons, opposed the writing down of "oral Torah." This is the most probable reason why Jesus never wrote anything or even imagined that any of his disciples ought to write down his teachings (i.e., his oral Torah).

Once this rule was broken, however, writings began to multiply.[17] When a Jew speaks of studying Torah, this is not a euphemism for "Bible study," as some Christians might imagine; rather, it is a way of directing attention to the systematic study of the books of "oral Torah," especially the *Mishnah* and the *Babylonian Talmud.* Jews commonly learned Hebrew (the language of the Five Books of Moses and of the synagogue prayers) and even some Aramaic (the everyday language of the rabbis) to enable them to examine Torah in the original languages. Today, however, these books have been made available in translation, which allows their

---

17. The short tractate *Pirke Abot,* appearing around 250 C.E., clarified the chain of authorities linking Moses with the rabbinic academy at Yavneh and related wisdom stories from each of the chief rabbis. Then, around 300 C.E., the *Tosephta,* a multivolume gathering of supplements to the *Mishnah,* was created. In the same period there appeared two systematic books of exegesis of the written Torah: *Sifra* on Leviticus and two volumes of *Sifrē,* one on Deuteronomy, the other on Numbers. Meanwhile, given the widespread use of the *Mishnah,* it became natural to use it as a general schema and to amend it. This was done by two different communities of rabbis, those in Palestine and those in Babylon. Thus the two great, multivolume commentaries on the *Mishnah* appeared, one called the *Talmud of the Land of Israel (Yerushalmi)* and the other the *Babylonian Talmud (Bavli).* The first was completed around 450, the second and larger collection around 600. Between the two Talmuds a collection of illustrative stories *(haggadah),* used by the rabbis to develop themes in Genesis and in Leviticus, was brought together. These collections were called *Genesis Rabbah* (ca. 400) and *Leviticus Rabbah* (ca. 450). Stepping back, one can see that the period from 200 to 600 C.E. represented a very fertile period for rabbinic Judaism. Behind each of these collections stands the remembered teaching (rules and stories) put forward by nearly a hundred named rabbis. The oral material was collected by association with the schema of topics already fleshed out in the *Mishnah* or by association with the flow of topics in an existing biblical book. All in all, these books (including a dozen more minor tracts not mentioned here) make up the literary corpus of formative Judaism and are used and reused by Jews to this very day.

use by Jews no longer prepared to study in the ancient tongues and by Christians who are even more seriously handicapped.

Many Christians have the mistaken notion that Jews today live rigorously by the rules Moses wrote down in the books of Exodus and Leviticus. These Christians are entirely unaware of the entire library of formative rabbinic materials that has interpreted, expanded, and deleted some of the original prescriptions of Moses. As regards deletion, let one example suffice. According to Moses a brother was obliged to marry the wife of his brother should he die childless. This became known as levirate marriage and, as can be supposed, it worked well in a society wherein the welfare of a childless widow was precarious and polygamy was practiced. Needless to say, the rabbis modified the application of this rule and, for some centuries now, have dispensed with it entirely. Thus it has been said by Resh Lakish, "There are times when the nullifying of the Torah may lead to the establishing of it" (*b. Menahot* 99a-b).

One might legitimately ask how Jews can imagine themselves to be faithful to God if they have changed the rules originally given to them through Moses. The answer to this comes in the form of a parable within a story told by an early modern teacher known as Elijah:

> Once, as I was walking along a road, a man accosted me. He came at me aggressively with the sort of argument that leads to heresy. It turned out that the man had [accepted] Scripture but not *Mishnah*. He asserted, "Scripture was given us from Mount Sinai but not *Mishnah*."
>
> I replied, "Were not both Scripture and *Mishnah* given by the Almighty? Does the fact that they are different from each other mean that both cannot have been given by him?
>
> "By what parable may the question be elucidated?
>
> "By the one of a mortal king who had two servants whom he loved with perfect love. To one he gave a measure of wheat, and to the other he gave a measure of wheat; to one [the first, he gave] a bundle of flax, and to the other a bundle of flax.
>
> "What did the clever one of the two do? He took the flax and wove it into a napkin. He took the wheat and made it into fine flour by sifting the grain and grinding it. Then he kneaded the dough and baked it, set the loaf of bread on the table, spread the napkin over the loaf, and left it to await the coming of the king.
>
> "But the foolish one of the two did not do anything at all.
>
> "After a while, the king came into his house and said to the two servants, 'My sons, bring me what I gave you.' One brought out the table with the loaf of bread baked of fine flour on it and with

the napkin spread over the bread. The other brought out his wheat in a basket with a bundle of flax over the wheat grains. 'What a shame! What a disgrace!'

"So, too, when the Holy One gave the Torah to Israel, he gave it as wheat to be turned into fine flour and as flax to be turned into cloth for garments." (*Seder Eliyyahu Zuta* 2)

This parable makes its point dramatically and no commentary is needed.

One can note, at this juncture, that the tradition of telling parables did not originate with Jesus, nor did it end with him. Some great rabbis are remembered exclusively through the poignant parables they told and retold to their disciples.[18] Unfortunately, as the Jesus movement separated itself from Judaism during the second century the art of creating teaching parables all but disappeared. A study of the Church Fathers demonstrates this vividly. The Shepherd of Hermas (150 C.E.) was perhaps the last great teacher who created and used parables. Athanasius, in his treatise *On the Incarnation* (325 C.E.), provides a half dozen designed to illustrate various facets of his christology. After him, however, original parables became very rare. The energy of the late Church Fathers was spent repeating and reinterpreting Jesus' parables. It never occurred to them to do what Jesus did.

Even God Was Required to Consult Experts in Torah

Once Christians understand the importance of the oral Torah and perceive how Jews have made concerted efforts to discern, in modern circumstances, what God would have them be and do today, it becomes very difficult to imagine Jews taking a lockstep and dehumanizing stand relative to the Mosaic Law. The rabbis tell the story of how even God has had to come to grips with the fact that, once he delivered Torah, and once he allowed that intelligent discernment was necessary for being faithful, even he could not dispense himself from consulting his sons when it came time to interpret Torah. Consider the following:

---

18. The rabbis, during the formative period of rabbinic Judaism, vigorously continued to create fresh parables in order to enhance and clarify key aspects of their teaching. Modern rabbis, sad to say, have been overcome by our print culture and seldom tell, much less originate, parables. Only among some select groups of Hasidim (ultra-conservative Jews following the tradition of the Baal Shem Tov originating in Poland) have I been able to discover an oral tradition of creating and teaching with parables.

> In the [rabbinic] session in the heavens, people were debating this question: If the bright spot [on the skin] came before the white hair, the person is [to be considered] clean. If the white hair came before the bright spot, he is clean. What about a case of doubt [as to which appeared first]?
> The Holy One, blessed be he, said, "Clean."
> And the rest of the fellowship of the heavens said, "Unclean."
> They said, "Who will settle this matter? It should be Rabbah ben Nahmani, for he is the one who said, 'I am an expert in the rules governing plagues. . . .'"
> A letter fell down from the sky to Pumbedita: "Rabbah ben Nahmani has been called up [to the heavens] by the academy of the heavens . . ." (*b. Baba Mesia* 86a)

In this story "God is represented in a heavenly session of the heavenly academy studying precisely those details of the Torah . . . as were mastered by the great sages of the day."[19] On a disputed question God takes a position over and against the consensus of the heavenly court. This, however, does not decide the matter. As in all complex affairs, preference must be given to the one who has the most experience in matters of this kind. Thus Rabbah ben Nahmani was called up because, even with God present, "heaven required the knowledge of the heroic sage."[20]

The Election of Israel as Grace

In the view of most Christians the supreme moment of grace is the dying and rising of our Lord Jesus Christ. Well and good. For Jews, what is their supreme moment of grace? Perhaps it is the mighty wonders that accompanied the liberation of God's people from the bondage in Egypt. Or, alternately, it may be the fact that God did not leave the children of Israel as orphans, but revealed to them his Torah and thus fulfilled his intention to father them. Or maybe the supreme moment of grace was when God gave the Israelites the land flowing with milk and honey. True, each of these events plays an important part in Jewish self-understanding and Jewish celebrations, yet the rabbis see all these things as the consequences of the central truth that God chose Israel to be his own people. The supreme grace, therefore, is the divine election of Israel.

The word "grace" comes from the Latin word *gratia* and signals a free gift. "In God's choosing Israel, the rabbis saw Israel's one claim

---

19. Jacob Neusner, *Incarnation of God*, 191.
20. Ibid.

to greatness."[21] "Why us?" the rabbis kept asking themselves. "What have we done to deserve God's love?" "Nothing." "How can one then explain why the Lord chose Israel and not some other nation?" The rabbis made various attempts to explain this. To begin with, R. Avira noted that "though the Lord is high, yet he takes note of the low" [Ps 138:6] (*b. Sotah* 5b). From this it follows:

> [Rabbi Yose said: The verse] "It was not because you were greater than any [other] people that the Lord set his love upon you and chose you, but because you were the humblest of all peoples" (Deut 7:7) means that the Holy One said to Israel, "I love you because even when I shower greatness upon you, you humble yourselves before me. I bestowed greatness upon Abraham, yet he said to me, 'I am but dust and ashes' (Gen 18:27). [I bestowed greatness] upon Moses and Aaron, yet they said, 'We are nothing' (Exod 16:8). [I bestowed greatness] upon David, yet he said, 'I am a worm and no man' (Ps 22:7)." (*b. Hullin* 89a)

When pushed, this is no explanation at all. One has only to examine the teachings of the rabbis to understand that, again and again, the very persons named were also sometimes proud and sometimes caused the Lord grief. The love affair between the Lord and Israel is not all roses; there is an abundance of thorns. The explanation of Rabbi Yose, therefore, functions more like a moral exhortation: "God chose us not because of any inherent worth; therefore, be humble." According to the rabbis, the Holy One himself was humble and, accordingly, chose the humble:

> Rabbi Joseph said, "A person should always learn from the attitude of his Creator, for lo, the Holy One, blessed be he, neglected all [the great] mountains and heights and brought his Presence to rest on [the little] Mount Sinai, and he neglected all valuable [towering] trees and brought his Presence to rest in the [burning] bush [of Moses]." (*b. Sotah* 5b)

Torah Study in the Presence of God

Rabbi Morris Kertzer, in his popular book, *What Is a Jew?* asks the central question: What do Jews believe about God? His answer is a profound summary of Jewish identity:

---

21. E. P. Sanders, *Paul and Palestinian Judaism* (Philadelphia: Fortress Press, 1977) 101.

Belief in one and only one God is central to Judaism as a religion. Judaism teaches also that God has done or will do three things.

First, God created the universe. Modern Jews believe that science best explains *how* the universe was born, but nonetheless, [Jews] see the hand of God in that process, in some way. Moreover, creation is a continuing process. . . .

Second, God revealed the Torah to Israel. Revelation is primarily associated with standing at Mount Sinai, but we believe also in continuing revelation thereafter. . . .

Third, we believe in redemption. Our God is not an impersonal force that began the world but does not care about it. We therefore believe that God intervened in history once to rescue the Israelites from Egypt, and that God will in some way redeem us all at the end of time.

Our God is thus a God of *creation, revelation,* and *redemption.*[22]

Rabbi Kertzer acknowledges that "very few Jews still believe that the Torah as we have it was handed down directly to Moses . . . or that the events as described in the book of Exodus are to be taken literally."[23] Nonetheless, even when Mount Sinai is received as a "symbolic event," Jews continue to acknowledge its centrality for defining "our commitment ever after to live a life of Torah, bringing ever nearer the dawn of God's reign on earth."[24]

Judaism and Christianity share an emphasis on *hearing* the Word of God, *interpreting* it, and *doing* it. For the rabbis, the act of occupying oneself with Torah was the event that mediated the experience of the presence of God:

Rabbi Halafta ben Dosa of Kefar Hananiah said: When ten men sit together and occupy themselves with Torah, the Presence [*Shekhinah*] abides among them, as it is said, "God abideth in the congregation of God" (Ps 82:1).

How do we know that this is true even when there are only five? Because it is said, "When a band [*aggadah*, held together by the five fingers of the hand] is his, he establishes [his Presence] upon the earth" (Am 9:6).

And from what do we infer that the same is true even when there are only three? From the verse, "In the midst of the judges [three being required], he judges" (Ps 82:1).

22. Rabbi Morris N. Kertzer, *What Is a Jew?* (New York: Macmillan, 1993) 111–12.
23. Ibid., 112.
24. Ibid., 113.

> How do we know that the same is true when there are only two? From the verse, "When they that fear the Lord spoke each to the other, the Lord hearkened and heard" (Mal 3:16).
>
> And how do we know that the same is true even of one [person occupied with Torah]? From the verse, "In every place where I hear my name mentioned, I will come to you and bless you" (Exod 20:24). (*Avot* 3:6)

Thus the study of Torah by the rabbis became a cherished moment in which the presence of the Lord was felt. This helps one to understand why the Torah scrolls receive such reverence during the synagogue service. Every Shabbat (Saturday morning), the rabbi or a reader takes the scroll of the Torah from the ark and makes a procession, bringing the Torah scrolls close to the members of the congregation. Those present reach out and touch the scroll with the fringes on their prayer shawls or with their prayer books and then they kiss the point of contact as a sign of reverence. Once the portion of the scrolls for the day is read, everyone sits, and the rabbi gives a commentary on the text just heard.

Michael Lerner, addressing Jews who have grown lukewarm regarding Torah study, tells them he still believes "that the world can be radically transformed, and that the Power that runs the universe is the power that makes that possible."[25] Especially in practical matters, Lerner advocates Torah study for its efficacy in "undermin[ing] the social basis for any system of oppression" (including the oppression of Palestinians by the modern state of Israel).[26] Yet Lerner is no starry-eyed idealist. He laments the fact that the study of Torah for many Jews has been a soul-deadening experience.[27] When he interviewed those who graduated with him in 1950 from Hebrew school, he discovered that "most of them looked back on Hebrew school as an ordeal that they went through to please their parents, and once they were free to make choices of their own, they ran from the Jewish world as fast as they could."[28] Most Catholics would find that many of their childhood friends would say approximately the same thing regarding the religious instruction they received as children. The failure of a religious tradition to take hold, consequently, is not a uniquely Jewish phenomenon.

25. Michael Lerner, *Jewish Renewal: A Path to Healing and Transformation* (New York: G. P. Putnam's Sons, 1994) 128.

26. Ibid., 224–64.

27. Ibid., 302–306.

28. Ibid., 1.

Salvation Comes to Israel Because of the Covenant

The identity of the people of Israel resides in their being chosen to be God's children, and because they were so chosen, it was necessary that they be given Torah. How could a father not give his *torah* to his own children? While Torah specifies what a child of God is expected to be and do, the failure to keep Torah does not break the covenant or result in God abandoning his people. How could a father abandon his own children? Some human fathers do abandon their children; for God, however, this is impossible. God is faithful (see, for example, Hos 11:1-4).

Yet God is not indifferent when his children ignore Torah and depart from his ways. As a responsible father, God chastises his people. They are chastised for major infractions such as the creation of the golden calf while Moses was on the mountain receiving the Torah (Exodus 32). When great calamities arrive, such as the destruction of the first Temple and the exile to Babylon (586 B.C.E.), the prophets account for this by saying that the Lord has withdrawn his protective presence from Israel because Israel has withdrawn itself from Torah.[29] With the destruction of the second Temple by the Romans in 70 C.E., the rabbis again felt constrained to interpret this as a repeat of the former destruction: The sins of Israel had brought on the tragedy (*b. Yoma* 9a).

Despite the sins of Israel, the Lord was committed to retaining them as his own (Deut 4:25-31; Heb 13:5). At times, however, the prophets themselves despaired. Jeremiah spoke for the Lord, saying, "I gave faithless Israel her certificate of divorce and sent her away because of all her adulteries" (3:8). The rabbis, in their turn, presented the prophet Hosea as even urging the Lord to abandon his people. The Lord, in this instance, defends his attachment to unfaithful Israel, using the prophet's own conduct as the teachable moment:

> Hosea said to the Holy One, blessed be he, "Your children have sinned." [If he had had his wits about him,] he should have said, "They are your children, children of those to whom you showed grace, children of Abraham, Isaac, and Jacob. [Accordingly] send your mercy to them."

---

29. It may appear foolish for the rabbis to discount social and political factors that led to the rise of the Babylonian empire. On the other hand, Jacob Neusner notes that "blaming one's own sins for what has happened carries a powerful message of hope: just as we did it to ourselves, so we can save ourselves" (*Messiah in Context: Israel's History and Destiny in Formative Judaism* [Philadelphia: Fortress Press, 1984] 185).

> It is not enough that he did not say the right thing, but he [also] said to him, "Lord of the world, the entire world is yours. Trade them in for some other nation."
>
> Said the Holy One, blessed be he, "What shall I then do with that elder [Hosea]? I shall tell him, 'Go, marry a whore and have children of prostitution.' [When he has done so] then I'll tell him, 'Divorce her.' If he can send her away, then I'll send away Israel."

The reader, of course, knows that the test involved depicts the very conduct of Hosea, for it was he who married a whore (Hos 1:1-11). Thus the story continues:

> After he [Hosea] had two sons and a daughter, the Holy One, blessed be he, said to Hosea, "Should you not have learned the lesson of your master Moses? Once I had entered into discourse with him, he separated from his wife [Exod 18:2]. So you too [ought to act likewise], take your leave of her."
>
> He [Hosea] said to him, "Lord of the world, I have children from her, and I simply cannot drive her out or divorce her."
>
> Said to him the Holy One, blessed be he, "Now if you—married to a whore with children of prostitution [such that] you don't even know whether they're yours or whether they come from some other fathers—are in such a state [of mind], then . . . how can you say to me, 'Trade them in for some other nation'?" (*b. Pesahim* 87a)

In the end the Lord himself dramatically refutes the advice of his own prophet. The rabbis even noted that the sarcastic name Hosea gave to his second son, "Not my people" (Hos 1:9), was later overturned, so that he was renamed as "Children-of-the-living-God" (*b. Pesahim* 87a).

Using imaginative teaching stories like these, the rabbis expressed their conviction that the Lord's mercy always overcomes his anger when it comes to his children. Thus one has in the following narrative a touching reflection on how God prays:

> Rabban Yohanan said in the name of Rabbi Yose, "How do we know that the Holy One, blessed be he, says prayers?"
>
> [Response] "Since it is said, 'Even them [the Gentiles] will I bring to my holy mountain and make them joyful in my house of prayer' (Isa 56:7). [Note that] 'their house of prayer' is not stated, but rather 'my house of prayer.' [Thus] on the basis of that usage we see that the Holy One, blessed be he, says prayers."
>
> "What prayers does he say?"

> [Response] Said Rabbi Zutra bar Tobiah [in the name of] Rab, "May it be my will that my mercy overcome my anger and that my mercy prevail over my attributes so that I may treat my children in accord with the trait of mercy and, in their regard, go beyond the strict measure of the law." (*b. Berakhot* 7a)

Accordingly, the rabbis put great stock in the notion that "his anger is but for a moment; his favor is for a lifetime" (Ps 30:5) (*b. Berakhot* 7a). Thus Jews find it incomprehensible when Christians speak of God as being unable (due to his anger) or unwilling (due to his justice) to forgive sins, from Adam onward, until Jesus willingly dies on the cross. I mention this here because the teachings of the rabbis so clearly come down in favor of God's mercy. The next chapter will treat this in detail.

In view of God's covenant and God's abundant mercy, pious Jews repeatedly pray that the Lord would come and gather the exiles and rebuild Jerusalem:

> Show yourself, Beloved, and cover me with the shelter of your
>   peace.
> Light up the world with your presence that we may exult and
> rejoice in you.
> Hurry, Loved One, the holy day [of our deliverance] has come:
>   show us grace as [you did] long ago.[30]

All good things have come to the people of Israel because God loved them. Even the bad things befalling the people were understood by the rabbis as due to the fact that God loved them enough to punish them for their failings. In the end, the day of deliverance will arrive when the Lord, the Beloved of Israel, will come and redeem them.

> In the future, when the time of redemption comes, the Holy One will say to Israel, "My children, I marvel that you were able to wait for me all those years." And Israel will reply, "Master of the Universe, but for your Torah you gave us, the nations of the earth would long since have caused us to feel that you were lost to us." (*Lam. R.* 3:21)

Christians share with Jews the expectation of God's coming to vanquish evil on the face of the earth, to raise the dead to life, to judge the whole world, and to gather the elect into his kingdom. The parables of waiting and expectation preached by Jesus are well known. The parables told by

---

30. *Gates of Prayer*, 159.

the rabbis regarding these same expectations are less well known. None-theless, what Christians need to recognize is that the future expectation preached by Jesus and Paul was part and parcel of Israel's expectation. Christians have added only footnotes to the heritage of Israel in this regard: (a) that the identity of the future Messiah is known to them and (b) that the Lord will gather not only the dispersed of Israel but also those Gentiles who, in the end-time, trust in the Lord. These things will be examined in chapter 5.

The Religious Quagmire After Auschwitz

The survivors of Auschwitz asked themselves what sense it makes to be chosen by God if "their Father" stood by inertly and ignored the prayers of hundreds of thousands of Jewish children beseeching him to save them and their beloved parents from the Nazi killing machine. Formerly, pious Jews imagined that bad things happen to good people if and only if they or their parents have committed some forgotten or unrecognized sin. Yet "there simply is no conceivable sin that could come close to justifying genocide."[31] Alternately, maybe God decided not to intervene in Auschwitz "because in the long run that would cripple us, perpetuate our childlike nature, make it impossible for us to develop the maturity and independence and autonomy that could allow us to be full partners with God in the healing and repairing of the world."[32] Yet even here there are problems:

> What kind of a parent, they ask, would allow their children to be murdered in front of their eyes? Perhaps a parent might endure watching some hurt befall a child—but if the parent saw the child being murdered, and *could* stop it, how could there be talk about allowing the child to develop its own maturity?[33]

Thus many Jews have become cynical about being chosen, being loved, being cared for by their Father in heaven. Others have become angry with the "God" whom they were trained to rely upon and to whom they en-trusted their children. So the conditions for finding the true God of Israel have become drastically different in this generation. A contemporary Jew struggling with the smoke of burning babies in his nostrils speaks:

31. Lerner, *Jewish Renewal*, 177.
32. Ibid., 178.
33. Ibid., 180.

I believe that anyone who wants to give God a chance needs to engage in a certain amount of "bitching" at the god [sic] they wish existed and who has let them down. Fully articulating one's bitterness and rage at this god, articulating the frustration and anger at those who think this god really does exist, is often an indispensable first step in the process of opening oneself to [an alternative experience of] God. And this is not accomplished once and for all.[34]

And after the rage burns through the tough barrier of "God's mysterious ways" and destroys all the outworn pious illusions, what then?

Another possibility remains for those of us who wish to testify to God's reality in the world: suggest that God cares very much, but simply lacks the power to intervene, or has constructed a world in which divine intervention is impossible. A God that has the wisdom to communicate truths about how we ought to live, truths which, if we lived by them, would make us able to accomplish a genuine *tikkun* ["repair"] of the world, would not be a useless God, though certainly less wish-fulfilling than a God who is our cosmic bellhop, doing our bidding if we behave right or if we offer the right sacrifices or right combination of prayers.[35]

Imagine yourself talking to a Jew who is choking on the stench of burning children in the camps. What might you say about God to such a person? Would it ring true, or would it sound hollow?

Some Jews believe that it is not permitted to question God's ways. But other Jews insist that they must question God's ways just as did their father Abraham (Gen 18:17-33). The rabbis, in response to God's impotence, related the following story:

Moses instituted the order of prayer for Israel when he said, "The great God, the mighty, the awesome" (Deut 10:17).

[A] Then came Jeremiah who said, "Heathen nations are battering at his temple hall—where are his awesome deeds [now]?" So he decided not to say, "The awesome God."

[B] Then came Daniel and said, "Heathen nations are enslaving his children—where are his mighty acts [now]?" So [in his order of prayer] Daniel decided not to say, "The mighty God."

[C] . . . But how dared flesh and blood [Jeremiah and Daniel] assert that God has limitations? "Because," so said Rabbi Isaac ben

34. Ibid., 412.
35. Ibid., 181.

Eleazar, "the prophets knew that their God demanded the truth, and they did not attempt to flatter him." (*b. Yoma* 69b)

It is not only that the Shoah creates a religious quagmire for Jews; Christians also have been touched by instances of senseless anguish and undeserved suffering. Why do two pious parents suffer through a seemingly endless series of miscarriages? Why does another mother give birth to a child severely deformed or one gripped by Down Syndrome? Why does a mother of five develop cancer of the breast and die a painful death? Why does a woman who has suffered under the hand of an abusive father find herself chained to an abusive husband? Why does a man who went to church every Sunday in his life suddenly begin losing every scrap of his memory and his dignity as his soul is gradually eaten away by Alzheimer's disease? Multiply all these instances a hundredfold and even a Christian might be ready to curse God or deny his existence entirely. Multiply them a thousandfold and one can glimpse how utterly abandoned by God and how utterly vulnerable most Jews feel when they remember the stench of the burning flesh in the camps.

Jacob Neusner once shocked a group of Christians in Cincinnati, Ohio, by telling them that Christian-Jewish dialogue has hardly begun. Talking about different religious celebrations and different notions of God has barely scratched the surface of polite conversation. "To know who I am, you have to know where I hurt," Neusner explained. Christians reading this book, therefore, have to be warned that most Jews living today carry the hidden pain of knowing that all the bleeding fists and tearful prayers of children in the camps did not move God to intervene. If you, the reader of this book, have not suffered at the hands of God, I would not advise you to even attempt to broach this issue with a Jew. If you have, you will know how to tread softly in an arena where one might not be welcome. In any case, it remains important for Christians to know that the quagmire of Auschwitz has profoundly shattered the warmth and safety afforded by the traditional Jewish experience of God.[36] Rabbi

36. For a revealing illustration of how Jews talk to Jews about the erosion of traditional beliefs within their communities see Rabbi Harold M. Schulweis, "Outreach To Jewish Secularists And Atheists, Yom Kippur 2004," *Valley Beth Shalom*, http://www.vbs .org/rabbi/hshulw/outreach.htm. According to the survey of Ephraim Yuchtman-Ya'ar ("Value Priorities in Israeli Society: An Examination of Inglehart's Theory of Modernization and Cultural Variation," in *Human Values and Social Change*, ed. Ronald Inglehart [Boston: Brill, 2003] 117–37), 54% of Israelis identify themselves as "secular." According to the survey of Arnold Dashefsky, et al., ("A Journey of the 'Straight Way' or the 'Roundabout Path:' Jewish Identity in the United States and Israel, " in Michele Dillon, ed., *Hand-*

Yannai is remembered, as far back as the second century, for having said, "We do not have in hand [an explanation] either for the prosperity of the wicked or for the suffering of the righteous" (*m. Abot* 4:15).

Whether Jews Are Superior to Everyone Else

From the standpoint of Jews, does the historical fact of their "chosenness" lead them to believe they are superior to everyone else on the face of the earth? To this question Michael Lerner provides a response with his usual frankness:

> Some Jews *do* think that they are better people than everyone else, which is only one of the many kinds of distortions that come from [suffering from] this [historic] oppression, as is the self-inflation that we sometimes use to resist the normal self-blaming that oppression engenders. But Jewish literature and Jewish humor are full of a deep awareness of how screwed up Jews can become. Chosenness doesn't mean being better.[37]

Needless to say, some Christians have also cultivated a notion of chosenness that, in their minds, gives them an unparalleled superiority in God's eyes. This distortion does not arise from suffering oppression; on the contrary, it has traditionally come from their attachment to the sufferings of one Jew, namely, Jesus. In former periods Christians have often enough pushed their chosenness even further by claiming that, since God wishes to punish the Jews for their crime in killing Jesus, Christians have been chosen as the scourge of God. Imagining that they had been "divinely chosen" for this task freed individuals from examining the bad faith driving their actions.

If Jews are not superior to all other peoples because of their divine chosenness, it does not follow that Jews are like everyone else. Far from it. Jews have been chosen by God to work with him for *tikkun haʾolam,* "healing/repairing the world."[38] Thus Jews are required, by virtue of

---

book of the Sociology of Religion [Cambridge and New York: Cambridge University Press, 2003] 240–61), 41% of Israelis identify themselves as "not religious." According to Peri Kedem ("Dimensions of Jewish Religiosity," in *Israeli Judaism,* ed. Shlomo Deshen, Charles Liebman, and Mishe Shokeid [London: Transaction Publishers, 1995] 33–62), 31% of Israelis do not believe in God, with an additional 6% choosing "don't know," for a total of 37% atheist or agnostic. (Source: Phil Zuckerman, "Atheism: Contemporary Rates and Patterns," http://www.pitzer.edu/academics/faculty/zuckerman/atheism.html.).

37. Lerner, *Jewish Renewal,* 294.
38. Ibid., 298.

their chosenness, to be different (not better). But to be truthful, many Jews, especially after the trauma of the Holocaust, want to blend in and not be or appear "different."[39]

> But if one has to testify to a God that does challenge a world of oppression, then one will surely feel a little conflicted about being "chosen" for this task. It may often seem as much of a curse as a blessing. . . . After the Holocaust, many Jews have challenged God to take back the chosenness. In their words and their actions they have said publicly: "We don't want it, we don't need it, we want out." Unfortunately there is no such possibility. A Jew who has gotten the message of Torah cannot *not* know the God who makes for the possibility of possibility.[40]

Thus, in a nutshell, being Jewish means standing up for God in today's world. This does not mean "preaching Judaism" or "making converts," as fundamentalist groups seem to think. Rather, it means being influenced by God to see the world as God does, to love the world as God does and, often enough, to stand with the oppressed against the oppressor. These, after all, are the words addressed to Moses from the burning bush:

> I have observed the misery of my people who are in Egypt; I have heard their cry. . . . Indeed, I know their sufferings, and I have come down to deliver them from the Egyptians, and to bring them up out of that land to a good and broad land, a land flowing with milk and honey. . . . So come, I will send you to Pharaoh to bring my people, the Israelites, out of Egypt. (Exod 3:7-8, 10)

Moses, it must be remembered, was being raised in the lap of luxury as "son of the Pharaoh." He knows, however, that he has been born a "son of Israel." Living within a conflicted self-identity, he learned by experience that his compassion for his people won out over his alliance with the Pharaoh. This happened on the day when he saw "an Egyptian beating a Hebrew, one of his kinsfolk" (Exod 2:11). He intervened and killed the Egyptian in the scuffle. When the event became known, Moses was forced to flee Egypt. Against this backdrop one can sense that Moses was well disposed to hear the message from the burning bush and that his sensibilities were already aligned with those of God. What Moses was not prepared for, however, was the necessity to confront Pharaoh and take action to mobilize the Israelites in preparation for their long

39. Ibid., 294–95.
40. Ibid., 295.

journey to freedom. From this narrative we can understand how Jews, in all times and places, are necessarily drawn into action once they align themselves with the Holy One who associates himself with the poor, the downtrodden, and the oppressed.

Jesus, from this perspective, was operating out of his Jewish instincts when he characterized his mission as directed toward accomplishing the words of Isaiah: "he has anointed me to bring good news to the poor. He has sent me to proclaim release to the captives and recovery of sight to the blind, to let the oppressed go free, to proclaim the year of the Lord's favor" (Isa 61:1-2 as cited in Luke 4:18-19). Thus, while Jews and Christians embrace variant and sometimes contradictory notions of their mission,[41] both are agreed that God has called them to accomplish God's work within the modern world. Often enough this mission is defined by the same texts, as we will see in what follows.

Conclusion

When one begins to find reasons to respect and admire Jews, a problem arises. In the Preface I told the story of how I, as an impressionable Catholic boy, was entirely disoriented when I was employed by a Jewish merchant. I explained how the justice and kindness of Mr. Martin served to soften my distrust and replace it with gratitude and admiration. At no point, though, did I have the good sense to transfer any of my gratitude and admiration for Mr. Martin to his Judaism. I already thought I knew about Judaism from my religious instruction classes. What I had learned was a caricature of Judaism. Even if the Christian Scriptures do represent the failings of many Jews in the first century, it never occurred to me that the Judaism of Mr. Martin had evolved for two thousand years and that, in that vast period of time, Judaism and the Jews had changed. What I have written in this chapter, therefore, is an antidote to some of the misinformation I had received.

Perhaps, you, the reader, have been unsettled by what I have written. I myself was unsettled when I discovered how much misinformation I had received as part of my upbringing. Know, then, that your anger and disappointment are not misplaced. If you wish, share them with other readers of this book at www.salvationisfromthejews.info. In the end, be assured that you have been about the work of doing what the bishops'

41. The Catholic-Jewish document, "Reflections on Covenant and Mission," will be examined in chapter 7.

guidelines of 1974 admonished you to do: "Christians must therefore strive to acquire a better knowledge of the basic components of the religious tradition of Judaism; they must strive to learn by what essential traits the Jews define themselves in the light of their own religious experience" (*Guidelines on Religious Relations with Jews*, Introduction).

Postscript: An Exercise in Rewriting

At the beginning of this chapter the reader encountered four representations of Judaism frequently found in Catholic textbooks and sermons. Each of these themes was fashioned by the perverse tendency of Christians to discredit Judaism by exalting Christianity. At the end of this chapter it should be possible for you to reformulate those statements in such a way that we can cherish who we are without engaging in misrepresentations of Judaism. The reader might want to take a piece of paper and endeavor to do this now.[42]

42. If you would like to share your reformulations or see what others have produced, go to www.salvationisfromthejews.info. Meanwhile, I offer sample reformulations of the first three. For the fourth, see chapter 5. These responses are not meant to be definitive; they are the firstfruits of someone seeking to redefine his faith and understanding in harmony with the "common spiritual heritage" and the "mutual understanding and appreciation" (*Nostra Aetate* 4) urged upon us by the bishops of Vatican II:

> 1. Both Jesus and the Pharisees adhered to Moses and the prophets. Accordingly, they knowingly spoke of the justice and judgment of God as a blueprint and a promise for God's reign here on earth. More often than not they both stressed the mercy, grace, and love of God.
> 2. Jesus presented God as a loving Father mightily caring for his children. This does not come as a surprise since he adhered to a tradition in which such notions and experiences were commonplace. The Pharisees of Jesus' day as well as their successors, the rabbis, were fond of emphasizing kindred notions of God.
> 3. Religious legalism has characterized segments of both the Christian and Jewish communities from time to time. Such legalism has serious consequences because it is born within a distortion of God and breathes through a misrepresentation of the very sources, whether Christian or rabbinic, that were designed to respect the dignity, the freedom, and the intelligence of adherents.

Appendix:
The Diverse Communities of Judaism in Modern Times

Since the Torah is the central and common heritage that defines Jewish identity, it was natural that communities of Jews would have different points of view when it came to interpreting and updating Torah. Furthermore, once ghettos and second-class citizenship were removed for European Jews in the early nineteenth century, Jews found themselves involved with the civic and secular life of the nations in which they resided. In due course three different strategies were developed to maintain faithfulness to God, on the one hand, and to address modernity on the other. These three strategies gave rise to the three principal Judaisms of modern times: Reform, Orthodox, and Conservative.

Reform Judaism came to expression in the early part of the nineteenth century. Reform Judaism recognized the legitimacy of making changes and regarded change as reform, thereby yielding "Reform" Judaism. The Reformers rejected important components of the Judaism of the Torah as interpreted by the rabbinic sages, and said so. The Reformers, for example, left it to the discretion of each Jew to decide whether God wanted them to retain the regulations regarding the selection and preparation of kosher foods. The Reformers also made room for the inclusion of modern-language prayers in their liturgy, since many Jews no longer had a facility in understanding Hebrew. In 2000, thirty-nine percent of American Jews identified themselves as Reform.

The first reactionary movement to Reform Judaism, called Orthodox Judaism, claimed continuity with the Judaism of the Torah as interpreted by the rabbinic sages. Orthodox Judaism reached its first systematic expression in the middle of the nineteenth century. It addressed the same issue, that of change, and held that Judaism lies beyond history; it is the work of God; it constitutes a fixed set of facts of the same order as the facts of nature. Thus traditional Hebrew prayers were to be retained and the traditional dietary rules were to be observed. Jews could live by the laws of the Torah and, within the limits imposed by those laws, could also participate as citizens in the politics and culture of their native countries. Orthodox Jews were expected not to drive their cars on the Sabbath because, for them, the modern automobile replaced the horse-driven carriage that traditionally "rested" on the Sabbath. Orthodox Jews are thus required to find homes near their synagogues. Similarly, in Orthodox synagogues separate sections are assigned to men and women (a tradition that, it should be noted, also prevailed in Christian assemblies until the nineteenth century). Orthodox Jews, moreover, are adamantly opposed to allowing their children to marry non-Jews and refuse to ordain women as rabbis. For them, the way of Torah does not permit such concessions to modernity. In 1990 only six percent of American Jews identified themselves as Orthodox—a decline of five percent from the eleven percent who so identified themselves in 1970. In 2000, however, twenty-one percent identified themselves as Orthodox.

The second response to Reform Judaism was Historical Judaism, known in America as Conservative Judaism. This Judaism occupied a center position between the two other Judaisms and maintained that legitimate change must be separated from illegitimate change. Contrary to Reform Judaism, Conservative Judaism refused to allow individual Jews to judge for themselves what elements of Torah applied today. Conservative Judaism formulated principles governing legitimate change through historical study. The formation of the Rabbinical Assembly guided by scholarly *Responsa* has ensured that an evolving and shared understanding of Torah guides the life of each community. In 2000, thirty-three percent of American Jews identified themselves as Conservative.

These Judaisms are alike in affirming the received oral Torah as interpreted through the ages. They are different in what they regard as enduring and in what they see as culturally conditioned and passing. While each is faithful to God and to the ancient rabbis, each expresses that fidelity according to different norms.

Three

The Story of Salvation:
The Return to Humility and Truth

> It ain't what you don't know that gets you into trouble.
> It's what you know for sure that just ain't so.
>
> —Mark Twain

When I was a young child, the story of salvation given to me by the Ursuline nuns at Holy Cross Grade School in Euclid, Ohio, was something so simple, so compelling, and so wonderful. Adam sinned and we inherited the consequences: God's grace dried up and the gates of heaven were sealed shut. For thousands of years people were dying, but no one was able to get into heaven. Everyone was waiting for God to send a redeemer. Then Jesus finally arrived and died for our sins on the cross. And, as my *Baltimore Catechism* so clearly demonstrated, at the moment when Jesus died on the cross, there, way up in the clouds, the gates of heaven were again opened. Finally the souls of all the good people who had died could enter into heaven and be with God for all eternity.

I was a graduate student in theology before I first discovered that Jews did not have the vaguest notion that the gates of heaven had been sealed shut because of the sin of Adam.[1] Jesus, needless to say, appears never to have made any reference to the gates of heaven or to original sin, nor is this doctrine found in any of the apostolic preaching. Paul's notion of death coming into the world through the first man (Rom 5:12) may be an initial step toward a doctrine of original sin, but it was never used by

---

1. See "Do Jews believe in the doctrine of original sin? http://www.jewsforjudaism.org/web/faq/faq123.html.

Paul to explain how the gates of heaven were closed and how forgiveness of sins was impossible during the entire period of Jewish history before Jesus.[2]

Salvation History that Overlooks God's History with Israel

Leaving these difficulties aside for the moment, an even greater defect appears from the vantage point of Jewish-Catholic dialogue. The drama of salvation incorporated in the *Baltimore Catechism* is entirely devoid of any reference to Jews and Judaism. Seemingly, eighteen hundred years of God's interactions with the sons and daughters of Abraham and Sarah amounted to nothing as far as salvation was concerned. This amounts to a form of destructive silence: saying nothing is tantamount to obliterating the significance of Israel in God's plan of salvation.

This destructive silence also has its modern counterparts. I offer two examples:

1. Rolf Rendtorff draws attention to Christian commentaries that treat the Hebrew Scriptures without taking note that they did belong and continue to belong to Israel:

> In the recent theologies of the Old Testament by Zimmerli (1972) and Westermann (1978), the heading "Judaism" is missing altogether in the index. For both these authors—and they are without any doubt representative of the trends that dominate Old Testament scholarship today—the Old Testament leads on to the New, but Judaism is not mentioned in the process.[3]

2. A website devoted to "Catholic Apologetics" recently posted a letter from Nina that politely objects to an oversight, namely that the history of the church presented on this website makes no reference to Judaism. John Salza, the owner of the website, defends his position even to the point of objecting to Nina's suggestion that Jesus fulfilled Judaism: "Judaism has been abolished, not fulfilled. The New Covenant has completely superseded the Old Covenant. The only thing that Christ has

---

2. Herbert Haag, *Is Original Sin in Scripture?* (New York: Sheed and Ward, 1969). By way of conclusion Haag notes that "the doctrine of original sin is not found in any of the writings of the Old Testament" and "certainly not in chapter one to three of Genesis" (p. 19). For an examination of the difficulties encountered by the classical doctrine of original sin see Roger Haight,"Sin and Grace," chapter 7 in *Systematic Theology: Roman Catholic Perspectives*, vol. 2, eds. Francis Schüssler Fiorenza and John Galvin (Minneapolis: Fortress Press, 1991).

3. Rolf Rendtorff, cited in Peter von der Osten-Sacken, *Christian-Jewish Dialogue* (Philadelphia: Fortress Press, 1986) 153–54.

brought to fulfillment is the fullness of His grace through the sacramental life of the Catholic Church. The Catholic Church has replaced the whole system of Jewry, with all of its legal, moral and ceremonial edicts."[4]

Contrary to this destructive silence and misrepresentation of Judaism, the Christian Scriptures situate the drama of salvation in relationship to Israel. This will be spelled out in detail later in this chapter. For the moment, however, let it suffice to note that the term "Israel"[5] appears in positive contexts no less than seventy times in the Christian Scriptures. Nor should it go unnoticed that when Paul begins to argue for the inclusion of Gentiles in the drama of salvation he does not fall back on any saying of Jesus but rather goes deep into the story of Abraham in order to argue that God, from the very beginning, had planned "to make him [Abraham] the ancestor of all who believe without being circumcised . . . and likewise the ancestor of the circumcised" (Rom 4:11-12). Paul, consequently, interprets his outreach to Gentiles as rooted within the origins of Israel. When the totality of Paul's writings is examined, it appears that "Paul does not talk about a 'new, true Israel' and would never have applied the name of Israel at all to a purely Gentile Christian church."[6] Nor should it go unnoticed that the bishops of Vatican II taught that "the church cannot forget that she received the revelation of the Old Testament by way of that people with whom God in his inexpressible mercy established the ancient covenant" (*Nostra Aetate* 3).

The early Church Fathers regarded the revelations of the Hebrew Scriptures and the revelations of the Son of God as made of the same cloth. Justin Martyr puts the matter succinctly: "Formerly he [the *Logos*]

---

4. John Salza, "MISCELLANEOUS—Q&A," http://www.scripturecatholic.com/misc_qa.html#oldcov. John Salza presents himself as defending the tradition of the current Catholic Church. In reality, however, the author is defending a position relative to Judaism that entirely denies the right of Judaism to exist after the establishment of the church. I myself am no stranger to this position. It follows quite naturally from the theology of the Catholic Church prior to Vatican II, but it has been repudiated by the Council and subsequent church teaching.

5. The term "Israel" never refers to the state of Israel (see Preface) or the land of Israel, but always to the people spiritually bound to the patriarchs and matriarchs, beginning with Abraham and Sarah. I say "spiritually bound" because it is evident that, in Israel's long history, many outsiders (Gentiles or *goyim*) have become insiders without any genetic roots. The classical case is that of Ruth who, even after the death of her husband, attaches herself to Naomi, saying, "Your people shall be my people, and your God my God" (Ruth 1:16). Ruth, in due course, becomes the great-grandmother of David. Even today, when outsiders embrace Judaism, water immersion (baptism in a *mikva*) is understood as a death (to their old life) and a rebirth (as a son or daughter of Abraham and Sarah).

6. Peter von der Osten-Sacken, *Christian-Jewish Dialogue*, 147.

appeared in the form of fire and the image of a bodiless being to Moses and the other prophets. But now . . . he was, as I have said, made man of a virgin" (*1 Apol.* 63.16). The history of salvation, consequently, spans the whole of human history. The drama begins with the *Logos* creating the world, then walking in the Garden with our first parents, then addressing the enmity between Cain and Abel, and so forth. Thus even before Abraham, Isaac, and Jacob enter the picture, the *oikonomia* ("household plan" or "economy") of our salvation was unrolling according to the divine plan. In this vision of things "the Incarnation represents only the high point of a permanent *oikonomia*."[7]

Irenaeus (130–200 C.E.), the bishop of Lyons, took the position of Justin and extended it by explaining that the work of salvation was a weighty endeavor that had to overcome difficulties on the part of humans and also difficulties on the part of the *Logos*. Humans had to progressively learn the ways of God and gradually conform their lives to them. The divine *Logos* had to familiarize himself with the ways of humans. Thus the progressive ascent of humankind has to be met with a progressive descent of the eternal *Logos*. In both instances the ascent and descent pass through the whole history of Israel.[8]

Irenaeus, consequently, had no difficulty understanding the synagogue as the mother of the church. In the synagogue the Torah "carried out the education of the soul" (*Adv. haer.* 4.13.2) in preparation for the freedom that would be revealed by Christ. Once it was revealed, however, Israel did not disappear. In fact, Irenaeus noted that "both slaves [Jews] and children [Christians] have a like devotion and obedience toward the head of the family; but the children have a greater boldness" (*Adv. haer.* 4.13.2).

For Irenaeus, consequently, the drama of salvation could not be told without telling the story of Israel. The divine *Logos* could not appear in human history without a progressive descent into the human condition. Judaism, in its turn, progressively pioneered the education of the soul in response to the *Logos* so that a people were ready to hear and to receive the advanced stage in spiritual evolution revealed by Jesus Christ. Just as it is arrogant and dangerous today for humans to ignore their dependence on their biological ancestors, in like fashion it is arrogant and dangerous for Christians to ignore their dependence on their spiritual ancestors.

---

7. Jean Danielou, *Gospel Message and Hellenistic Culture* (Philadelphia: Westminster, 1973) 161.

8. For details of the descent and ascent in Irenaeus see ibid., 168–82.

For over fifteen hundred years Catholics were forbidden to enter a synagogue and, with even greater force, were forbidden to pray with Jews. In 1986, John Paul II broke a longstanding barrier when he visited the principal synagogue in Rome. It was on this occasion that he spoke of the "common spiritual patrimony that exists between Jews and Christians" (a theme already present in *Nostra Aetate*) and then confirmed, for those Jews present, that "you are our dearly beloved brothers, and in a certain way, it could be said that you are our elder brothers."[9]

Thesis One: *The Christian churches, misled by their triumphalism, have imagined that salvation history begins with the fall in the Garden and then jumps immediately to the birth of Jesus Christ. This is the heresy of the Gentiles whereby the importance of Jews and Judaism in God's plan of salvation has been either systematically distorted or passed over in silence. Fidelity to Jesus and to the early church requires that Christians return to their roots (a) by embracing Abraham and Sarah as our spiritual ancestors and (b) by acknowledging the salvation history of Israel as the* sine qua non *for the descent of the* Logos *into humanity and our ascent to the holiness of the children of God.*

Exploring Universal Claims Relative to Jesus' Death

While the Catholic Church has not officially endorsed any specific soteriology,[10] the most popular by far is the theology whereby God forgives

---

9. *New York Times*, April 14, 1986, Section 1. Michael S. Kogan rightly noted that "the pope's statement recognized both that the validity of Christianity rests upon the prior validity of Judaism and that the two faiths remain siblings today in a unique relationship that clearly must involve the mutual recognition of the continuing validity of each" (*JTS* 26 [1989] 704).

10. Soteriology seeks to make sense of how God offers salvation to his/her people. Jesus and his immediate disciples anticipated the coming of God from heaven to gather the Jewish exiles and to establish his kingdom on earth. The Church Fathers preferred to think that the divine *Logos* had become human in order to establish that humans could, by successive stages, attain to that divinization to which they were destined by God. During the medieval period Christians were preoccupied with sin: Adam failed God in the Garden and accordingly all his children were conceived in sin and destined for eternal damnation. Jesus, the Son of God, however, became human so that a human could make complete satisfaction by his death on the cross for all the sins of the world. Whether God is envisioned as bringing the kingdom or as restoring human access to divinization or as providing satisfaction for sins makes a big difference in how God is understood and how Jesus relates to God and to our salvation. Interested readers might consult Karen Armstrong, *A History of God* (New York: Ballantine Books, 1993).

all sins due to the merits of Christ's Passion on the cross. During my eight years at Holy Cross Grade School in Euclid, Ohio, I recall vividly how we knelt on the wooden floor next to our benches every morning and faced the large crucifix above the blackboard as we recited our morning prayers. On Fridays in Lent we were herded into the church and confronted with an even more vivid reminder of the drama of our salvation. The Stations of the Cross consisted of fourteen graphically depicted sufferings of Jesus, which covered the sidewalls of Holy Cross Church. At the beginning of each station Fr. McMonigle, vested in his somber black cope, called out in a loud voice, "We adore thee, O Christ, and we bless thee." All of us children then dropped to our knees and answered in a deafening chorus, "Because by thy holy cross thou hast redeemed the world!"

The Church Fathers had no uniform way of accounting for the efficacy of Jesus' death. Athanasius (d. 363), for example, depicted Jesus as entering into a wrestling match with the devil. At the end of the match Jesus was done in by the devil, but, given the ferociousness of the match, the devil was considerably weakened and exhausted—thereby allowing the disciples of Jesus to overcome him (*De Incarnatione* 8, 24, 27). Augustine (d. 430) depicted the devil as tempting Jesus, becoming frustrated, and savagely killing his body because he could not touch his soul. Yet this was a divine plot to lure the devil into overstepping his proper rights by killing the innocent. God, consequently, was then free to legally penalize the devil by taking from him those persons whom he had claimed as his own (*On Free Will* 3.10.31).

Anselm of Canterbury (d. 1109) formulated a soteriology based on the claim that all sins in every time and in every place were forgiven *exclusively* through the passion and death of Jesus. Anselm was a pastor doing pastoral theology. In his day Anselm was disturbed by the prevailing notion that the devil had a central role in the drama of salvation, and he set out to use the medieval notions of honor and fealty to reconstruct the drama of salvation. In this drama the devil was no longer the chief antagonist, but it was the offended honor of God the Father that had to be appeased. Anselm's theological speculation and intellectual persuasiveness, key traits of the nascent scholastic method, proved so compelling that his account of the efficacy of the cross held the field.[11]

---

11. In both Catholic and Protestant circles today some form of substitutionary atonement is generally accepted as the principal mode for accounting for the importance of Jesus as redeemer. Only in the Eastern Orthodox Churches does one find a primacy

Thomas Aquinas, working more than a century later, spoke of the merits and the efficacy associated with the incarnation and the preaching of Jesus, yet when it came to considering the Passion he slipped entirely into the path of penal substitution that Anselm had trod before him. Thus, according to Aquinas, "If he [God] had willed to free man from sin without any satisfaction, he would have acted against justice" (*S.T.* III 46, 6, ad 3). While the Middle Ages had invented gruesome forms of prolonged torture, Aquinas had no difficulty in affirming that "Christ's passion was the greatest pain ever suffered" (*S.T.* III 46, 6). In the end, therefore, "Christ's passion was not only sufficient but superabundant atonement for the sins of the human race" (*S.T.* III 48, 2).

While the late Middle Ages saw the creation of numerous dogmatic syntheses, the *Summa Theologica* of Thomas Aquinas gradually came to be preferred in most circles. The *Roman Catechism* produced in 1568 following the Council of Trent was thus massively dependent on Aquinas. The *Baltimore Catechism* produced in the United States in 1858, in its turn, presented the penal atonement theory of Anselm as the sole explanatory matrix for delineating Jesus' identity and purpose. Protestant catechisms invariably assimilated variations of this and, accordingly, have also focused their attention on Jesus' death for our sins.

Expansions in the Number of those Rescued from Hades

At first the efficacy of Jesus' preaching and healing mission was limited to those living persons who had encountered him or his first disciples and responded to "the Good News of God." With time, the death of Jesus was seen to have some benefit for everyone then living: "He [Jesus Christ] is the atoning sacrifice for our sins, and not for ours only but also for the sins of the whole world" (1 John 2:2). By the opening of the second century some sectors of Christianity went even further and explored ways to extend the benefits of Jesus to those who had already died. In these scenarios Jesus' death afforded the occasion for him to be able to offer his message to those who had died and were abiding in Hades awaiting the general resurrection of the dead on the last day. Hades was the mythical abode of the dead—a borrowing from Hellenistic culture—and should be understood as quite distinct from what the medievalists identified as "hell." The original intent of "he was not abandoned to Hades" in a

---

given to the incarnational theologies of the Church Fathers and the continued insistence that "Christ became human in order that humans may become divine."

sermon in Acts (2:31) was to reinforce the reality of the death of Jesus before his resurrection. In 1 Peter, however, one finds the phrase "Christ also suffered for sins" (3:18) being used in connection with the explanation that "he was put to death in the flesh . . . and made a proclamation to the spirits in prison" (3:18-19). Those to whom he preached, however, are expressly limited to those who "did not obey, when God waited patiently in the days of Noah, during the building of the ark" (3:20). The suffering and death of Jesus thus afforded him a few days in Hades wherein he "made a proclamation" to those who drowned at the time of Noah's flood. The implied meaning here appears to be that those who died in the flood without the benefit of a prophet's warning were now permitted to benefit from the Jewish prophet Jesus.

In the mid-first century Justin Martyr again makes reference of Jesus' mission to those who had died. In this case, however, it is not the sinners of Noah's generation who are recipients of the Good News, but the Jews who had died: "The Lord God remembered his dead people of Israel who lay in their graves, and he descended to preach to them his salvation" (*Dial.* 72.4). In the early second century Clement of Alexandria further extended the mission to the dead. In his way of thinking Jesus preached his Good News to the righteous Jews in Hades (as just noted), and the apostles, following their deaths, preached to the philosophers who had lived righteous lives (*Strom.* VI, 6.45, 5). Thus 1 Peter, Justin Martyr, and Clement of Alexandria form something like stepping-stones whereby the efficacy of Jesus' preaching in Hades was gradually understood to have reached backward in time to liberate those imprisoned there. At each step the outreach is extended.

The third-century *Gospel of Bartholomew* dramatizes Jesus' foray into Hades. This gospel portrays the King of Glory as menacingly descending a thousand steps into the underworld. Hades, the god of the underworld, trembles as he descends. Having arrived, Jesus "shattered the iron bars," pummeled Hades "with a hundred blows and bound him with fetters that cannot be loosed" (19). Here one has a commando rescue operation designed to save "Adam and all the patriarchs" (9). Jesus specifically says to Adam: "I was hung upon the cross for your sake and for the sake of your children" (22). Jesus' death is here understood not as penal substitution but as the necessary means for gaining access to the underworld so that he might destroy the power of Hades and release those imprisoned by demonic powers. Hades is the pagan god guarding the underworld. By destroying Hades, Jesus is able to release not only the generation of Noah but also all generations going all the way back to

Adam himself. The intent of this narrative appears to be that those who died were not to be forever disadvantaged because they did not have a chance to hear Jesus' preaching. Furthermore, the narrative shows that Hades has been defeated and those who have died need no longer live in despair (since the bars of their imprisonment have been destroyed). This does not mean, of course, that everyone at the final judgment will be admitted into Paradise since, even on earth, only a small number of the living who heard the message of Jesus reformed their lives and anticipated the coming kingdom of God. The *Gospel of Bartholomew* marks a high point insofar as the scope of Jesus' message has been extended backward all the way to Adam. This would seemingly imply that those who do not hear the Good News during their lifetimes have the opportunity to hear it in the afterlife. It was with this intent that "he descended into Hades" was added to the Apostles' Creed during the fourth century.[12] The outreach of Jesus' preaching of the Good News was thus extended all the way back in time to the first humans.

What is plain to observe is that the *Gospel of Bartholomew* firmly centers the efficacy of Jesus in his preaching mission—"that I might come down on earth to heal the sin of the ignorant and give to men the truth of God" (65). Jesus' death serves only for giving him access to those who had died and liberating those imprisoned by Hades. Second, *Bartholomew* knows nothing of inherited sin or of the gates of Paradise being forever closed. As the Church Fathers indicated, it was the gates of Hades that needed to be broken down in order for God's plan of liberation to be fulfilled. Jesus, in this scenario, is not the atoning victim on the cross but the one who mounts a commando raid to smash the gates of Death. Finally, what is evident, however, is that the fall of the angels is now part of the backdrop for understanding how those angels who refused to worship Adam (the critical test, 51-58) as the Lord commanded would, as a result of their expulsion from heaven to earth, become the sworn enemies of Adam and his race. The stage is thus being set to perceive the temptation in the Garden as being the choice of serving God or serving Satan.

---

12. The Apostles' Creed represents the church's second-century summary statement of belief. Rufinus, in *The Exposition of the Creed* (ca. 400 c.e.), makes note of the fact that "descended into Hades" did not exist in the Roman version of the Creed. Hence this phrase must have been added to the Apostles' Creed sometime in the fourth century. This would place it in the same era as the *Gospel of Bartholomew*.

The Medieval Synthesis of Thomas Aquinas

Thomas Aquinas (d. 1274), along with other medieval theologians, attempted to consolidate and harmonize the diverse traditions of the first five centuries. According to Aquinas, Jesus descends into the underworld not to break the bonds of those imprisoned there, but to gather the elect and lead them to the gates of heaven that have been opened by his atoning death on the cross. The underworld, at this point, is still being understood as the abode of all the dead, both righteous and sinners. Now, however, fiery torments are introduced. The souls of those who are damned are already in torment. The souls of those destined to be saved by Jesus experience only a temporal punishment calculated to purify them from their former sins. Fire for them is purgatorial and, in due course, later centuries will make a clear distinction in place between those in purgatory and those in hell. This need not concern us here. For our purposes we need only to note that Jesus' descent into Hades/hell has come full circle. Jesus comes not just to preach to the generation of the flood as in 1 Peter. Nor does Jesus mount a commando raid to break down the gates of Hades. Rather, Jesus' death opens the gates of heaven, and his descent into hell is specifically to take those who have lived righteously and carry them up, with him, into heaven. In Acts, Jesus ascends alone into heaven and waits, at the right hand of God, for the time of his return. In Aquinas all the righteous, from Adam onward, are carried by the resurrected Jesus into heaven where they can enjoy the Beatific Vision. When Jesus returns at the end-time all these saints will come to earth with him, their bodies will be resurrected from the grave, and both the living and the dead will be judged at the final judgment. Then the righteous will enter into eternal joy and the unrighteous into eternal torment.

According to the medieval tradition the mythical "gates of heaven" were permanently closed following the sin of Adam (*S.T.* II-II 164, 2). This reinforces Anselm's logic pertaining to the universality of sin (both original and actual) and the utter inability of anyone to atone for his or her own sins. But then salvation arrives: "The gate of heaven's kingdom is thrown open to us through Christ's passion" (*S.T.* III 49, 5). Here again Aquinas notes that not even the Jewish patriarchs who were sinless were able to enter heaven: "The holy fathers were detained in hell for the reason that, owing to our first parent's sin, the approach to the life of glory was not open" (*S.T.* III 52, 5).

Aquinas not only presents Jesus as descending into hell to rescue the righteous; he also has Jesus achieving on the cross those infinite merits that are required for the universal atonement of all sins, from Adam's first sin to the last sin on earth at the end of time.[13] Even relative to the Jews, Aquinas says: "The holy fathers [of Israel], by doing works of justice, merited to enter the heavenly kingdom through faith in Christ's passion . . ." (*S.T.* III 49, 5, ad 1). The deliverance of the Jewish patriarchs, consequently, was not due to their assimilation of the faith of Abraham or their lifelong fidelity to God; rather, it is "through faith and charity [that they] were united to Christ's passion" (*S.T.* III 52, 7). Jesus' death, consequently, provides a store of merits that reach backward in time and serve to justify the Jewish saints. No one can gain entrance into heaven without faith in Christ's Passion—Jews included.

Whether Jews Know Forgiveness Apart From Jesus

Such a scheme of things reinforces the utter bankruptcy of Judaism. Without saying it in so many words, the synthesis of Thomas Aquinas takes the entire tradition of the Hebrew Scriptures regarding the readiness of God to forgive and turns it on its head. Consider, for example, Psalm 32:

> Happy are those whose transgression is forgiven,
>> whose sin is covered.
> Happy are those to whom the LORD imputes no iniquity,
>> and in whose spirit there is no deceit.
> While I kept silence, my body wasted away
>> through my groaning all day long.
> For day and night your hand was heavy upon me;
>> my strength was dried up as by the heat of summer.
> Then I acknowledged my sin to you,
>> and I did not hide my iniquity;
> I said, "I will confess my transgressions to the LORD,"
>> and you forgave the guilt of my sin. (Ps 32:1-5)

---

13. The *Roman Catechism* endorsed the Thomistic perspective, saying: "Christ the Lord descended into hell that, having seized the spoils of the devils, he might conduct into heaven those holy fathers and other pious souls liberated from prison" (1.6.q.6). The *Catechism of the Catholic Church* repeats the message of Trent, emphasizing the fact that "the Gospel was preached even to the dead" (sec. 632 & 634, following 1 Pet 4:6). This event is interpreted in universal and eschatological terms: "This is the last phase of Jesus' messianic mission, a phase which is condensed in time but vast in its real significance: the spread of Christ's redemptive work to all men [and women] of all times and places . . ." (sec. 634). The implication here appears to be that when Christ returns on the Last Day and releases the dead from the prison of death in order to hear the Good News, this will be the final realization of the universal mission of Christ implied in the earlier "condensed in time" descent into hell following his death on the cross.

What one discovers here is the assurance of forgiveness for those who turn back to the Lord and acknowledge their sin. Quite independent of any question of the efficacy of sacrificial rites or acts of atonement (by oneself or by another), Israel has always believed that the act of *teshuvah* ("turning back") insures God's forgiveness.[14] The classical Christian tradition, however, would say the psalmist was sorely mistaken.[15]

In the Hebrew Scriptures one finds hundreds of instances of forgiveness of sin. In the case of David one remembers how the prophet Nathan confronted the king with the parable that served to expose his treachery in having Uriah killed in battle so that David could lay claim to his wife (2 Sam 12:2-4). David responds quickly and unambiguously: "I have sinned against the Lord" (2 Sam 12:13). Once David has confessed his guilt, the prophet offers God's consolation: "Now the Lord has put away your sin . . ." (2 Sam 2:13b). The classical Christian tradition, however, would say that the prophet Nathan was misled by a deceiving spirit, for no sin was forgiven for any Jew, David included, prior to or independent of the death of Jesus. Alternately, a Christian might want to say that David was truly forgiven, but only insofar as God anticipated the atoning death of Jesus, which came a thousand years later. Either way, the message is clear—the Hebrew Scriptures are false and need to be reinterpreted by the atoning death of Jesus.

Whether the Gospels Speak of Forgiveness Apart from Jesus

In the gospels one also finds a challenge to the theology of the atoning death. When they speak of John "proclaiming a baptism of repentance for the forgiveness of sins" (Luke 3:3 par.), this accords well with the prevailing Jewish tradition of forgiveness following repentance. Yet no

14. E. P. Sanders, after making an extensive study of this topic, summarizes by noting that "the universal view [of the rabbis] is that *every individual Israelite* who indicates his [or her] intention to remain in the covenant by repenting, observing the Day of Atonement and the like, will be *forgiven* for all his transgressions" (*Paul and Palestinian Judaism* [Philadelphia: Fortress Press, 1977] 182).

15. Within Judaism sins were understood as freely forgiven by God. According to Anselm's *Cur Deus Homo*, God was not free to forgive sins unless some suitable satisfaction was made for the loss of honor inflicted on the deity. While the early Church Fathers would have understood sorrow and penance as serving to effect satisfaction, Anselm argued that such deeds done by humans were already expected by God and were thus incapable of restoring the lost honor. In an absolute sense, therefore, Anselm argued that no sin (along with the satisfaction due to sin) could be forgiven without appealing to and transferring the merits of Christ's death on the cross.

mention of Jesus' death is made in this place. Later, even Jesus said to the man who was a paralytic, "Friend, your sins are forgiven you" (5:20). In this instance, if Jesus had studied the *Baltimore Catechism* he should have said, "Friend, your sins will be forgiven once the Son of Man is lifted up on the cross."

As for Jesus' parables of the kingdom, none of them makes any mention of the fall of Adam in the Garden and the impossibility of attaining forgiveness of sins before Jesus' death. In fact, none of them focuses on the Passion of Jesus as opening the gates of heaven. The parable of the Prodigal Son goes to the extreme of having the son who squandered half his father's resources with loose women return home to find his father running to him and pardoning him even before he gets a chance to confess his failings. According to the terms of this parable, the son feels that his sins are unpardonable, and he can only expect, at best, to get a job: "Father, I have sinned against heaven and before you; I am no longer worthy to be called your son; treat me like one of your hired hands" (Luke 15:18-19). Jesus' parable, however, demonstrates that the love of our Father in heaven exceeds the weight of our sense of being beyond forgiveness. In its essence Jesus' parable dramatizes the Jewish notion that God is and has always been ready to forgive his children. Parables from the rabbis capture the same lesson.[16] When all is said and done, therefore, the classical Christian tradition would have to say that even Jesus was sorely mistaken when it came to the issue of forgiveness of Jewish sins.

E. P. Sanders, more than any other scholar, has taken a hard look at the host of distortions that crowd into Christian literature. Some Christians have tried to reconcile the problems within the classical tradition by emphasizing that God is always ready to forgive but that atonement—understood as satisfaction of the penal suffering due to every sin—can never be made without the merits of Christ. Within the rabbinic tradition one finds various opportunities for atonement: (a) "repentance effects atonement," (b) "the Day of Atonement effects atonement," (c) "death effects atonement," (d) "almsgiving effects atonement," and (d) "chastisements (in this life or in Gehenna) effect atonement."[17] In none

---

16. There have been many fine studies of how the rabbis taught in parables in much the same way as did Jesus. Especially noteworthy are the following: Harvey K. McArthur, et al., *They Also Taught in Parables* (Grand Rapids: Zondervan, 1990); Clemens Thoma, et al., eds., *Parable and Story in Judaism and Christianity* (New York: Paulist Press, 1989); Brad H. Young, *Jesus and His Jewish Parables* (New York: Paulist Press, 1989).

17. E. P. Sanders, *Paul and Palestinian Judaism*, 158.

of these cases, however, is atonement understood as "automatic" or "earned." It is always a graced occasion:

> Their way of phrasing the sentences about atonement may mislead readers into thinking that they conceived the process of atonement to be automatic. The Rabbis doubtless had confidence that God would forgive those who did what was appropriate for atonement, but they did not suppose that atonement would be effective apart from the reconciling forgiveness of God. They pictured God as always ready to forgive, and so had no need of saying "repentance atones if God chooses to forgive."[18]

Recovering God's Grief at the Death of the Son

Atonement theories have the effect of wiping away the shame of the cross and presenting Jesus' death as the brightest moment in salvation history. According to the Synoptics, however, it is the darkest: "From noon on, darkness came over the whole land until three in the afternoon" (Matt 27:45 par.). Such "darkness" points to lamentation. The prophet Amos, for example, speaks of the darkness with which the Lord will cover the earth on the last day as "turn[ing] your feasts into mourning, and all your songs into lamentation . . . like the mourning for [the death of] an only son" (8:10). Robert Gundry cites a long list of parallels.[19]

Popular theology has sometimes associated this "darkness" with "the fearful concept of Jesus 'bearing,' even actually 'becoming' our sin."[20] This interpretation of the "darkness," however, is determined by the projection of atonement motifs into the Passion narrative: "Nowhere in Mark is Jesus said to bear the sins of others; so Mark's audience could hardly be expected to interpret the darkness thus."[21]

My childhood Catechism presents the image of the gates of heaven being thrown open at the moment of Jesus' death, after having been locked ever since the sin of Adam and Eve. According to the Synoptics, however, it is the Temple veil that is rent in two "from top to bottom" (Matt 27:51 par.). In most instances this rending of the veil has been interpreted to signal that the crime of the priests was so grievous that God

---

18. Ibid., 161.
19. Robert H. Gundry, *Mark: A Commentary on His Apology for the Cross* (Grand Rapids: Eerdmans, 1993) 963.
20. John R. W. Stott, *The Cross of Christ* (Downers Grove, IL: InterVarsity Press, 1986) 79.
21. Gundry, *Mark,* 964.

abandoned the Holy of Holies—tearing through the Temple veil as he exited. Such an interpretation fails to take into account that the disciples of Jesus in Jerusalem went to the Temple daily to pray and teach (Acts 2:46; 3:1; 5:42). Other scholars have suggested that this tearing "originally represented Jesus' death" and later became a "supernatural portent of Jesus' deity."[22] But why represent Jesus' death symbolically when the event itself was just narrated? Hebrews makes an oblique reference to "the new and living way that he opened for us through the [Temple] curtain" (Heb 10:20), but it would be risky to transpose the theology of Hebrews back into the Synoptics.

Finally, in an unexpected moment I chanced upon an explanation by David Daube,[23] a Jewish scholar. The moment I heard it, all the clues of the text snapped into place.

> One has to be aware of the modes of expressing grief then current among the Jewish people. When a father of Jesus' day would hear of the death of a son, he would invariably rend his garment by grabbing it at the neck and tearing it from top to bottom [see, e.g., Gen 27:34; Job 1:20; *b. Moed Qatqan* 25a, *b. Menahot* 48a]. This is precisely the gesture suggested by the particulars of Matthew's text: "The veil of the Temple was torn in two from top to bottom" (27:51). In truth, God is Spirit. Symbolically, however, the presence of God within the holy of holies was rendered secure from prying eyes by the veil which surrounded that place. As such, the veil conceals the "nakedness" of God. It is this "garment" which the grief-stricken Father of Jesus tears from top to bottom when he hears the final death-cry of his beloved son. Even for the Father, therefore, the death of Jesus is bitter tragedy and heartfelt grief.[24]

This interpretation has the merit of paying attention to the form of the tearing ("from top to bottom") and of harmonizing completely with the "darkness" that preceded it. Both symbols, consequently, serve to signal to the Jewish reader the grief and rage of God at the death of his/her Son. At the same time, these symbols serve as a point of departure for reeducating ourselves as to how we might recapture our own suppressed

---

22. Robert H. Gundry, *Matthew: A Commentary on His Handbook for a Mixed Church under Persecution* (Grand Rapids: Eerdmans, 1994) 575.

23. David Daube, *The New Testament and Rabbinic Judaism* (London: Athlone Press, 1956) 23–26.

24. Aaron Milavec, *To Empower as Jesus Did: Acquiring Spiritual Power Through Apprenticeship* (Lewiston: Edwin Mellen, 1982) 57.

rage and indignation[25] at the needless suffering of Jesus. Finally, this reading of the Passion allowed me to weep for Jesus—tears that had been blocked so long by a theology bent on sugarcoating his death.

Recent Criticism of Substitutionary Atonement

Within the last twenty years the soteriology of the atoning death has fallen on hard times.[26] To begin with, God's threat of death (Gen 2:17) directed toward his own children in the Garden strikes modern ears as a cruel and excessive punishment for the single infraction of eating the forbidden fruit.[27] Furthermore, studies by Herbert Haag demonstrate

25. After writing this, I experienced, firsthand, the rage and indignation of Kathy, a Catholic teenager, on viewing the film "Jesus Christ Superstar." She stomped out of the theater visibly angry and told her mother how she hated "the bully" (Caiaphas) and that "stupid queer" (Annas) who "hurt Jesus." In the face of her fury, her mother calmly proceeded to explain to her how it was necessary that Jesus should suffer in order to atone for our sins. At that moment I saw clearly how Anselm had so thoroughly subverted even the ability of this mother to sympathize with the appropriate rage of her daughter. Yet how would Anselm explain to this child how such a disgusting crime was part of God's eternal plan to redeem the world? If we ourselves are prohibited from using an evil means to accomplish a good end, how can our Father continue to be revered when he is reputed to sanction the torture of the innocent in order to forgive the guilty? For further details see Milavec, "Is God Arbitrary and Sadistic?"

26. The theological, biblical, and pastoral deficiencies of substitutionary atonement form an immense topic. In what follows I can only touch the surface. Readers who want an in-depth and very readable introduction to the subject might want to go to David Heim, "Rethinking the Death of Jesus," *The Christian Century* (March 22, 2005) 20–25, available at http://www.religion-online.org/showarticle.asp?title=3167.

27. Some of the early Church Fathers (Irenaeus, Origen) regarded Adam and Eve as literally children growing up in their parent's garden. Because they were children, the fruit of the "tree of the knowledge of good and evil" (Gen 2:17) was naturally inaccessible to them, yet God planted this tree in the middle of the Garden because he definitely wanted them to eat of it when he discerned that they were ready. As often happens, however, children rush ahead and seize adult ways prematurely. According to Origen, Eve's initiative merely represents the well-known fact that girls mature earlier than boys. The serpent in this narrative is not what will later be identified as Satan in disguise (Wis 2:24; Rev 20:2) but the Wisdom figure of ancient cultures. The serpent, accordingly, quite rightly reveals to Eve that touching the fruit will not cause her to die—on the contrary, "God knows that when you eat of it your eyes will be opened [so as to discern good and evil], and you will be like God" (Gen 3:5). They ate and "the eyes of both were opened" (Gen 3:7)—just as the serpent revealed. The fact that they notice, for the first time, that they are naked only demonstrates that they are indeed seeing with adult eyes (and have lost the innocence of childhood). Then, once God discovers what has happened, he does not curse them. How could he? Rather, God says, "See, the man [lit., "earthling"] has become like one of us, knowing good and evil" (Gen 3:22). Thus God excludes them from the Garden where

that "the idea that Adam's descendants are automatically sinners because of the sin of their ancestor . . . is foreign to Holy Scripture."[28] As Martin Buber would have it, the descendants of Adam sinned "as Adam sinned and not because Adam sinned."[29] Furthermore, the notion that forgiveness for the guilty must be achieved at the price of torturing the innocent runs the risk of supporting a very dubious and unbiblical notion of divine justice. Accordingly, Stephen Finlan notes quite pointedly: "It does us no good to perceive Jesus as heroic if we are forced to view God as sadistic."[30] Richard Rohr, meanwhile, in his retreats and homilies tells his hearers: "As our own Franciscan scholar John Duns Scotus taught, Jesus did not need to die. There was no debt to be paid. Jesus died to reveal the nature of the heart of God."[31] Feminist theologians, for their part, alert us that classical soteriology espouses a sadistic case of "divine child abuse."[32] Edward Schillebeeckx, in equally telling terms, concludes his study of the topic of suffering by saying, "First of all, we must say that we are not redeemed thanks to the death of Jesus but despite it."[33]

Parallel critiques can be heard within Protestant circles. Wolfhart Pannenberg, a leading Lutheran theologian, notes that "Anselm's conception . . . was also taken over by the dogmatics of Protestant orthodoxy in the

---

they might also eat of the tree of life and live forever. In so doing, God, acting like a good father, gets Adam ready for the curses of farming, and Eve is prepared for the curses of childbearing. In brief, Adam and Eve enter into the adult world wherein their parent will no longer do everything for them. This reading of Genesis (which prevails today within the Eastern Orthodox Churches and in many Jewish circles as well) captures much more of the deep nuances of the ancient narrative than do those later readings that imagine Adam and Eve were tempted by Satan and committed a grievous sin worthy of death. Anselm regarded the crime as one of unpardonable treason since the children of God had taken the side of God's enemy against him. In Anselm's day the punishment for treason was death, not only for the guilty participants in the crime but for their children as well. It thus seemed natural that the death penalty imposed ("spiritual death") fell not only on our first parents but on all their future children as well.

28. Herbert Haag, *Is Original Sin in Scripture?* (New York: Sheed and Ward, 1969) 106.

29. Martin Buber, *Two Types of Faith* (New York: Macmillan, 1951) 158.

30. Stephen Finlan, *Problems with Atonement* (Collegeville, MN: Liturgical Press, 2005) 97. Finlan's citation is in the context of capturing the critique of Michael Winter.

31. Richard Rohr, o.f.m., "Learning From the Cross," *Every Day Catholic* (March 2001), available at http://www.americancatholic.org/Newsletters/EDC/ag0301.asp. For more details on Duns Scotus see http://www.franciscans.org.uk/2001jan-mulholland.html.

32. See, for example, Rita Nakashima Brock, "And a Little Child Will Lead Us: Christology and Child Abuse," in *Christianity, Patriarchy, and Abuse: A Feminist Critique*, ed. Joanne Carlson Brown and Carol R. Bohn (New York: Pilgrim Press, 1989) 42–61.

33. Edward Schillebeeckx, *Christ: The Experience of Jesus as Lord* (New York: Seabury, 1980) 729.

seventeenth century, although its primary concern is foreign to the authentically evangelical understanding of salvation."[34] John T. Carroll and Joel B. Green, meanwhile, conclude their extensive study of Paul with this caution: "Paul uses an almost inexhaustible series of metaphors[35] to represent the significance of Jesus' death, and penal substitution (at least as popularly defined) is not one of them."[36] Measuring the pastoral impact of the atonement theory, a recent book closes with a strong cautionary note: "We believe that the popular fascination with and commitment to penal substitutionary atonement has had ill effects in the life of the church in the United States and has little to offer the global church and mission by way of understanding or embodying the message of Jesus Christ."[37]

Rabbi Tovia Singer, in response to a Christian inquiry, reminds his questioner that, after all is said and done, the notion that Jesus' death on the cross was a "sacrifice" would have been abhorrent to God "since the Jewish people were strictly prohibited from offering human sacrifices under any circumstances."[38] To this one might add that, in Jewish circles,

---

34. Wolfhart Pannenberg, *Jesus—God and Man* (Philadelphia: Westminster, 1968) 43.

35. Among the metaphors used by Paul to account for the saving activity of Jesus are the following: (a) "justification" as understood within a court of law, (b) "redemption" as a commercial transaction, (c) "reconciliation" between individuals and groups, (d) "sacrifice" in the context of ancient worship, and (e) "triumph over evil" as a battleground image. None of these metaphors taken individually or collectively adds up to Anselm's theory of substitutionary atonement. Only when substitutionary atonement is read back into all the metaphors of Paul does everything appear to come together into a unified theory. Yet when one examines the particulars, problems persist. An example: Why does Paul say that Jesus "was handed over to death for our trespasses and was raised for our justification" (Rom 4:25) or "If Christ has not been raised, your faith is futile and you are still in your sins" (1 Cor 15:17)? Substitutionary atonement theories do not know how to give due importance to the resurrection of Jesus. Another example: Paul sometimes presents Jesus' death as a sacrifice, but he also urges believers to "present your bodies as a living sacrifice" (Rom 12:1), and he refers to his own preaching the gospel as his "priestly [i.e., sacrificial] service" (Rom 15:16). Atonement theories do not know how to give due importance to these other "sacrifices." For details see Robert J. Daly, *The Origin of the Christian Doctrine of Sacrifice* (Philadelphia: Fortress Press, 1978).

36. John T. Carroll and Joel B. Green, eds., *The Death of Jesus in Early Christianity* (Peabody, MA: Hendrickson, 1993) 263.

37. Joel B. Green and Mark D. Baker, *Recovering the Scandal of the Cross: Atonement in New Testament and Contemporary Contexts* (Downers Grove, IL: InterVarsity Press, 2000) 220. For a clear and insightful examination of the "saving death" interpreted within its cultural context see Stephen J. Patterson, *Beyond the Passion: Rethinking the Death and Life of Jesus* (Minneapolis: Fortress Press, 2004).

38. Rabbi Tovia Singer, "Could Jesus' Death Atone for Any Kind of Sin?" on the site *Outreach Judaism: Judaism's Response to Christian Missionaries,* www.outreachjudaism.org/jesusdeath.html. Muslims also have difficulties with the atoning death of Jesus. See, for

any true sacrifice had to be offered by a Jewish priest in the Jerusalem Temple.[39] On these grounds alone one can be certain that whenever Paul speaks of Jesus' death as a sacrifice he is using a metaphor that cannot be taken literally. We can also be certain that however Paul is understood as affirming that "we have been justified by his blood" (Rom 5:9), this cannot be interpreted to negate the clear and unambiguous assurances of forgiveness that play out in the Hebrew Scriptures and in the parables of Jesus wherein absolutely no appeal is made to an atoning death. Rabbi Gerald Sigal speaks for contemporary Jews as follows:

> God forgave sin before Jesus' appearance and continues to forgive without any assistance from the latter. It is no wonder that many centuries before the time of Jesus, Isaiah declared: "Israel is saved by the Lord with an everlasting salvation" (Isa 45:17). . . . This is true at all times and in all places.[40]

Thesis Two: *Classical substitutionary atonement theories, ignoring the Jewish experience of God as a benevolent father, have imagined that God was somehow unwilling or unable to forgive sins beginning with the sin of Adam and going all the way to the moment when his beloved Son, Jesus Christ, died on the cross. Furthermore, both Catholic and Protestant churches have exaggerated the universal significance of Jesus' death by imagining that no sin, whether original or actual, could ever be entirely forgiven and atoned for without appeal, in faith, to the infinite merits of Jesus. This is the heresy of the Gentiles that emerged as Christianity broke free of the guidance and wisdom of Israel. Fidelity to Jesus and to the early church require that Christians return to their sources in order to again reenvision God as lavishly open to forgiveness without any reference to*

---

example, Sam Shamoun, "Islam's Doctrine of Substitutionary Atonement and the Ransoming of Sinners," on the site *Answering Islam: A Christian-Muslim Dialogue* (Nov. 2006), at http://answering-islam.org.uk/Shamoun/ransom.htm.

39. After the destruction of the Temple the rabbis designed substitutes for Temple sacrifices. The descendants of Eli, accordingly, could find no atonement by sacrifice and meat-offering, but they might receive pardon through occupation with the study of the Torah and acts of loving-kindness (*b. Rosh Hashanah* 18a). According to another tradition "the Holy One, blessed be he, foresaw that the Holy Temple would be destroyed and promised Israel that the words of the Torah, which is likened unto sacrifices, will, after the destruction of the Temple, be accepted as a substitute for sacrifices" (*Tanḥuma ahri,* 10; *Midrash Tanḥuma,* 3.85a).

40. Gerald Sigal, "Jews for Judaism: Reference Section," #081, http://jewsforjudaism .org/j4j-2000/html/reflib/tri081.html.

> the death of Jesus. Even the parables and activities of Jesus reinforce such
> a view. As for Gentiles, it is entirely understandable that they celebrate
> their own graced teshuvah as coming to them entirely due to the life,
> death, and resurrection of Jesus. They should not be deceived into imagin-
> ing, however, that the atonement of Jewish sins must always and every-
> where be funneled through the name, the person, and the merits of Jesus
> Christ.[41]

The Priority of Israel's Salvation in the Message of Jesus

Just as the saving activity of Jesus cannot be narrowly limited to the
few hours he hung on the cross, in like fashion the very character of salvation cannot be reduced merely to the "forgiveness of sins." In fact,
Catholic biblical scholarship has shown that Jesus' own perspective on
salvation was focused on the coming of the reign of God on earth. Faced
with this final event of salvation, conversion of life with the attendant
forgiveness of sins stands only as the remote preparation for the Lord's
coming. Final salvation remains a future event. Jesus lived and died as
a Jew, and his Jewish followers lived out their Judaism against the backdrop of accepting Jesus as the suffering Messiah, the son of David, whom
God had raised from the dead, thereby preparing for his second coming
in glory to usher in the reign of God. All in all, these are all Jewish expectations being worked out within a Jewish populace.

Following the landmark study of Joachim Jeremias, we are forced to
recognize that the ministry of the historical Jesus was exclusively to and
for Israel.[42] What would happen to the Gentiles in the end times was an

---

41. In brief, the failure of Ratzinger's *Dominus Jesus* does not lie in its endeavor to
explain how it is that divine grace appears outside the visible boundaries of the church.
Rather, having done so, this treatise makes the error of imagining that (a) God's redemption can be entirely captured by the atonement for sins and (b) the death of Jesus alone
can accomplish this atonement. It then follows that divine grace outside the visible
boundaries of the church must *always and everywhere* be the grace of Christ. In the case of
early Israel, therefore, one has to further imagine that the sins of Israel were forgiven due
to the *anticipated merits* of Jesus Christ. The moment (a) that God's forgiveness is received
independent of Jesus and (b) that Israel is seen as the first recipient of salvation, the whole
argument of *Dominus Jesus* falls like a house of cards.

42. Joachim Jeremias, *Jesus' Promise to the Nations* (Philadelphia: Fortress Press, 1982)
11–39.

open question.[43] According to some prophetic texts all Gentiles were going to be utterly destroyed by the Lord at his coming (Mic 5:9, 15). Still other texts proposed that some Gentile nations would survive, but only for the purpose of serving Israel—Gentile kings and queens "shall bow down to you, and lick the dust of your feet" (Isa 49:23; Mic 7:16-17). Then there are a few prophetic texts in which the Lord proposes that some Gentiles would join with Israel and become part of the final ingathering:

> The foreigners who join themselves to the Lord, to minister to him, to love the name of the Lord . . . these I will bring to my holy mountain, and make them joyful in my house of prayer; their burnt offerings and their sacrifices will be accepted on my altar; for my house shall be called a house of prayer for all peoples. Thus says the Lord God, who gathers the outcasts of Israel, I will gather others to them besides those already gathered. (Isa 56:6-8)

Following the careful study of Paula Fredriksen, two things were thus absolutely necessary for the Gentile mission: (1) the conviction that the end times had already begun and (2) the assurance that the Lord was prepared not to destroy or humiliate but to graciously embrace Gentiles in the final ingathering.[44] Both these convictions deeply marked the Jesus movement. On the one hand Jesus proclaimed the reign of God as close at hand, and his resurrection from the dead was seen as the "first fruits" of the general resurrection. On the other hand, Jesus' association with the marginalized (prostitutes and tax collectors) in Israel may have paved the way for his disciples to extend this outreach to the Gentiles. Moreover, Jesus paved the way for a benevolent vision of the Gentiles within his Judaism when he "removed vengeance on the Gentiles from the picture of the future."[45]

Based on this understanding, it becomes clear why Gentile inclusion was based on abandoning idolatry and adhering to the Lord God of Israel. Gentiles were to be included in the final ingathering as Gentiles and not as Jewish proselytes.[46] Paul had it right, therefore, when he described the Gentiles as being grafted on the root that is Israel. Only to the extent

---

43. E. P. Sanders, *Jesus and Judaism* (Philadelphia: Fortress Press, 1985) 212–21, provides an excellent discussion of the fate of the Gentiles.

44. Paula Fredriksen, "Judaism, the Circumcision of Gentiles, and Apocalyptic Hope," *JTS* 42 (1991) 533–58.

45. Jeremias, *Jesus' Promise*, 45.

46. Fredriksen, "Judaism," 547.

that the salvation promised to Israel was realized would the Gentiles have a hope of being received by the Lord.

The Priority of Israel's Salvation in Luke-Acts

If one examines the Hebrew Scriptures one is assured that final salvation is squarely centered on Israel: "*Our Redeemer*—the LORD of hosts is his name—is the Holy One of Israel" (Isa 47:4; emphasis added). What has generally been overlooked, however, is that this same perspective holds true within our Christian Scriptures. Here are seven examples:

1. According to Acts, when the disciples came together during the forty days following his Passion, Jesus was "appearing to them . . . and speaking about the kingdom of God" (Acts 1:3). During these meetings his disciples naturally asked him, "Lord, is this the time when you will restore the kingdom to Israel?" (Acts 1:6). Such a question indicates clearly that the figure of Jesus was wedded to the destiny of Israel.

2. Luke, in his gospel, offers the prophetic words of John's father as anticipating that "the Lord God of Israel" would soon raise up a savior to redeem the Jewish people:

> Then his father Zechariah was filled with the Holy Spirit and spoke this prophecy: "Blessed be *the Lord God of Israel,* for he has looked favorably on *his people* and *redeemed them.* He has raised up a mighty savior for us in the house of his servant David, as he spoke through the mouth of his holy prophets from of old, that *we [Jews] would be saved from our enemies and from the hand of all who hate us.* Thus he has shown the mercy promised to our ancestors, and has remembered his holy covenant, the oath that he swore to our ancestor Abraham, to grant us that *we, being rescued from the hands of our enemies, might serve him without fear,* in holiness and righteousness before him all our days. (Luke 1:67-74, emphasis added)

3. Later, at the purification, the prophetic words of Simeon enforce this expectation:

> Now there was a man in Jerusalem whose name was Simeon; this man was righteous and devout, looking forward to *the consolation of Israel,* and the Holy Spirit rested on him. It had been revealed to him by the Holy Spirit that he would not see death before he had seen the Lord's Messiah. Guided by the Spirit, Simeon came into the temple; and when the parents brought in the child Jesus, to do for him what was customary under the law, Simeon took him in

his arms and praised God, saying, "Master, now you are dismiss-
ing your servant in peace, according to your word; for *my eyes have
seen your salvation,* which you have prepared in the presence of all
peoples, a light for revelation to the Gentiles and for glory to your
people Israel." (Luke 2:29-32; emphasis added)

The work of the Messiah is understood here as effecting "the consolation of Israel." Once this salvation arrives "in the presence of all peoples,"
the Messiah and/or the salvation of God will be a "light" that will function in two ways: (a) "for revelation to the Gentiles" and (b) "for glory
to your people Israel." Here, in Luke's gospel, one hears for the first time
that at least some Gentiles will benefit from the salvation of Israel.

4. The Canaanite woman in Matthew's gospel imagines that "the dogs"
(= Gentiles) could expect only to get some crumbs that fall from the table
of "the children" (= Jews) (Matt 15:26-27).[47] This accords with Matthew's
insistence that Jesus originally intended that his disciples were to center
their attention exclusively on "the lost sheep of the house of Israel" (Matt
10:6). One has to wait until the end of the gospel before the risen Lord
expands this missionary directive.

5. Even when one examines the missionary journeys of Paul in Acts, one
discovers that he and Barnabas are not called first to convert Gentiles. In
fact, everywhere they go they always present their message initially in the
synagogue—the place where Jews are assembled (Acts 13:5, 14; 14:1; 16:13;
17:1, 10, 17; 18:4, 19; 19:8; 28:17, 26-28). In every place, furthermore, Paul
and Barnabas approach Gentiles *only after* the Jews have rejected their message. In the first instance of this Luke spells out the policy completely:

> "It was necessary that the word of God should be spoken first to
> you. Since you [Jews] reject it and judge yourselves to be unworthy
> of eternal life, we are now turning to the Gentiles. For so the Lord
> has commanded us, saying, 'I have set you to be a light for the
> Gentiles, so that you [Israel] may bring salvation to the ends of the
> earth.'" (Acts 13:46-47)

The use of the passive, "it was necessary," points toward the divine plan.
The message of salvation is addressed first to Jews. Jewish resistance,
however, releases the apostles to abide by another divine imperative—

---

47. Matthew omits Mark's saying, "Let the children first be fed full." Thus for Matthew
there can never be the surmise that the Gentiles will receive their bread of Torah only when
the children of Israel have been fed. Rather, the supposition is that Jesus never envisions a
time for favor to fall on the Gentiles. See, e.g., Robert H. Gundry, *Matthew,* 314–16.

namely, that Israel is called to be "a light for the Gentiles." In this case it is not any commissioning on the part of Jesus following his resurrection as in Matthew, but the mandate of the Lord found on the lips of Isaiah. Even in Isa 49:5, however, the first mission of the servant is "to bring Jacob back to him [the Lord], and that Israel might be gathered to him [the Lord]." Only after "[raising] up the tribes of Jacob" and restoring the "survivors of Israel" does the Lord direct his servant Israel to be a "light to the nations" (Isa 49:6). This priority of the mission to the Jews found here is paralleled in Paul's letters, where he says quite plainly that he brings the Gospel "to the Jew first" (Rom 1:16; 2:9-10; 3:2).

6. One hears this same priority of the mission to Israel in the words of James at the Jerusalem council:

> James replied, "My brothers, listen to me. Simeon has related how God first looked favorably on the Gentiles, to take from among them a people for his name. This agrees with the words of the prophets, as it is written,
>> 'After this I [the Lord God] will return, and I will rebuild the dwelling of David, which has fallen; from its ruins I will rebuild it, and I will set it up, so that all other peoples may seek the Lord[48]—even all the Gentiles over whom my name has been called. Thus says the Lord, who has been making these things known from long ago.'" (Acts 15:13-18)

"The words of the prophets" here conflates Amos 9:11-12, Jer 12:15, and Isa 45:21. "The dwelling of David" must originally have referred to the Davidic monarchy, yet in this context it might also be intended to include "the story of Jesus, culminating in the Resurrection, in which the promise made to David [Acts 2:24-28] is fulfilled."[49] Thus, by implication, the Gentiles will find the Lord only after God has reestablished the Davidic kingdom on earth. When the prophetic text says "I will return," this refers to the return of the Lord God to gather in the exiles and to restore Israel along with "the Gentiles over whom my name has been called." The mission to the Gentiles, consequently, is again intimately associated with the end of days, when the Lord will restore the fortunes of Israel.[50]

---

48. Clearly the Septuagint is used here. The Hebrew text at this point asserts that "the House of David shall reestablish its authority over the nations that were ruled by David" (*TANAKH* [Philadelphia: Jewish Publication Society, 1985] note on Amos 9:13).

49. Ernst Haenchen, *The Acts of the Apostles* (Oxford: Basil Blackwell, 1973) 448.

50. See Isa 45:22; 56:6-8; Zech 2:11; 8:20-23; Tob 14:6-7. Even according to Jesus, the Ninevites, the Queen of Sheba, the inhabitants of Tyre and Sidon, even those of Sodom and

7. Paul's letter to the Romans specifically traces the roots of Gentile inclusion in the legacy of Israel by using the figure of Abraham as father of the circumcised and the uncircumcised. Later in this letter Paul names Christ as *"a servant of the circumcised* on behalf of the truth of God." How so?

> [A] *in order that he might confirm the promises* given to the patriarchs, and
>
> [B] *in order that the Gentiles might glorify God for his mercy.*
>
>> [1] As it is written, "Therefore I will confess you among the Gentiles, and sing praises to your name" [Ps 18:49; 2 Sam 22:50];
>> [2] and again he says, "Rejoice, O Gentiles, with his people" [Deut 32:43 LXX];
>> [3] and again, "Praise the Lord, all you Gentiles, and let all the peoples praise him" [Ps 117:1];
>> [4] and again Isaiah [11:10] says, "The root of Jesse shall come, the one who rises to rule the Gentiles; in him the Gentiles shall hope." (Rom 15:8-12)

One can note here that Paul appeals exclusively to prophetic texts in the Hebrew Scriptures that suggest Gentiles will find inclusion within Israel. Apparently Paul knows nothing of importance that Jesus might have said or done in this regard. The only important thing is that Jesus has been raised and the time for the ingathering is close at hand. Thus while Paul's Good News to the Jews is that their final redemption is about to arrive, the Good News delivered to the Gentiles is that some of them will be called to participate in the salvation given to Israel. If so, then these Gentiles might be expected to pay an honorary tribute to Israel in recognition of the gift they have received:

> For Macedonia and Achaia have been pleased to share their resources with the poor among the saints at Jerusalem. They were pleased to do this, and indeed they owe it to them; for *if the Gentiles*

Gomorrah will take part in the final resurrection and testify against Israel (Matt 10:15; 11:22; 12:41-42 *par.*). Luke 4:25-27 even goes so far as to relate how, already in the days of Elijah, God sent the prophet to a Gentile (even though there were many widows in Israel), and how, already in the days of Elisha, Naaman the Syrian was healed (even though there were many lepers in Israel). Thus for Jesus the end times would disclose that "many [Gentiles] will come from east and west and will eat with Abraham and Isaac and Jacob in the kingdom of heaven, while the heirs of the kingdom will be thrown into the outer darkness" (Matt 8:11-12 *par.*). In each of these cases it will be noted that the inclusion of righteous Gentiles is only envisioned after the general resurrection. See Jeremias, *Jesus' Promise,* 40–54.

have come to share in their [Israel's] spiritual blessings, they ought also to be of service to them in material things. (Rom 15:26-27; emphasis added)

A review of these texts allows one to see how, even within our Christian Scriptures, the salvation of Gentiles is unequivocally bound within God's destiny for Israel. In the first few generations the Jewish followers of Jesus became persuaded that the God of David would appoint Jesus as the messianic king following his restoration of Israel. Gentile inclusion was envisioned as a secondary offshoot of God's abiding love for Israel. By the fourth and fifth generations, however, the number of Jewish adherents in the Jesus movement was dwarfed by the overwhelming influx of Gentiles. In this new environment everything got turned around. Whereas the Hebrew prophets assured Israel that God was coming to save them and that the Gentiles, for the most part, would receive his wrath, the Gentile church was now selectively quoting these same Hebrew prophets to assure Gentile Christians that God was reaching out to bless them and that, due to Israel's unfaithfulness, his wrath was reserved for them. In a nutshell, this is the root of the anti-Jewish poison that came to contaminate the faith of the primitive church, and it will not be successfully rooted out until such time as the priority of Israel is again recognized as the core of the Good News.

> **Thesis 3:** *In its current theology, the church perceives itself as the recipient of salvation outside of and independent of the fate of Israel. This is the heresy of the Gentiles that Paul first exposed in his letter to the Romans when he challenged the Gentiles to "remember that it is not you that support the root, but the root that supports you" (Rom 11:18). Fidelity to Jesus and to the early church, therefore, requires that Christians repent of their arrogance and return to the Lord's choice of Israel as the source and the center of God's redemptive love for the Gentiles.*

Conclusion

My conclusions are disturbing even to myself. How far I have come from the teenager joining in the roar of the crowd that proclaimed ". . . by thy holy cross thou hast redeemed the world!" The *Baltimore Catechism* that I then used entirely passed over two thousand years of salvation history. Jews were seen not as "the first to believe" but as "the first to betray" God. Salvation, meanwhile, was narrowly rescripted to mean "the forgiveness of sins" and the "opening of the gates of heaven," realities that were given central and universal importance, completely ignoring God's abiding love and enduring promises to Israel. In this climate it was easy and natural for me, an impressionable Catholic youth, to pity (and even to despise) Jews.

I take courage from the fact that Vatican II began to extract the poison that infected my church. It is not enough, however, to acknowledge with Paul that "Jews remain very dear to God" and to insist that we share "a common spiritual heritage" (*Nostra Aetate* 4) when, as this chapter makes clear, Catholics have hardly begun to gauge the carefully disguised ways in which our ancestors have distorted the faith of the early church in favor of a false gospel. The three theses in this chapter (a) expose how the preaching of the Gospel has been poisoned and (b) suggest remedial steps whereby this poison can be purged. For far too long the salvation history of the Christian church has been truncated and the abundant forgiveness of God has been falsified.

It is not enough for Christian churches to recover the Jewishness of Jesus; rather, we must recover the Jewish mindset of Jesus when he prayed that the reign of God would come on earth and that sins would be forgiven "despite the death of Jesus." On this score so much remains to be done. I pray to God that you, the reader of these pages, would meditate on these things in your heart, that you would apply to your life those truths that set your heart free, and that your life would become God's faithful leaven that transforms the way in which the Good News of God's salvation is being passed on.[51]

51. If you would like to share your reflections or see what others have produced, go to www.salvationisfromthejews.info.

Four

Parting of the Ways:
The Emergence of the Church
out of Judaism

> We have ample evidence for characterizing as a family quarrel
> the relationship between the two great religious traditions of the West.
>
> —Jacob Neusner

Eight years ago I was invited to be a visiting professor at a Christian liberal arts college, where I offered classes in the New Testament. During the second week of classes we began to systematically work through the Gospel of Mark. I opened the class by reading out loud the following: "And they went into Capernaum; and immediately on the Sabbath he entered the synagogue and taught. And they were astonished at his teaching . . ." (Mark 1:21-22). Then I asked my students: "I can't figure this out. Why should Jesus have gone into a synagogue on the Sabbath? Why didn't he wait for Sunday and go to a Christian church?" My students were dumbfounded. They admitted that they had never thought about that before. Then a young woman blurted out, "Wasn't Jesus a Jew?" So I asked the entire class, "How many of you think of Jesus as a practicing Jew?" Only three raised their hands. Then a young man asked for clarification, "Wasn't Jesus born a Jew but then, at some point, he became a Christian?"

At this point I knew that my real work had begun. So I got out my own *Baltimore Catechism*, which was the mainstay of Catholic education in the United States and had been my own handbook of formation when I was a youth. In this *Catechism* much attention is given to the divine and human natures of Christ, but nothing is said about the Jewish nature of

Jesus. Even when texts like "You have heard it said . . . but I say to you . . ." are considered, the reader gets the impression that Jesus is setting out the higher Christian morality over and against the inferior ethics of the Jews. At no point do the authors of the *Catechism* regard Jesus as a committed Jew wrestling with the task of making sense out of his own Jewish tradition. Rather, as my student correctly hinted, Jesus appears to be founding a new religion, Christianity.

Initial Assessment

Rabbi Jacob Neusner has given a lot of attention to the split between the synagogue and the church. How could two religious movements emerging out of the same common heritage end up being such fierce antagonists? Here is Rabbi Neusner's conclusion:

> We have ample evidence for characterizing as a family quarrel the relationship between the two great religious traditions of the West. Only brothers can hate so deeply, yet accept and tolerate so impassively, as have Judaic and Christian brethren both hated, and yet taken for granted the presence of, one another.[1]

In this "family quarrel" two boundaries are very clear. The first is that Jesus was personally committed to Judaism; he trained his disciples to live Torah in anticipation of the reign of God that was just about to break into history. At no point did Jesus or his first disciples renounce their Judaism in favor of establishing a new religion. Rather, their purpose was "to fulfill the Torah," i.e., to achieve righteousness, not through any appeal to the merits of the death of Jesus (as the medieval Christians, citing Paul, would have it) but through a complete and heartfelt observance of what God would have them be and do. Matthew, persuaded that Jesus took this position, does not hesitate to put it squarely on his lips:

> Do not think that I have come to abolish the law [Torah] or the prophets; I have come not to abolish but to fulfill. . . . Therefore, whoever annuls one of the least of these commandments, and teaches others to do the same, will be called least in the kingdom of heaven; but whoever does them and teaches them will be called great in the kingdom of heaven. (Matt 5:17, 19, NRSV alt.)

---

1. Jacob Neusner, "The Jewish-Christian Argument in the First Century: Different People Talking About Different Things to Different People," *Religious Studies and Theology* 6 (1986) 9.

If the Jesus movement had consistently lived according to these words of Jesus it would undoubtedly have remained a subgroup within Judaism to this very day. But it did not.

This brings us to the second clear boundary. By the end of the first century Gentile-dominated segments of the Jesus movement wanted to retain their own self-definition as "the true Israel" while at the same time rejecting all forms of Judaism that were not absorbed into their own movement. Ignatius (ca. 35–107), the bishop of Antioch, gives expression to this in the letter he wrote to the church at Magnesia while he was under Roman guard on his way to Rome:

> Be not seduced by strange doctrines or by antiquated fables, which are profitless. For if . . . we live after the manner of Judaism, we avow that we have not received grace: for the divine prophets lived after [the manner of] Christ Jesus. . . . It is monstrous to talk of Jesus Christ and to practice Judaism.[2]

Here, at the opening of the second century, one finds a clear pastoral formulation of the great reversal. Bishop Ignatius advances the principle that the "new" renders the "old" unreliable, unworthy of adherence, and even "vile." He even asserts that "it is monstrous to talk of Jesus Christ and to practice Judaism"—an assertion that completely nullifies Jesus' words about "whoever annuls one of the least of these commandments," quoted above. Even if one interprets these words as directed entirely to Gentile believers, they still do a grave injustice to Jesus and his Jewish followers by maligning their sacred traditions.

The *Epistle of Barnabas* contributes to the great reversal, using a markedly different route. This treatise was written sometime between 70 and 135 by an anonymous author (whom we, following tradition, shall call "Barnabas") from the church at Alexandria. It makes the claim that Jews have misinterpreted circumcision, Sabbath, and food regulations by imagining that they were to be literally practiced rather than spiritually observed. Then, going further, Barnabas demonstrates that the "new" people whom the Lord "redeemed out of darkness" (*Barn.* 14) have a priority over the older people of Israel. To drive this point home, Barnabas cites the Lord's words to Rebecca found in Genesis: "Two nations are in your womb, and two peoples in your belly, and one people shall vanquish the other, and the greater shall serve the lesser" (*Barn.* 13). Barnabas interprets these words as referring prophetically to the Christian-Jewish struggle.

2. Ign. *Magn.* 8-10.

The same goes for Isaac's error in giving his final blessing to his second and younger son and later lamenting that "the greater shall serve the lesser" (*Barn.* 13). Barnabas seemingly finds nothing in the words of Jesus to defend his stand. He reaches back in time, therefore, and uses a Jewish-style midrash to demonstrate that "the greater [Israel] shall serve the lesser [Christians]." Unlike Paul, who used midrash to show how Abraham was the father of both "the circumcised" and "the uncircumcised" (Romans 4) or how Abraham's two sons represent the "two covenants" (Gal 4:24) of unequal value, Barnabas affirms that the Jews wrongly claim to have the covenant for, in God's eyes, that covenant now belongs exclusively to Christians. Not only does the "new" render the "old" unreliable (as Ignatius would have it), but the great reversal is now complete: (a) the greater Israel serves the lesser church and (b) covenantal love is withdrawn from the older Israel and conferred on the younger church.

Once again the two boundaries are clear. In the beginning Jesus clearly affirmed his own Judaism and even limited his mission to the house of Israel. In the course of three generations after Jesus, however, the Gentiles who had attached themselves to the Jewish movement Jesus left behind claimed all the blessings of God for themselves and rejected Judaism as bereft of any further participation in God's plans. From this point it requires only a small step to imagine that Jesus himself or, at any rate, his immediate disciples broke with Judaism and founded a new religion. This is what later generations of Christians came to think and what the young man in my theology class had learned from his teachers. This is what John Salza, the author of the website "Catholic Apologetics," is still preaching today. It remains necessary, consequently, to take a closer look at some of the early evidence and come to an informed position respecting when and why the church was established (outside of Judaism).

Whether Jesus Intended to Found a Church

Traditional fundamental theology, among both Catholics and Protestants, presupposed that Jesus' direct intention and explicit will was to found the Christian church. This was understood to have taken place in three stages:

> In the first, Jesus *prepared* for the foundation. During his lifetime he did not institute the Church itself but laid its foundations: he assembled a group of believers, he selected apostles, he promised the primacy to Peter, and he even instituted the sacraments of baptism and Eucharist.

> The second stage, the actual *institution*, took place after the resur-
> rection. . . . Only then did he give the power to teach, sanctify, and
> rule to the apostolic college. Only then did the Church come into
> existence. . . .
> The final stage was the *promulgation* of the Church's existence,
> which took place at Pentecost. At this time the Church became nec-
> essary for the salvation of humankind.[3]

The impression conveyed here is that Jesus found Judaism wanting and,
accordingly, he founded the only one and true religion *outside* of Judaism.

This thinking first got into serious trouble as a result of the German
Lutheran quest for the historical Jesus during the second half of the
nineteenth century. Critical scholarship demonstrated that only in one
gospel and on one occasion was Jesus reported to have said, using the
future tense, "I will build my church" (Matt 16:18). On the other hand,
those participating in the quest for the historical Jesus were increasingly
persuaded that Jesus' central concern was not establishing a new religion
but heralding the reign of God as close at hand. These are the terms in
which the gospels themselves summarize the message and purpose of
Jesus (Matt 4:17 par.) and, according to Matthew, the message and purpose of John the Baptizer as well (Matt 3:2). The parables of Jesus, meanwhile, deal extensively with the inbreaking of the kingdom and offer not
the slightest insight or information regarding the foundation or growth
of the Christian church. In 1900, Adolph von Harnack, the leading Lutheran church historian, delivered a series of lectures at the University
of Berlin in which he summarized the impact of the new biblical studies.[4]
Harnack's aim was to find the basis for Christianity in the teaching of
the historical Jesus, apart from later dogmatic developments. He considered dogma a Greek construct, though in the case of Christian doctrine
it was grounded in the gospel.

Harnack's conclusion was initially greeted with profound skepticism
by most Roman Catholics. It was disturbing to imagine that Jesus did
not directly and immediately establish the church and the papacy and
the seven sacraments they cherished. A French Roman Catholic scholar,
Alfred Loisy, attempted to refute Harnack's analysis by making use of
the exegetical principles by which Harnack arrived at his conclusions.
Loisy maintained that the essence of Christianity was found in the faith

---

3. Francis Schüssler Fiorenza, *Foundational Theology: Jesus and the Church* (New York: Crossroad, 1984) 75.

4. Adolph von Harnack, *The Essence of Christianity* (New York: Harper, 1957).

of the developed church, expanded under the guidance of the Holy Spirit. That Jesus did not found a church or institute the sacraments did not make them less essential to Christian life.[5] Pius X, distressed by the exegetical principles used by Harnack as well as by Loisy, put into effect a campaign against the new forms of biblical scholarship that effectively purged from Catholic circles all persons and writings that endorsed modern biblical studies. Thus Catholics had to wait until the mid-1950s before they were allowed to reinvestigate and publish their modern studies regarding Jesus' intention with respect to the church.

Before the 1950s, Catholics lived an academic life quite separate from Protestants. They had their own journals, their own professional societies, their own institutes, their own universities. In the 70s and 80s this changed drastically. Now even the official church was encouraging Catholics to join with Protestants in collaborative biblical studies. Catholics were being hired in Protestant institutions; Protestants were teaching in Catholic institutions (even seminaries). As a result, Catholics today share with liberal Protestants a love of the Bible and a commitment to exploring its meanings using historical-critical methods.

Relative to studies of the foundation of the church, Francis Schüssler Fiorenza summarized the situation within Catholic scholarship prevailing in the mid-80s as follows:

> Although the traditional historical [approach] is still very much alive and although some new approaches have developed . . . one characteristic is decisive for most of these contemporary approaches: they seek to take seriously the criticisms and weaknesses of the historical demonstration, to acknowledge the eschatological dimension of Jesus' proclamation of God's reign, and to reject an oversimplified harmonization of diverse historical data about the origin of the Church.[6]

As for Jesus' intention regarding the church, a developmental or salvation-history approach was embraced as having the most promise. This approach begins by acknowledging that the historical Jesus was preoccupied with heralding the forthcoming reign of God to Israel (see, e.g., Acts 10:36) without making any plans to found an institution outside Judaism. The Synoptic Gospels, it must be remembered, never imagined that Jesus was ever

5. There is a good brief summary of the differences between Harnack and Loisy in F. L. Cross, ed., *The Oxford Dictionary of the Christian Church* (3d ed. E. A. Livingstone; Oxford: Oxford University Press, 1997) 993.

6. Francis Schüssler Fiorenza, *Foundational Theology*, 91.

officially expelled from the local synagogues despite his bad press from the Pharisees. The same thing can be said for Paul as he visited the towns of the Diaspora and consistently found a hearing within their local synagogues. He meets resistance (just as did Jesus), yet at no time does Paul encounter a blanket expulsion from the synagogues that would have necessitated establishing independent institutional structures.

In the case of the Gentiles, we do find Paul initiating *ad hoc* operating procedures relative to their worship, the resolution of internal disputes, and their code of conduct. The letters of Paul even openly address "the church *(ekklēsia)* of the Thessalonians" (1 Thess 1:1; 2 Thess 1:1), "the church *(ekklēsia)* of God that is in Corinth" (1 Cor 1:2; 2 Cor 1:1), etc. Paul's repeated use of the Greek term *ekklēsia* clearly demonstrates that these "churches" were not buildings but "local assemblies" meeting in private homes. At no point does Paul claim that he established these "assemblies" due to some direct and immediate intention of Jesus Christ, nor does Paul at any point claim that he or any other circumcised Christians were intending to found a new religion the moment these "churches" were brought into existence.

All in all, the newer Catholic approaches to fundamental theology agree that the separation of the Jesus movement from Judaism did come eventually; however, when it came it does not hinge on any clear mandate on the part of Jesus to establish his "church" (singular, Matt 16:18) outside of Judaism. What, then, were the circumstances that provoked this separation? The remainder of this chapter will explore them and draw conclusions at the end.

Whether the Church Emerged at Pentecost

Pentecost has traditionally been regarded as "the birthday of the church" by both Catholics and Protestants. In the sermons preached on Pentecost each year, believers routinely hear this presented to them by their priests and ministers. Here are brief excerpts from two preachers, one Catholic and one Protestant:

> Pentecost is the birthday of the church. This day, which saw the coming of the Spirit upon the apostles and Mary, formally inaugurates the mission of the Church to preach the Good News to all peoples.[7]

7. James A. Verrecchia, "Gospel Commentary: The Birthday of the Church," *Guest Column* of the *Catholic Herald*, May 28, 1998. Verrecchia mentioned Mary because Pentecost coincided with the Visitation of Mary (May 31) in 1998.

Acts 2 celebrates the birthday of the church. It took place during the feast of Pentecost. Pentecost is a [Jewish] harvest festival, fifty days after Passover. During this particular festival, a new kind of harvest was reaped: 3000 souls were gathered in the Kingdom of God. That harvest day began a reaping process that is still going on worldwide. The Spirit of God continues the work he began in Acts 2. He will never stop working until the Lord comes to ring down the final curtain of time.[8]

An examination of the text being read in the churches on Pentecost (Acts 2) moves in quite a different direction. For starters, the sacred text says nothing about "the birthday of the church." Pentecost was a long-established Jewish feast (as the Protestant preacher rightly notices). Hence one might begin by allowing that the gathering of the 120 on Pentecost signals (at least in the mind of Luke) their continued attachment to Jewish festivals following the death of Jesus. In any case we have no evidence that a Christian feast of Pentecost was celebrated annually at the time that Luke wrote Acts. Next, one must take notice that those who gathered in Jerusalem for this feast were not Gentiles but "Jews from every nation under heaven" (Acts 2:5). Accordingly, it comes as no surprise that Peter addresses them as "men of Judaea," as "Israelites," and as "the entire house of Israel" (Acts 2:14, 22, 36). Essentially, Acts 2 envisions no Gentile mission whatsoever. Peter's discourse is strictly a Jew-to-Jew exchange.

Given the current understanding of the theology of baptism within the churches, some Christians might be inclined to imagine that the three thousand Jews who were baptized (Acts 2:37-38) were leaving their Judaism behind in order to join the church of Jesus Christ. Acts, in sharp contrast, makes it quite clear that "the gift of the Holy Spirit" (Acts 2:38) offers an early warning sign of the end times (Acts 2:17-21, citing Joel 2:28-32). The resurrection of Jesus from the dead offers an additional sign: God has chosen his *moshiach* (2:22-36). Many hearers are "cut to the heart" (2:37) by these signs of the approaching end times, and Peter accordingly invites them to "repent, and be baptized" (2:38). Baptism at this point has much the same character as John's baptism—those anticipating the reign of God (following John's preaching) confessed their sins, were immersed in the river Jordan, and returned home to live out their Jewish lives in anticipation of God's coming. Nothing in Acts remotely

---

8. Pastor Glen Pettigrove, "Birthday of the Church," *Sermon Notes*, September 30, 2001.

suggests that these Jews who were baptized withdrew from Jewish assemblies from that day forward. The Good News offered them, after all, was the fulfillment of the destiny of Israel "for the promise is for you, for your children . . ."(2:39).

After Pentecost, Acts specifically says that the disciples and those who had joined with them (a) pooled their resources on behalf of those who were needy (2:44), (b) "spent much time together in the temple" (2:46), and (c) "broke bread at home and ate their food with glad and generous hearts" (2:46). Immediately thereafter, Peter and John are presented as visiting the temple "at the hour of prayer" (3:1). There is nothing here to suggest that the disciples of Jesus had "Christian worship services" in the Jewish temple or that they "set themselves apart" and deliberately avoided participating in the regular public prayers in the temple.[9] As for "the breaking of bread," many scholars and preachers have wanted to imagine this as signaling "the reenactment of the Lord's Supper." At this point in Acts there is no clear indication of when, where, and how often the Eucharist was being celebrated (if at all). Thus "the breaking of the bread" could merely refer to the Jewish tradition of giving thanks before ordinary eating. The phrase "ate their food with glad and generous hearts" (2:46) would enforce this understanding. For the sake of argument, however, let us suppose that we are to think of the Lord's Supper here. Are we to imagine that the three thousand Jews baptized on Pentecost were assigned to eucharistic assemblies in private homes? Even if thirty could be crowded into each home, this would require coordinating huge food preparations and finding one hundred homes with large dining tables. There is no way to imagine that the apostles, who had only come to Jerusalem eight weeks earlier, could have garnered these resources. Furthermore, since the three thousand baptized were themselves visitors who came to Jerusalem for the feast, it has to be recognized that nearly all of them would have plans to return home shortly afterward. What Luke wants to communicate is that, following Pentecost, some of the three thousand did eat with the apostles, did share their resources, and did return home marveling at the signs (Jesus' resurrection and the outpouring of the Holy Spirit) that the "last days" (2:17) were upon them. We can even imagine that many or most of them, on arriving at home, shared their fresh discoveries with

9. Luke clearly wants his readers to associate the parents of John and Jesus (Luke 1–3) as well as those Jews baptized on Pentecost with traditional temple piety (Acts 2:46, 3:1, 5:42). In the Roman world Luke is addressing, piety toward the gods, piety toward the family, and piety toward the homeland go hand in hand.

family and friends who did not make the pilgrimage to Jerusalem for the feast. Nothing, however, should incline us to think that they somehow imagined themselves cut off from their Judaism, baptized into a new religion, and impelled to found household churches.

Within Acts, therefore, far from being the originating date ("the birthday") for the Christian church, Pentecost stands as the decisive moment when the frightened Jewish followers of Jesus began boldly to continue the mission he had given them when he trained them in Galilee (Matt 10:1-5 par.). Those who responded to Peter's message were Jews living in the far-flung nations of the earth where they had never had a chance to know or to hear Jesus. The parting of the tongues of fire in Luke's narrative calls to mind the Jewish midrash whereby, during the original Pentecost on Mount Sinai, God's voice thundered and flashed on the mountain and spread out over the entire earth as seventy tongues of fire.[10] Each tongue symbolized one of the seventy world languages. Thus Jewish midrash signaled that God wanted to deliver his Torah not just to Israel assembled at the base of the mountain, but to all peoples in their own languages spread out over the entire face of the earth. Hence, while no Gentile participation is named or intended at this point, Luke appears to be creatively weaving in themes from this Jewish midrash to suggest that Pentecost was the first step in God's primordial plan for sanctifying all the nations of the world. Nonetheless, Luke makes us wait for Acts 10 before Peter baptizes his first Gentile. For the moment, Jesus' message of the coming kingdom has been accepted by Jews who would return to their homes and praise God in most of the languages of the Mediterranean world. This is something to be marveled at, but it is decidedly not the "birthday of the church."

---

10. According to the Jewish midrash: "When God gave the Torah on Sinai, He displayed untold marvels to Israel with His Voice. What happened? God spoke and the Voice reverberated throughout the world. It says, And all the people witnessed the thunderings (Exod 18:15). Note that it does not say "the thunder," but "the thunderings"; wherefore, R. Johanan said that God's Voice, as it was uttered, split into seventy voices, in seventy languages, so that all the nations should understand. When each nation heard the Voice in their own vernacular, their soul departed (i.e., they were in fear), save Israel, who heard but who were not hurt" (*Exodus Rabbah* 5.9). According to Exod 20:18, as literally translated: "All the people saw the voices and the flames." Philo interpreted this to mean that when God spoke "the people seemed rather to be seeing it than hearing it" (*Decalogue* 45). Thus seeing the flames and hearing the seventy voices merged. In Hebrew, "tongue" is often used for "language" (as in the English idiom "my native tongue"). Hence in Luke seventy "tongues of fire" are the visible aspect of all the languages spoken on the face of the earth.

Whether the Church Originated When Jesus Was Named as Messiah

Some scholars believe that the church emerged as a direct result of the recognition that Jesus was the Messiah. Matthew 16:18, when carefully examined, might well suggest that on "this rock" (i.e., the profession of Peter) the church *will* be built. Meanwhile, Peter, when defending himself before the Sanhedrin, specifically speaks of "Jesus Christ" as "the stone that was rejected by you, the builders; it has become the cornerstone " (Acts 4:11). Peter's allusion to Psalm 118 critically links David with Jesus:

> The psalm is about David, and therefore inferentially about the Messiah. It is a Passover psalm and therefore relates to the re-demption theme. David is the pattern of the redeemer. . . . David, though a younger brother and lacking in prestige, was chosen to effect that ancient redemption [from the Philistine menace]. The specialists, even Samuel, David's own family, Goliath, then Saul and others rejected and overlooked him. Yet he was chosen, evidently by God. . . . The psalmist emphasizes that the junior and the unlikely [candidate] can (as frequently [happens] in Jewish history) be the means of God's purpose.[11]

John's gospel contains an instructive story about Jesus healing a man born blind. Having received his sight, the man is subsequently examined by the Pharisees (John 9:13, 15, 16). Unable to gain a satisfactory answer, they bring in the parents of the man. The parents plead ignorance. Why? John explains: "His parents said this because they were afraid of the Jews; for the Jews had already agreed that anyone who confessed Jesus to be the Messiah would be put out of the synagogue" (John 9:22). Scholars generally agree that the threat of exclusion from the synagogue does not fit the actual situation at the time of Jesus.[12] The Synoptics, for their part, represent Jesus himself as encountering resistance in the synagogues of Galilee. At no time, however, are either Jesus or his disciples excluded from the synagogue. More than likely, therefore, the story in John's gospel has been "updated" to include a threat of what was known to be happening in John's community, namely, that Jews attached to the way of Jesus were excluded from the synagogue precisely because they proclaimed him as Messiah.

---

11. J. Duncan M. Derrett, *Studies in the New Testament* (Leiden: Brill, 1978) 2:61–62.

12. Raymond E. Brown, *The Gospel According to John.* AB 29, 29A. (Garden City, NY: Doubleday, 1966) 380.

I must admit that I myself was firmly convinced for a long time that the parting of the ways was principally due to the profession of Jesus as the Messiah. However, after I began to read the rabbinic materials I was astonished to find a wide range of messianic speculation that was openly tolerated among the rabbis. Yohanan ben Zakkai, for instance, a contemporary of Jesus, was reported to have trained his disciples to await the return of King Hezekiah as Messiah. R. Hillel (1st c. B.C.E.), in contrast, was reported to have "maintained that there will be no Messiah for Israel, since they have already enjoyed him during the reign of Hezekiah" (*b. Sanh.* 98b). King Hezekiah (d. 687 B.C.E.) figures in messianic speculations because he was a model, reforming king who ushered in the Deuteronomic revival. What is unusual, however, is to have a rabbi suggesting that the Messiah has already come and, it would seem to follow, another was not to be expected. What then? Perhaps, as Isaiah implies, God alone would come to redeem Israel (Isa 47:4).

R. Eliezer (fl. ca. 80–110 C.E.) taught his disciples that even the final redemption of Israel was conditional: "If Israel repent, they will be redeemed; if not, they will not be redeemed" (*b. Sanh.* 97b). To this R. Joshua objected: "If they do not repent, they will not be redeemed! But the Holy One, blessed be he, will set up a king over them whose decrees shall be as cruel as Haman's, whereby Israel shall engage in repentance, and he will thus bring them back to the right path" (*b. Sanh.* 97b). In effect, if Israel repents voluntarily God will send them a holy and wise Messiah to redeem them. If not, God will anoint a cruel and inept Messiah who will cause so much hardship that Israel will be forced to repent. In other words, Israel would return to the Lord's ways either by the stick or the carrot.

Beyond this diversity of thought, it would appear that rival schools of disciples were fond of naming their own master as God's candidate for Messiah:

> What is his [the Messiah's] name? The School of R. Shila said, "His name is Shiloh, for it is written 'until Shiloh come' [Gen 49:10]." The School of R. Yanni said, "His name is Yinnon, for it is written, 'His name shall endure forever: e'er the sun was, his name is Yinnon' [Ps 72:17]." The School of R. Haninah maintained, "His name is Haninah, as it is written, 'Where I will give you Haninah' [Jer 16:13]. . ." (*b. Sanh.* 99a)

Not only did formative Judaism tolerate rival schools, it would even tolerate a dominant rabbi naming a false Messiah. This happened when the renowned R. Aqiba identified Simon ben Kosiba (called "Bar Kochba," "son of the star," by his adherents) as "the King Messiah" during the Jewish revolt against Rome in 132–135 C.E. (*y. Taan.* 4:5). The revolt was brutally crushed by the Romans. As a result, Bar Kochba was given the nickname "Bar Kozeba" (i.e., "Son of Disappointment" or "Son of the Lie") by the rabbis. But this did not prevent these same rabbis from continuing to honor R. Aqiba as one of the greatest lights for Israel. Indeed, his judgments on numerous issues were credited in both Talmuds.

All things considered, while it is impossible to know precisely what was the degree of tolerance within the synagogues of the first century, one can safely say that the messianic speculation within the rabbinic sources points to such a large range of diversity as to easily accommodate the messianic claim of the Jesus movement. Most probably, therefore, naming Jesus as the Messiah could not have been the decisive cause either for universal exclusion from the synagogues or for the establishment of the church outside Judaism.

Whether the Church Originated Because of the Synagogue Curse

The synagogue prayers that have come down to us only date back to the medieval period. One cannot be certain what prayers were used in the first century. In 1898 a fragment from the storehouse (*geniza*) of a synagogue in old Cairo was published. It contained a very early version of the "Eighteen Benedictions" (*Amidah*), a prayer traditionally recited three times each day and used in the synagogue. What interested Christian scholars was the twelfth benediction within this Geniza Fragment:

> [1] For the apostates, let there be no hope. [2] And let the arrogant government [of Rome] be speedily uprooted in our days. [3] Let the Nazarenes [*nosrim*] and heretics [*minim*] be destroyed in a moment. [4] And let them be blotted out of the Book of Life and not be inscribed together with the righteous. [5] Blessed are you, O Lord, who humble the arrogant.

There is no easy resolution of all the difficulties involved in unraveling this text. We have evidence that, shortly after the siege and destruction of Jerusalem in 70 C.E., Rabban Gamaliel reformulated the *Amidah* in order to condemn "apostates," i.e., Jewish defectors during the time of the war with the Romans. Then the petition for uprooting the arrogant Roman government follows, and after it the petition against the "Nazarenes and heretics." The term "Nazarenes" was likely the one used by Jewish followers of Jesus, as evidenced by Acts 24:5 where Paul is called "a ringleader of the sect of the Nazarenes." Since members of the Jesus movement had a pacifist bent and a well-developed mission to attract and convert Romans, it can be presumed that Nazarenes had little incentive to take up arms against the Romans. Thus the prayer against "apostates" and "the arrogant government" naturally led to a curse on those Jewish groups who were unwilling to oppose Roman rule and defend God's sanctuary.

Reuven Kimelman has carefully explored the meaning of *nosrim* and *minim* since there is uncertainty as to whether either of these terms was being applied to Christians. He concludes, on the basis of Palestinian rabbinic materials, that "*minim* had a Jewish sectarian denotation and was not used to refer to Gentiles."[13] Thus such a term could have included Jewish Christians but would not have been expected to refer to Gentiles attached to the Jesus movement. The term *nosrim*, meanwhile, appears to be a later addition[14] and, from the rabbinic material, one only learns that Jews in temple times did not fast on Sundays because of them: "R. Yohanan [ben Zakkai] said, 'On account of the *nosrim*'" (*b. Taan.* 27b). In addition to Acts 24:5, Kimelman notes that some Church Fathers offer more information regarding this group.[15] Jerome, for instance, writes:

> Until now a heresy is to be found in all parts of the East where Jews have their synagogues; it is called "of the Minaeans" and cursed by Pharisees up to now. Usually they are named Nazoraeans. They believe in Christ . . . but since they want to be both Jews and Christians, they are neither Jews nor Christians. (*Ep.* 112.13)

From this one can conclude that, whenever the prayer cited above was used, it did not have the force of excluding or condemning Gentile Christians but was rather directed toward Jews who attached themselves to Jesus of Nazareth. Since both terms point in the same direction, Kimelman suggests that the second term is explicative and could read: "the Nazoraeans who are the heretics."[16]

---

13. R. Reuven Kimelman, "Birkat Ha-Minim and the Lack of Evidence for an Anti-Christian Jewish Prayer in Late Antiquity," in E. P. Sanders, ed., *Jewish and Christian Self-Definition* (London: SCM Press, 1981) 2:230.
14. Ibid., 234.
15. Ibid., 237–38.
16. Ibid., 244.

The twelfth benediction may have been introduced to thwart continued participation of Jewish Christians within the synagogue. But it remains to be seen why they were excluded. Was it because they refused to fight the Romans in the war of 66–70 C.E.? The juxtaposition of the second and third themes in the prayer above might suggest this. Or was it because this group had identified Jesus as the one to return as Messiah? From the discussion above it appears doubtful that this alone could have excluded anyone from the synagogue. On the other hand, a group persuaded that the end times were close at hand and that God was poised to "[bring] down the powerful from their thrones, and [lift] up the lowly" (Luke 1:53) would be disposed to wait for their Savior rather than to prematurely take up arms. If this is the case, then the twelfth benediction would gain a unity of perspective from beginning to end.

When and how widely this twelfth benediction was used remains an open question. If it had been used broadly for an extended period of time one would expect that the rabbis might have registered a complaint against the Nazareans as pacifists ("yellow-bellies") in the time of Israel's greatest peril and that such a complaint would have found its way into one of the rabbinic collections. Since nothing like this is found, it remains unclear when, where, and how often it was used. In the end, therefore, the Geniza Fragment is not able to shed any sure light on the separation of the church and the synagogue due to unresolvable uncertainties surrounding the dating, the extent of usage, and the definitive meaning of the twelfth benediction.

Whether the Church Emerged Because of Distrust of Temple Worship

In the ancient world the sight of priests offering animal sacrifices within a temple was entirely commonplace. "Sacrifice permeated the ancient world, and it was a fact of life."[17] Both Jews and Gentiles lived in a cultural milieu in which such things were divinely sanctioned and routinely practiced. Various expressions of Judaism in favor of the temple cult can be found scattered throughout its literature. The *Mishnah* asserts that "the land of Israel is holier than all lands" and that "the temple mount is more holy than it" (*m. Kelim* 1:6, 8). Even in Luke's gospel one finds the opening chapters espousing the romantic notion that the parents of John and of Jesus were firmly attached to the temple cult. One

---

17. Kenneth Stevenson, *Eucharist and Offering* (New York: Pueblo, 1986) 11.

might even expect that the reader of Luke's gospel would be supposed to envy Anna who "never left the temple, but worshiped there with fasting and prayer night and day" (Luke 2:37).

Gerd Theissen and Annette Merz, on the other hand, assert that the Christian sources portray both positive and negative assessments of temple sacrifice and that Jesus, near the end of his life, deliberately created a rite to displace such sacrifices. On the positive side Theissen and Merz note that Jesus recognized "the holiness of the temple and priestly control in the case of the healing of lepers . . . and of the payment of the temple tax by his followers [Mark 1:44-45 par.; Matt 17:24-27; 23:16-22, 35-36; Luke 11:50-51]."[18] On the negative side, Theissen and Merz note that significant sayings of Jesus indicate a critical attitude toward the temple cult:

> Here the tendency is always to set the moral above the cultic: care of parents has priority over assigning goods to the temple (Mark 7:6ff.); tithing cooking herbs is not on the same level as a concern for law, mercy and faith (Matt 23:23f.); love of God and neighbor are more important than sacrifice (Mark 12:32-34—this conclusion is drawn by a scribe and Jesus acknowledges it in 12:35); and a sacrifice is worthless unless it has been preceded by reconciliation between the parties in a dispute (Matt 5:23f.).[19]

It is no coincidence, consequently, that Jesus is said to appeal to Hosea 6:6—"For I desire steadfast love and not sacrifice." While the prophets generally were critical of temple sacrifice, this is one of those rare prophetic sayings that presents God as positively declaring "this and not that."

Jesus' deeds go even further. According to Theissen and Merz, Jesus ignored the purification rites necessary for those entering the temple (see Num 9:9; John 13:10; 18:28; 𝔓Ox 840; *Gospel of the Ebionites,* fragment 6).[20] In addition, Jesus anticipated the destruction of the temple with the understanding that "God will erect another in its place."[21]

James D. G. Dunn, in assessing when and how there was a parting of the ways between Christianity and Judaism, takes as his starting point the curious fact that, according to Acts, the Jerusalem church of the 30s

---

18. Gerd Theissen and Annette Merz, *The Historical Jesus: A Comprehensive Guide*, trans. John Bowden (Minneapolis: Fortress Press, 1998) 602.

19. Ibid.

20. Ibid., 432.

21. Ibid.

"remained very focused on the temple."[22] However, Stephen, a leader of the Hellenized Jews within the Jesus movement, disturbed this status quo by speaking out strongly against the temple (Acts 6:11, 14). If Acts 7 can be taken as representing the crisis Stephen provoked, it is understandable that his outspoken views might have triggered a "lynch mob" that led to a general persecution (Acts 8:1). As a result, Dunn concludes that "Stephen marks the beginning of a radical critique of the temple on the part of the infant Christian movement."[23]

Following this line of reasoning, Dunn discerns a split within the early Jesus movement itself regarding the role of the temple. Over and against the pro-temple stance of the Peter Christians, the Stephen Christians hammered out a self-definition that refused to give the temple and its sacrificial system any role whatsoever in their religious identity. Since this was the group primarily expelled from Jerusalem (Acts 8:1), it is no mystery that, once the Stephen branch of the Jesus movement predominated, Christians favoring an amalgamation of Jesus' message with traditional temple piety were in the slim minority.

E. P. Sanders[24] and John Dominic Crossan[25] go even further and conclude that Jesus' prophetic actions against the temple set in motion the very forces that led to his death. Dunn believes that Jesus' unfavorable sayings toward the temple may not have originated with him but were created later and projected on him by Hellenistic Jews like Stephen. In any case, all three scholars find an anti-temple platform within the early layers of the Jesus movement.

Only a fraction of Jews living in Diaspora were able to make the long and dangerous pilgrimage to Jerusalem three times each year (Exod 23:14-17)—for *Pesach* (Passover), for *Shavuot* (Pentecost), and for *Sukkot* ("Tabernacles"). Some contented themselves with substituting table rites within their homes and commemorative readings within their synagogues.[26] Diaspora Jews who did these things, needless to say, did not imagine that they were somehow no longer Jewish. The Stephen Chris-

---

22. James D. G. Dunn, *Partings of the Ways Between Christianity and Judaism and their Significance for the Character of Christianity* (London: SCM Press; Philadelphia: Trinity Press International, 1991) 57.

23. Ibid., 67.

24. E. P. Sanders, *Jesus and Judaism* (Philadelphia: Fortress Press, 1985) 61–75.

25. John Dominic Crossan, *Who Killed Jesus?* (San Francisco: HarperSanFrancisco, 1995) 50–65.

26. Details for understanding the Pharisaic revolution in these terms can be found in the Appendix at the end of this chapter.

tians within the Jesus movement, consequently, should not be understood as stepping outside Judaism because of the fact that they vigorously opposed the temple cult.[27]

Whether the Church Emerged Because of the Circumcision Controversy

The Jesus movement was initially composed entirely of Jews. Under these circumstances the issue of circumcision never arose because all the men in the movement were circumcised, just as Jesus was. Male circumcision was understood as a sign of the covenant between God and Abraham, for God had said to Abraham: "You shall circumcise the flesh of your foreskins, and it shall be a sign of the covenant between me and you. . . . Any uncircumcised male who is not circumcised in the flesh of his foreskin shall be cut off from his people" (Gen 17:11, 14). This rule seems perfectly clear. Why, then, did Peter and Paul admit Gentile men into the Jesus movement by baptism alone without circumcision? And what happened in the early 50s to bring the issue of circumcision to a boil within the Jesus movement (Gal 2:1-6; Acts 15:1-5)?

James D. G. Dunn has studied this issue. According to Dunn,[28] Cornelius and other early converts were effectively already monotheists and practicing many of the traditions of Israel (Acts 10:2). Dunn postulates that in the beginning baptism marked the commitment of both Jews and Gentiles to follow the way of Jesus and "even the more traditional Jerusalem believers might also have been content for the time being to allow such Gentiles to remain in an anomalous status,"[29] since they were en

27. After the destruction of the temple by the Romans in 70 C.E., all Jews were required to make do with table and synagogue rites as substitutes for the former temple sacrifices. The strain did not entirely disappear, however. The Peter Christians (along with the synagogue Jews) anticipated that the Lord would rebuild the temple when he came; the Stephen Christians did not. This controversy continues to divide both Christians and Jews to this day. When I searched the web with the keywords "rebuilding the temple," no less than 60,600 hits turned up. A significant number of these sites are devoted to programs for destroying the mosque on the Temple Mount and rebuilding the temple in all its former glory. Others, however, caution that this "rebuilding" must wait for the coming of the Messiah. Still others envision that the new Jerusalem that will come down from heaven in the last days will have no temple at all (see Rev 21:10, 22).

28. Dunn, *Partings of the Ways*, 124–27.

29. Ibid., 126.

route to full inclusion that would eventually be marked by circumcision (for the men).[30]

But then something changed. Dunn points to "the deteriorating political situation in Judaea"[31] beginning with Emperor Caligula's attempt to have a statue of himself set up in the temple (40 C.E.). A succession of subsequent power struggles[32] edged the nation toward hostilities with the Romans. During this period "any factors perceived as a threat to national identity would make it necessary for both national and religious boundaries to be defended with vigor."[33] Hence Dunn estimates that in the early 50s zealous Christians from Jerusalem began challenging the relaxed boundaries hitherto surrounding Gentile converts: "It is necessary for them to be circumcised and ordered to keep the [entire] law of Moses" (Acts 15:5).

We know the results. The Jerusalem community met and reached the decision "that we should not trouble those Gentiles who are turning toward God" (Acts 15:19). Paul, in his own earlier missionary journeys, never required circumcision for Gentiles. When the Gentile Titus visited Jerusalem with Paul and "was not compelled to be circumcised" (Gal 2:3), Paul regarded this as a confirmation that he "was not running . . . in vain" (Gal 2:2). Later Paul would create a theological fortress to justify his stance by affirming that "a person is a Jew who is one inwardly, and real circumcision is a matter of the heart" (Rom 2:29) and by showing that Abraham was pronounced righteous *before* he was circumcised (Rom 4:1-12).

When the early church gradually moved from delayed male circumcision to no male circumcision whatsoever, one might think that this would have signaled to all Jews that the Jesus movement was stepping outside Judaism. Before one comes down hard on this issue, however, one must know that even within Judaism the mandate for circumcision did have some notable exceptions. To begin with, fifty-one percent of all Jews are not circumcised—namely, the women. Even for men, however, the Jew Paul spoke of circumcision as "a matter of the heart" (Rom 2:29), knowing full well that

30. Dunn fails to take into account a critical difference within the Jesus movement due to its eschatological posture. Dunn's account, accordingly, needs to be corrected and supplemented with Paula Fredriksen's insights that come near the end of this chapter. In effect it was the delay of the *parousia* that raised the issue of the adequacy of baptism for Gentile adherents. In the early period the shortness of the time remaining allowed Gentiles to find inclusion as Gentiles.

31. Dunn, *Partings of the Ways,* 126.

32. Ibid., 127.

33. Ibid.

this symbolic understanding of circumcision was part of his Jewish heritage (e.g., Lev 26:41; Deut 10:16; 30:6; Jer 4:4; 9:25; Ezek 44:7, 9).

Philo, a Jewish contemporary of Paul in Alexandria, argued that "in reality the proselyte is one who circumcises not his uncircumcision but his desires and sensual pleasures and the other passions of the soul for, in Egypt, the Hebrew nation was not circumcised" (*Questions and Answers on Exodus* 2.2). Scholars are unsure whether Philo is correct on this point since, according to Exod 4:22-26, Moses was not circumcised until shortly before the Exodus. On the other hand, Josh 5:5 says that "all the people who came out had been circumcised, yet all the people born on the journey through the wilderness . . . had not been circumcised." In any case, Philo correctly argues that since the entire Hebrew nation was at one time or another uncircumcised, it is not physical circumcision that makes a Jew, but mastery over sensual desires.

Josephus, another contemporary, recounts the history of Izates, the crown prince of the house of Adiabene, who, on embracing Judaism, was persuaded not to be circumcised lest it cause political unrest. Ananias, his Jewish mentor, responded that "he might worship God without being circumcised" and that "God would forgive him . . . while it was omitted out of necessity and for fear of his subjects" (*Ant.* 20.41-42).

While Philo gives circumcision a spiritual meaning and Josephus records an exceptional case of conversion without circumcision, neither of these authors would have gone as far as Paul did when he taught all male Gentile converts to avoid circumcision. Nonetheless, what is important to recognize here is that Paul made his case "against circumcision" on the basis of his Jewish midrashic argument. Essentially he was a Jew arguing with Jews on a Jewish question. In the end they might not agree, yet no Jew could accuse Paul of stubbornly rejecting a key ingredient of Judaism without due cause. After all, did not his contemporaries, Philo and Josephus, do the same thing? The circumcision controversy, consequently, was not the place where either Paul or the Council of Jerusalem stepped outside Judaism. This will become more evident in what follows.

Whether the Church Emerged Because of Negation of the Sabbath

The Roman year of 365 days (366 every fourth year) was divided into twelve months. No provisions were made for a weekly cycle of seven days. Jews, on the other hand, understood their seven-day week as rooted in creation (Gen 2:2-3) and divinely sanctioned in the Decalogue

(Exod 20:8-11). Keeping the Sabbath was consequently a visible sign of adherence to the covenant (Exod 31:16-17; Deut 5:15; Isa 56:6). Deliberately violating the Sabbath was often perceived as abandoning the covenant (1 Macc 1:43; Josephus, *Ant.* 2.346; Philo, *Vit. Mos.* 2.213-220) and was, at least in earlier periods, punished by stoning (Num 15:32-36). Every inadvertent violation of the Sabbath required a sin offering in the temple (Lev 4:27-35). So important was this observance that Jews living outside Palestine had petitioned and received a special dispensation to gather for synagogue worship on the Sabbath even if it happened that Roman clubs and associations were prohibited from meeting on that day according to the Roman calendar (Philo, *Gaius* 155-159; Josephus, *Ant.* 14.241-246, 258, 263-264). Furthermore, Jews had even gained a special exemption from military service on the grounds that the Sabbath rendered them incapable of serving in the imperial armies (Josephus, *Ant.* 13.252, 14.237).

Given the importance of the Sabbath rest, it is curious that nowhere in the New Testament does one find any universal rule to cease from working on any fixed day of the Jewish week. Even when the seven-day week was introduced into the Roman calendar in the late first century, and "Sunday" was taken as the day when Christians met to celebrate the Eucharist in the mid-second century, this day remained an ordinary workday unless it accidentally fell on a civil holiday in the Roman calendar. Not until 321 C.E. do we find the Emperor Constantine declaring "the day of the sun" to be commemorated by the closing of the civil courts and the workshops in the city. Later emperors prohibited slaves from working on that day, and the Germanic kings, following their conversion, banned hard labor on Sundays by everyone.

In effect the emergence of the Sabbath rest came very gradually. During its formative period, moreover, the Gentile church appears to have disregarded the Lord's command to "remember the sabbath day, and keep it holy" (Exod 20:8). Jewish Christians and Jews in general faithfully observed the Sabbath rest during this entire period. They, of course, had the imperial freedom to do so. All others were forced to follow the Roman calendar when it came to days of work and days of rest.

When the Synoptic Gospels were written, Jesus was remembered to have disturbed pious Jews by his infractions of the Sabbath rest (Mark 2:23–3:6 par.). Even these narratives, however, presuppose that Jesus regarded the Sabbath as the day of rest mandated by the Lord God. The Jesus of Mark, however, goes so far as to say that "the sabbath was made for humankind and not humankind for the sabbath" (2:27). This reinterpretation clearly puts human considerations in the driver's seat (as was shown in chapter 2). Matthew and Luke, understandably, removed this from their gospels. The Jesus of Mark was clearly too liberal relative to Sabbath rest.

The apostle Paul, for his part, discouraged those Gentiles who had begun to observe "special days, and months, and seasons [within the Jewish calendar]" (Gal 4:10; Col 2:16) from continuing to do so. In his letter to the Romans, on the other hand, Paul puts forward a more moderate position on this matter. He now takes the stand that, in order to eliminate needless quarreling (14:1), members of the Jesus movement should recognize that there exists a lawful diversity in such matters.

> Some judge one day [the Sabbath] to be better than another, while others judge all days to be alike. Let all be fully convinced in their own minds. Those who observe the day [of the Lord] observe it [the Sabbath] in honor of the Lord. Also those who eat [on a Jewish day of fasting] eat in honor of the Lord . . . while those who abstain, abstain in honor of the Lord . . . (Rom 14:5-6)

One might suspect that Paul was aware that some of the Christians in the Roman church did keep the Sabbath and that this observance also included some Gentiles. Knowing this, Paul here argues that those who keep the Sabbath rest "honor the Lord [God]." Likewise, those who "judge all days to be alike" can also regard their "working" on the Sabbath as honoring the Lord. Notice that Paul does not specifically say that the former rule applies to Jewish Christians while the latter rule applies to Gentile Christians:[34] quite the contrary. Paul leaves the matter open. Most Jews, needless to say, would have been habituated from birth not to work on the Sabbath. In so doing they felt they honored the Lord. Some Romans voluntarily kept the Sabbath rest with the Jews because they admired their practice or kept it for superstitious reasons.[35] Paul

---

34. The Jew Trypho, after learning that Christ dispensed Christians from Sabbath observances, asked whether a Christian could keep the Sabbath if he wished to. Justin Martyr (100–165 c.e.) knew of some Jewish Christians who kept the Sabbath and replied, "Yes, as long as he doesn't try to force other Christians to keep the law of Moses" (Justin, *Dialogue with Trypho*, 47).

35. The Romans were cautious about going out or beginning any new enterprise on "the day of Saturn." This may in part be due to Jewish custom and in part to the astrological interpretation of Saturn as a "maleficent planet" (Willy Rordorf, *Sunday: The History of the Day of Rest and Worship in the Earliest Centuries of the Christian Church*, trans. A. A. K. Graham [Philadelphia: Westminster, 1968] 29).

seems to be allowing that Gentiles in the Roman church could be firm Sabbath keepers (contrary to what he wrote in Gal 4:10 and what is said in Col 2:16).

In fact, we have no firm evidence that allows us to know how rigorously Jews in the first-century Diaspora kept the Sabbath rest. The observance must have been quite deliberate, however, given the fact that Jewish communities had petitioned and gained Roman exemptions in these matters. Whether a man was circumcised or not was hidden by his clothes. Whether a man worked on the Sabbath, however, was evident for all to see. The blurring or even the outright abandonment of the Sabbath rest would consequently signal to neighbors that one was no longer a practicing Jew. On the other hand, neighbors would be on solid ground if they refused to regard Gentile Christians as part of a "Jewish" movement if they routinely ignored the Sabbath rest. If asked, they might explain that they were fully incorporated into the faith and hope of Israel,[36] but "as Gentiles" they did not need to act or live "as Jews" (in fact, they were sometimes even openly discouraged from it). The whole issue of Sabbath rest, consequently, may have been a thorny issue within the Jesus movement, but it is hard to imagine how it could have been the pivotal litmus test that separated the church from the synagogue, since Jewish Christians normally kept the Sabbath.

Whether the Church Emerged Out of the Jewish Wars with Rome

Josephus details confrontation after confrontation between Romans and Jews. Illustrative was the affair wherein Cumanus, Roman procurator from 48–52 C.E., caused ten thousand Jews to die in the temple courts. As Josephus reports it, the whole affair began during the Passover when a Roman soldier, after discreetly defecating, decided to moon the Jewish pilgrims using "such words as you might expect upon such a posture" (Josephus, *Bell.* 2.224). Thus it would appear that a Roman soldier, surprised at being spotted relieving himself next to a city wall, endeavored to turn his embarrassment around by mooning the crowd. Since an of-

---

36. In fact, it seems that many synagogues had Gentile sympathizers like the Roman centurion Cornelius in Acts, who was perceived as "a devout man who feared God . . . gave alms generously . . . and prayed constantly [in the synagogue?]" (10:1). Josephus writes that "[the Antiochian Jews] were constantly attracting to their religious ceremonies multitudes of Greeks, and these they had in some measure incorporated with themselves (*Bell.* 7.45). If this is the case, the presence of Gentile sympathizers within the Jewish Jesus movement would not have been unthinkable or even irregular in the first century.

fense against honor had transpired, a Jewish delegation met with the procurator to ask that the soldier be punished. Cumanus hesitated. Hot-headed Jewish youths, meanwhile, threw stones at Roman soldiers, who were quite numerous in and around the temple during the time of the feast (*Bell*. 2.224). In a reckless show of force Cumanus sent his troops into the crowded temple courts with orders to beat the pilgrims gathered there. In their panic the pilgrims charged for the exits: "the violence with which they crowded to get out was so great, that they trod upon each other and squeezed one another till ten thousand of them were killed" (*Bell*. 2.227). Josephus may be inflating the numbers. Nonetheless, he was quite correct in showing that the temple was a rallying point for Jewish malcontents restless under the Roman occupation of Jerusalem. Every few years open violence broke out. Each event set the stage for a slow burn until the next conflagration took place. Josephus summarizes: "The flame [of open conflict] was every day more and more blown up, till it came to direct war" (*Bell*. 2.265).

In the year 66, guerilla raids on Roman barracks intensified. The Roman fortress in Jerusalem was overrun and the survivors were lynched. War with the Romans was inevitable. Vespasian swept down through Galilee with his Roman legions and surrounded Jerusalem. Over a period of almost two years, nearly a million Jews were slowly starved to death by the Roman blockade of Jerusalem. Then the Romans breached the walls and burned the temple to the ground, killing all who resisted. Ninety-seven thousand survivors were sold into slavery, a standard Roman practice whose purpose was to recoup the cost of the expensive siege.

Both during and after this war, Jews were regarded suspiciously by the Romans as a rebellious and stiff-necked people. While Jewish resistance to imperial domination rankled many Romans, the Jewish religion seemed to be an even more potent cause for Roman distrust. This can be seen from the fact that, while the Romans were normally tolerant of foreign religions, "it is in relation to Jews that we find imperial initiatives to discourage anyone choosing to become a Jew or to be known as one."[37] Jews were despised as "atheists" insofar as Romans recognized that Jews regarded all the Roman gods as vulgar products of a warped imagination. All the other peoples conquered by Rome were seemingly able to give a nod of approval to the Roman religion; the Jews, in contrast, fiercely opposed any contact whatsoever with Roman rites and deities.

---

37. James McLaren, "From Jewish Movement to Gentile Church," *Jewish-Christian Relations*, http://www.jcrelations.net/en/?item=768.

This manifest intolerance was regarded by many Romans as "suspect" and "dangerous," especially because a significant number of Romans had themselves abandoned their ancestral religion in order to join their "atheism."[38]

During this same period Jewish Christians scattered throughout the empire were undoubtedly anxious to distance themselves from any association with "rebels" against Rome. Gentile Christians, as a result, would have been careful to play down or even to deny Jewish sympathies. Furthermore, since Christians were also recruiting Romans away from their ancestral religion, Christians quickly became marked for intimidation and even outright persecution. The fact that Christians were able to offer Romans incorporation into the "true Israel" without male circumcision, food regulations, and Sabbath rest, however, undoubtedly also worked to appeal to potential Roman converts at the same time that it served to differentiate Christians from Jews.

The war with Rome that resulted in the destruction of the temple in Jerusalem had a massive impact within Judaism. No longer would Judaism be associated with centralized temple worship and the rule of priests. There was thus a power vacuum within Judaism itself. The Pharisees who had survived the siege and had regrouped at Yavneh were intent on promoting their own Jewish spirituality to fill this power vacuum. "The goal was not the triumph over other sects [of Judaism] but the elimination of the need for sectarianism itself."[39] The Pharisees were always innovators in tension with the temple priesthood; they were bent on lay learning and lay rites that escaped the narrow strictures of the temple priests (see Appendix). With the temple gone, the Pharisees were destined to flourish and to fashion a rabbinic religious identity that would become the dominant surviving form of Judaism to the present day. During this period the synagogues abandoned receptivity to Gentiles in favor of getting their own house in order. Meanwhile, the Jesus movement, with its growing sympathy for Gentiles, would undoubtedly have been seen as counterproductive and divisive. When one reads the Synoptic Gospels, consequently, one finds Jesus' conflicts with the Pharisees holding a central place, whereas during the actual ministry of Jesus

---

38. Romans both admired and distrusted the Jews. For a detailed study of these two aspects see John G. Gager, *The Origins of Anti-Semitism* (Oxford: Oxford University Press, 1985) 35–102.

39. Shaye J. D. Cohen, "The Significance of Yavneh: Pharisees, Rabbis, and the End of Jewish Sectarianism," *HUCA* 55 (1984) 29.

it is quite possible that Jesus had little or no contact with Pharisees in Galilee.[40] The Synoptic Gospels, consequently, reflect the condition of Christians in the postwar situation and advise Christians to distance themselves from the "yeast of the Pharisees" (Mark 8:15) as it existed after 70 C.E.[41] The rabbis, needless to say, were also distancing themselves from the yeast of the Christians.

Whether the Church Emerged Because of the Abrogation of the Torah

Christians sometimes imagine that Jesus abandoned the Torah that defined his Jewish covenant with the Lord. Nothing could be further from the truth. The Sermon on the Mount, when closely examined, does not displace the Torah; rather, Jesus shows that in all areas his disciples must interpret the Torah more broadly so that "your righteousness exceeds that of the scribes and Pharisees" (Matt 5:20). In the case of the prohibition against murder, for example, Jesus regards insults and name-calling as meriting as much severity as deliberate killing (Matt 5:17-20). This is a strong indication that the Jewish Christians in Matthew's community kept the entire Torah. It is even probable that the Gentiles who were being embraced by this community were also destined, in gradual and even doses, to be entirely trained and initiated as Jews. Jesus, after all, was a Jew and, for many, following Jesus meant embracing his Judaism.

Christians sometimes imagine that Jesus gave his disciples the Law of Love that entirely replaced the Law of Moses. The key passage in Matthew normally used to support such a view is Jesus' response to the Pharisee who inquired about the greatest commandment: "'You shall love the Lord your God with all your heart, and with all your soul, and with all your mind.' This is the greatest and first commandment. And a second is like it: 'You shall love your neighbor as yourself.' On these two

---

40. The ascendancy of synagogue Judaism under the direction of rabbis who are the spiritual descendants of the Pharisees left the mistaken historical impression that the Pharisees determined normative Judaism in Galilee prior to the destruction of the temple. While our historical records are thin, it would appear that few if any Pharisees lived in Galilee before the late first century. For an overview of this issue see David Goodblatt, "The Place of the Pharisees in First Century Judaism: The State of the Debate," *JSJ* 20/1 (1989) 12–30.

41. Michael J. Cook, in "Jesus and the Pharisees—The Problem as it Stands Today," *JES* 15 (1978) 441–60, makes the point that neither the Christian gospels nor the rabbinic materials provide any sure historical information respecting the practices, location, and influence of the Pharisees during the pre-70 period.

commandments hang all the law and the prophets" (Matt 22:37-40). The so-called double love commandment that Jesus offers the lawyer does not replace the Torah given by Moses. Quite the opposite: it serves as a statement of the "greatest commandment," which governs all the other commandments of the Torah and the prophets.

The joining of love for God and for neighbor was also understood to be foundational within Judaism. In the first century *Testaments of the Twelve Patriarchs,* Dan teaches his sons, "Love the Lord throughout your life and one another with a true heart" (*T. Dan* 5:3), and Issachar teaches his sons, "Love the Lord and your neighbor" (*T. Iss.* 5:2). Philo, when describing the special commandments given to the Jews by God, notes that everything can be divided into two categories: (1) "the regulating of one's conduct towards God by the rules of piety and holiness" and (2) "[the regulating of] one's conduct towards men [women] by the rules of humanity and justice" (*Spec. Leg.* 2.63).

The Golden Rule is found in Lev 19:18 where, after a list of numerous deeds to be avoided (Lev 19:11-18), it forms a kind of conclusion: "But [on the contrary], you shall love your neighbor as yourself." In Matthew 22:39 these words are found on the lips of Jesus and, as a result, many well-meaning Christian scholars have attempted to demonstrate the superiority of the positive Golden Rule over the negative formulation that appears to be more common in Jewish sources and in the *Didachē.* E. P. Sanders, however, notes that the negative formulation has a distinctively stronger force.[42] The negative formulation of the Golden Rule has a special place in rabbinic Judaism because, according to the first-century school of Hillel, it served as a comprehensive summary of the Torah that a convert needed to know when approaching Judaism. In the rabbinic story an unnamed proselyte approaches Hillel and challenges him to teach him the whole of Judaism while standing on one foot. Hillel, who is not put off by this brash proposal, responds: "What is hateful to you, do not do to your neighbor. This is the whole Torah; the rest is commentary" (*b. Shab.* 31a).

Most interpretations of Paul endeavor to contrast justification by the Law[43] with justification by grace. The implication is that Judaism is

---

42. Sanders, *Jewish Law from Jesus to the Mishnah: Five Studies* (London: SCM Press; Philadelphia: Trinity Press International, 1990) 71.

43. As for "justification through the law," Paul "says nothing to imply that this is the normal Jewish understanding of the covenant" (Neil Elliott, *Liberating Paul: The Justice of God and the Politics of the Apostle* [Maryknoll, NY: Orbis, 1994] 134). In fact, careful examination of Jewish sources demonstrates that Israel always relied on a future made possible by the Lord and not on their good works. Daniel, for example, prays: "Incline your ear, O

wrong-minded because it tries to achieve righteousness by personal conformity to the Law. According to Paul this is a self-defeating impossibility because "all, both Jews and Greeks, are under the power of sin" (Rom 3:9). What, then, is to be done? Paul explains his thesis:

> We hold that a person is justified by faith apart from works prescribed by the law. Or is God the God of Jews only? Is he not the God of Gentiles also? Yes, of Gentiles also, since God is one; and he will justify the circumcised on the ground of faith and the uncircumcised through that same faith. *Do we then overthrow the law [Torah] by this faith? By no means!* On the contrary, we uphold the law [Torah]. (Rom 3:28-31, emphasis added)

This is the contrast in Paul's theology of inclusion. In these latter times God has made way for the Gentiles to be justified by virtue of their faith in the future of God. Jews and Gentiles, consequently, are both justified and saved by this same faith.

Many scholars have been puzzled that Paul was engaged in such a vigorous debate respecting the status of the Gentiles in the 50s. Should not this debate have originated and been settled in the late 30s when the Gentile outreach first began? A very attractive explanation for this delay has been offered by Paula Fredriksen. Her solution may be summarized in three points:

1. The early Jesus movement emerged out of Jesus' heralding the kingdom of God as close at hand. The prophets frequently declared that all Gentiles would be destroyed along with their idols when the Lord comes (e.g., Mic 5:9, 15) and that their cities would be either devastated or repopulated by Israel (e.g., Isa 54:3; Zeph 2:1-3, 8). Jesus and his disciples, on the other hand, embraced "the positive extreme" within the prophetic tradition. According to this rather thin strand of prophetic vision, Gentiles in the last days would abandon idolatry and attach themselves to exiled Jews in their midst and join them in worshiping the God of Jacob (Isa 2:2-4; Mic 4:1-3) and together both Jews and Gentiles would eat the feast that the Lord would prepare for them in Jerusalem (Isa 25:6).

2. Within the Jesus movement, Jews prepared for the Lord's coming by turning in faith to a heartfelt observance of the Torah; Gentiles, on the other hand, were to *"turn from* idolatry (and the sins associated with it)

---

my God, and hear. Open your eyes and look at our desolation and the city that bears your name. We do not present our supplications before you on the grounds of our righteousness, but on the grounds of your great mercies. O Lord, hear; O Lord, forgive; O Lord, listen and act and do not delay!" (Dan 9:18-19).

and *turn to* the living God." Thus male circumcision, Sabbath keeping, and kosher foods were required of Jews but not of Gentiles since "Gentiles are saved as Gentiles: they do not, eschatologically, become Jews."

3. This situation prevailed during the 30s and 40s and allowed Jews and Gentiles to be joined in faith and fellowship, bound together in the same hope. Then a critical stress point emerged: "By mid-century, surely all these Christians must have realized that their expectations [of the imminent coming of the Lord] had not been fulfilled. . . . Gentiles continued to join the movement in numbers; the mission to Israel, however, had foundered."[44]

In response to this crisis some Jewish Christians began to advocate that, given the delay in the Lord's coming, Gentiles ought to completely convert to Judaism so as to ensure their place in the world to come. Others, like Paul, strenuously insisted that the old policy of admitting Gentiles "with only the requirement of moral, not halachic, conversion" be maintained: "This meant no idols. It also meant no circumcision."[45]

The value of Fredriksen's reconstruction is that she is able to explain how and why the early church was of one mind in regarding male circumcision, Sabbath observance, and kosher foods as unnecessary and inappropriate for Gentiles who waited on the Lord. Then, as the feverish expectation of the coming of the Lord cooled and the mission to the Jews was drying up, there was an internal drive to bring Gentiles into a full Jewish identity and practice. In part this could be motivated by anxiety regarding the salvation of those Gentiles who died before the coming of the Lord (as reflected in 1 Thess 4:13-18). In part it could also be motivated by fear, on the part of some, that the Jewish identity of the church was in danger of being lost as the influx of Gentile adherents increased while the addition of Jewish members nearly ceased. Whatever the complex motivations, the early 50s mark the emergence of bitter internal quarrels regarding the status of Gentile adherents among the people of God when the Lord comes to establish his kingdom on earth.

Conclusion

Stepping back, one can see that there was no one event (such as Pentecost) and no single cause (such as naming Jesus as Messiah) that led to the final break. Progressively, however, the way of life and the faith

44. Paula Fredriksen, "Judaism, the Circumcision of Gentiles, and Apocalyptic Hope." *JTS* n.s. 42 (1991) 532–64, at 531.
45. Ibid.

orientation of the church grew in directions that differentiated it and later even set it in opposition to the synagogue. In examining these points of opposition one can see that they cluster around the Gentile mission of the church. At various times and in various places Jews embraced a Gentile outreach,[46] so the outreach cannot be imagined as, in itself, incompatible with Judaism. Nonetheless, the Gentile mission was a factor that progressively aggravated the rifts between the Judaism of the Jesus movement and the Judaism of the synagogue of the late first century. Without the Gentile mission it is entirely possible that Christianity would have remained a form of Judaism. With the success of the Gentile mission, however, it was only a matter of time before a Gentile majority within the churches themselves began to actually oppose male circumcision, observance of the Torah, keeping the Sabbath, holding to the (old) covenant, and maintaining the centrality of Jerusalem as though these things were somehow foreign to their fundamental faith.[47] The argument of this chapter has been that these same things were very much at the core of the Jesus movement precisely because the salvation of Gentiles was always entirely contingent on the salvation of Israel. The Jewish wars with Rome, in their turn, cemented the determination of the church to safeguard its mission to the Gentiles by distancing itself from the "rebellious" Jews.

When the origins of this break are investigated, one can see that it was not Jesus or Paul or Barnabas who wanted this to happen. The sad and true words of Jacob Neusner cited earlier, therefore, aptly bring this chapter to a close:

> We have ample evidence for characterizing as a family quarrel the relationship between the two great religious traditions of the West. Only brothers can hate so deeply, yet accept and tolerate so impassively, as have Judaic and Christian brethren both hated, and yet taken for granted the presence of, one another.[48]

---

46. From 170 B.C.E. to 70 C.E., for example, "Judaism showed itself to be a virile missionary faith, seeking to win not only renegade Jews but also Gentile sinners to faith in the true God" (David S. Russell, *The Method and Message of Jewish Apocalyptic: 200 BC–AD 100* [Philadelphia: Westminster, 1964] 298).

47. The *Letter of Barnabas* cited earlier in this chapter and the writings of Justin Martyr clearly demonstrate this position.

48. Neusner, "The Jewish-Christian Argument," 9. If you would like to share your reflections on this chapter or see what others have produced, go to www.salvationisfromthejews .info.

Appendix: The Pharisaic Revolution as Mother of the Church

The Jesus movement emerged out of the Pharisaic revolution, which had transformed Jewish identity. Many Christians will find this strange. After all, don't the Synoptic Gospels portray the Pharisees as the enemies and rivals of the Jesus movement? Precisely. But it was because the church emerged out of the synagogue (and not out of the temple) that it inherited a system of thought liberated from the temple cult as defining worship and from the Aaronide priesthood as defining conduct. Ellis Rivkin, in his fascinating book, *The Shaping of Jewish History*,[49] offers the following portrait of how the Pharisees turned temple Judaism on its head:

1. Instead of relying on the temple cult managed by the priests to define worship, the Pharisees gave every Jew the right and the obligation to address God. Thus daily prayers and simple rituals conducted by ordinary individuals served "to bring the individual into direct communion with God" (58). Furthermore, these prayers and rites were performed not in the divinely ordained holy temple, but within the ordinary spaces of home and synagogue.

> This was a truly revolutionary step, for nowhere in the Pentateuch is prayer obligatory. . . . The Pharisees were therefore once again going off on a highly original tack when they made mandatory the saying of the *Shema*—"Hear O Israel, the Lord is our God, the Lord is one"—in the morning and evening, and when they introduced the recitation of the prayer now called the *Amidah* or *Shemoneh Esreh* as the prayer par excellence; when they required each individual to utter benedictions before meals, after meals, and on other occasions; and when they established fixed readings from the Pentateuch and the prophets on the Sabbath. And although the synagogue may at first have been a place where Scripture was read and only later a house of prayer, the Pharisees were its creators.[50]

Furthermore, the Pharisees enabled ordinary Jews to celebrate the Jewish holidays within their homes, thereby making their homes "sacred space." The mother and father officiated at simple rites within the family without any need to be a priest or to call upon a priest. This transformation paved the way for Jews to live out their entire lives independent of the temple

---

49. Ellis Rivkin, *The Shaping of Jewish History* (New York: Charles Scribner's Sons, 1971). Subsequent scholarship has muted some of Rivkin's generalizations.

50. Ibid., 58–59.

cult—a situation that became a permanent reality following the Roman destruction of the temple in 70 C.E.

2. Instead of having the priests direct the reading and the interpretation of Torah, the Pharisees gave every male Jew the right and the obligation to read and interpret the Torah for himself, guided by the oral traditions handed down by the rabbis. The assertion that there was a binding oral tradition alongside the binding written scroll separated the Pharisees from the Aaronide priesthood. By taking charge of their own interpretation, the Pharisees declared their intellectual and spiritual independence from the priests. "The Pharisees even went so far as to allow discussion, debate, and even alternate renderings of the Law [Torah]. This too was revolutionary innovation."[51] The Pharisees made it possible for living oral traditions to expand and contract their sense of what God would have them be and do—something that, according to the priests, was frozen in the Scriptures. When it came to the discussions and debates with Jesus and his disciples, the Pharisees sometimes took issue with their understanding and application of the Scriptures, yet they never contested the right of non-priests to read and interpret Torah as such. This was their shared heritage.

3. Instead of allowing the centralized and centralizing temple to dominate Jewish religious existence, the Pharisaic revolution generated pinpoints of light throughout the Roman world. In local synagogues (which were frequently in private homes or in open spaces), ordinary Jews experienced greater responsibility and involvement in the shape and the shaping of their way of life. In contrast to the centrist policies of the Jewish priesthood ". . . the triumph of the Pharisees was the triumph of universalism. Now the vital issue was salvation, not the land and the cult. . . . The Pharisaic revolution thus made it possible for the Diaspora to become a generating force free of the dependence on the land of Israel."[52]

In sum, when these three aspects of the Pharisaic revolution are taken together they provide insights as to how the Hellenized Jews within the Jesus movement were the first to gainsay the centrality of the temple and the first to extend the way of Jesus to outsiders (see Acts 6:8–8:8). All in all, therefore, the Pharisaic revolution served as the springboard for both rabbinic Judaism and the Jesus movement.

51. Ibid., 60.
52. Ibid., 85–86.

Five

Jesus as Messiah:
Christian Humility in the Face of Jewish
Objections

> Any messiah in whose name men are tortured is a false messiah.
>
> —Elie Wiesel

As the dialogue between Jews and Christians continues, sooner or later one arrives at the hard issues. Here, most emphatically, the exchange is strained. The Jewish partners in the dialogue may find the graciousness to honor Jesus as a rabbi, even a prophet, but never as the Messiah ordained by God to usher in the reign of God. So, too, for Catholic participants Mary might be understood as a dedicated Jewish mother who heroically stood by her son even at the cross, yet this woman cannot be understood by Jews as having a favored position among all women since she is the mother of the divine redeemer and mediator of grace for all her spiritual children. Protestants, of course, would join with Jews in feeling a distaste for the exalted place that Catholic piety has given to Mary and would turn away from any hint that prayers addressed "through the Mother" might find a better reception than those addressed directly to God. Finally, the Jewish participants would find themselves at a complete loss as to how to make sense of the Trinity—a doctrine that, in Jewish ears, sounds suspect and, at best, appears to be a border-line flirtation with polytheism (despite repeated Christian affirmations that they are strict monotheists).

A strained dialogue does not mean no dialogue at all. To begin with, it helps if the Christian partners can try to account for their position in such a way that Jews might be able to make sense of it. It does no good to present the Christian position in terms that are absolutely foreign or nonsensical to Jews. After all, it was Jews who first crafted most Christian positions, and they knew at the time that their positions harmonized with rather than grating against Jewish sensibilities. Hence, as in every deep conversation, one has to take increasingly into account the horizon of understanding employed by the person to whom one is speaking. In the end one does not expect to gain an adherent; rather, one hopes only to reduce the needless obstacles to mutual understanding. This will become clearer as the separate issues are considered.

Jesus' Message: The Kingdom Is Coming

Before we consider the conflicts that have arisen over the identity and function of the Messiah, it is necessary to remember that Judaism and Christianity share a common hope[1] in the coming of the reign of God. In dialogue between Christians and Jews, both sets of participants would do well to begin with this and, after all the controversies have been considered, to return to it as the basis for what we hold in common.

According to the Synoptics, the coming kingdom was the central metaphor dominating Jesus' public ministry:

> The central aspect of the teaching of Jesus was that concerning the Kingdom of God. Of this there can be no doubt and today no scholar does, in fact, doubt it. Jesus appeared as one who proclaimed the Kingdom; all else in his message and ministry serves a function in relation to that proclamation and derives its meaning from it.[2]

In Matthew's gospel, for instance, Jesus' public ministry is summarized by saying that "Jesus went throughout Galilee, teaching in their synagogues and proclaiming the good news of the *kingdom*. . ." (Matt 4:23 par.; emphasis added). Again, when Jesus is presented as anticipating the future it is summarized in these terms: "This good news of the *kingdom* will be proclaimed throughout the world, as a testimony to all the

---

1. The expectation that God will come to gather the exiles and establish his reign has already been indicated in chapters 2 and 3. This theme was first sounded in the synagogue Sabbath prayer: "Hurry, Loved One, the holy day [of our deliverance] has come: show us grace as [you did] long ago." Next it appeared in our analysis of the Jewish character of the opening phrases of the Lord's Prayer. Finally, it was spelled out in detail in the section entitled "The Priority of Israel's Salvation in the Message of Jesus," in chapter. 3.

2. Norman Perrin, *Rediscovering the Teaching of Jesus* (New York: Harper & Row, 1967) 54.

nations; and then the end will come" (Matt 24:14). The "end" referred to here is the passing of this present era in order to make way for the reign of God.

Heralding the kingdom did not bring it into existence; rather, it served to prepare God's people to get ready for God's arrival. Most of Jesus' parables are really metaphors of getting ready. For the women Jesus tells the parable of how ten virgins, friends of the bride, kept their lamps burning as they awaited the arrival of the groom with his buddies who, it seems, completely lose track of time and arrive after midnight (Matt 25:1-13). For the men Jesus tells the parable of how the male servants need to keep busy (literally, "keep their loins girt") while their master is away at a wedding feast and could arrive home at any moment. When the master returns he surprises those who are ready by girding himself, setting a table, and waiting personally on his faithful servants (Luke 12:35-40). Parables such as these emphasize that God is coming to gather Israel into his reign (the feast), that the moment of his arrival is uncertain, that he will arrive in the dead of night (when evil is afoot), and that those awaiting him need to keep busy (about their Father's business) until then.

The first Passover marked the night when God entered into history to liberate his people; thus for many Jews there was the anticipation that God's final entrance into history might well overtake them as they celebrated Passover "again this year." In this spirit, therefore, Jesus said to his disciples, "I have eagerly desired to eat this Passover with you" (Luke 22:15), and after drinking the cup he said, "From now on I will not drink of the fruit of the vine until the kingdom of God comes" (Luke 22:18). Jesus went to his death, tragically, without seeing the kingdom he had so ardently preached and longed for.

The Acts of the Apostles makes it clear that the proclamation of the kingdom continued to form the central agenda of the early church. Philip, one of the Seven ordained by the Twelve, is presented as reaching out to the Samaritans: "he proclaimed the good news about the *kingdom* of God and the name of Jesus Christ" (Acts 8:12). Likewise, Luke characterized the mission of Paul in these same terms: "he entered the synagogue and for three months spoke out boldly, arguing persuasively about the *kingdom* of God" (Acts 19:8). The whole of Acts closes with this summary of Paul's final mission to the Romans: "he [Paul] lived there [in Rome] two whole years . . . proclaiming the *kingdom* of God and teaching about the Lord Jesus Christ with all boldness and without hindrance" (Acts 28:31). In sum, what Luke presents to us is that, at the time he wrote Acts, the proclamation of the coming reign of God was the Good News that formed the focal message of Jesus and the early disciples. Furthermore, Luke also makes plain that at the time when Jesus' importance in the drama of salvation was being expanded, Jesus' role was always integrated within and subordinated to God's reign.[3]

Jesus' Kingdom Expectation as Central to His Jewish Faith

According to the Synoptics, Jesus never specifically defined the reign of God, nor do the evangelists. Given the centrality of this concept, we must suppose that in each case hearers would have been familiar with "the kingdom." Jews were familiar with the notion that their Lord and God acted powerfully within history to forward the cause of justice and righteousness. The "kingdom/reign of God," therefore, was not a place, not a title, not an office, not a church—it was God acting within society and the world.

The American Catholic scholar John P. Meier speaks of "the kingdom" as "an abstract way of speaking of God ruling powerfully as king."[4] What may surprise Christians is that Jesus and his Jewish contemporaries thought of this kingdom as "coming here on earth" (as opposed to our "going to heaven" after death).[5] The Jewish prophets seldom used the phrase "kingdom of God," but they repeatedly used near equivalents. For example, Isaiah says to Israel: "Be strong, do not fear! Here is your

---

3. In Acts 19:8, for instance, only the kingdom preaching is mentioned. In Acts 8:12 and 28:31 the kingdom preaching is named first, and only then "teaching about the Lord Jesus Christ." A detailed analysis of the sermons in Acts would also show this same relationship, but it is beyond the scope of this book. For a detailed and highly readable study of how the expectation of God's coming as Savior was gradually overlaid with the saving acts of the Messiah see John A. T. Robinson, *Jesus and His Coming* (Philadelphia: Westminster, 1979).

4. John P. Meier, *A Marginal Jew: Rethinking the Historical Jesus* (New York: Doubleday, 1994) 2:298.

5. During the first millennium Christian expectation moved from (a) God's coming to earth to establish his kingdom to (b) having our souls leave behind this earth at death in order to be with God in heaven. The later view also embraced the notion of "the return of Jesus" and "the resurrection of the body" in the end times, but these aspects were lost sight of in the concentration on "going to heaven." When the liturgical renewal in the late 60s introduced the eucharistic acclamation "Christ has died, Christ has risen, Christ will come again," most Catholics were surprised to learn that their church believed that Jesus Christ was returning in the last days. They were also surprised to discover that their church not only believed in "saving souls" but that Catholics were committed to living the way of Jesus in order to prepare for God's reign of justice and peace on earth. This will be presented in greater detail in this chapter and in chapter 7.

God. . . . He will come and save you" (35:4). And when God does come
on the last day, Zechariah describes in great detail how he "will become
king over all the earth" (Zech 14:9). According to the vision of Daniel,
when the Lord comes he will destroy all evil rulers who exploit and af-
flict their subjects; then he will put "the holy ones" in their place as benevolent and just leaders (Dan 7:18, 22, 27; see Luke 1:52).

The Jewish prophets seldom, if ever, speak of the coming of the Messiah (*moshiach* in Hebrew). On the other hand, Jesus and his Jewish contemporaries were very familiar with the idea that the Lord God was
getting ready to come to earth to destroy evil and gather his elect. Once
this was accomplished, many expected God to appoint a righteous king
(the Messiah, the son of David) to rule over his people with justice and
peace. The role of the Messiah was always integrated within and subordinated to God's coming to save Israel.[6]

The early Jewish Christians, when they spoke of Jesus having been
raised and taken into heaven by God, never imagined that Jesus was
content to stay in heaven or that they were someday destined to join him
there. Quite the contrary, as Peter explains to his Jewish audience: Jesus
"must remain in heaven [only] until the time of universal restoration [of
Israel] that God announced long ago through his holy prophets" (Acts
3:21). In those last days, when the "times of refreshing may come from
the presence of the Lord [God]," he will "send [to earth] the Messiah
appointed for you, that is, Jesus" (Acts 3:20). In sum, Peter assures his
hearers that God was preparing to bring Jesus back to earth when it came
time for him to establish his kingdom on earth. If the kingdom comes to
us, then Jesus has to be in the right place (namely, on earth) in order to
function as the just king (the Messiah).

Jews, for their part, celebrate every Passover by setting a place for the
prophet Elijah. In some instances the children are even sent out into the
streets to see if Elijah has come. Elijah, it will be remembered, was taken
up into heaven by a "chariot of fire" and "a whirlwind" (2 Kgs 2:11). But

6. The eschatological trajectory within Judaism was, in its early phases, without any
messianic age; in its later phases the mighty works of God were given over to his Messiah. The transition from God alone as the expected Savior to God and his Messiah joining forces, and then on to the coming (alternatively the "return") of the Messiah, eclipsing
God's coming, can be traced within the Jewish literature of Middle Judaism. During this
same period the Jesus movement was fashioning its own eschatology as well. For a brief
examination of this development see Milavec, *The Didache: Faith, Hope, and Life of the Earliest Christian Communities, 50–70 C.E.* (New York: Paulist, 2003) 676–82. For a book-length
examination see Robinson, *Jesus and His Coming.*

no one stays in heaven. Elijah was taken up because God wanted him to be ready to return in the last days. The Septuagint closes with these words: "Lo, I [the Lord-God] will send you the prophet Elijah before the great and terrible day of the Lord comes" (Mal 4:5). This helps explain why Jesus in the Synoptics informs his disciples that John the Baptizer is Elijah returned (Mark 9:13; Matt 11:13-14; 17:12-13). In John's gospel, on the other hand, when John the Baptizer is asked point-blank whether he is Elijah, he denies it (John 1:21).

Jesus' Kingdom Prayer

Jesus' prayer addressed the "Father" and petitioned that his "kingdom come." This prayer admirably captures the central core of Jesus' preaching. Having studied this prayer, Joachim Jeremias concluded that the first two petitions in the Lord's Prayer were not "newly constructed by Jesus, but come from the Jewish liturgy, namely from the Kaddish, the 'holy' prayer with which the synagogue liturgy ended and which was familiar to Jesus from childhood."[7] James D. G. Dunn, writing twenty years later, came to this same conclusion (seemingly independently) when he noted how "striking" it was that the Lord's Prayer "was so closely modeled on Jewish prayers of the time—particularly the Kaddish."[8] The *Kaddish* used in the synagogue during the time of Jesus was surmised[9] to be as follows:

7. Joachim Jeremias, *New Testament Theology: The Proclamation of Jesus*, trans. John Bowden (New York: Charles Scribner's Sons, 1971) 198.

8. James D. G. Dunn, *The Partings of the Ways Between Christianity and Judaism and their Significance for the Character of Christianity* (London: SCM Press, 1991) 38.

9. Paul F. Bradshaw, in his *Search for the Origins of Christian Worship* (Oxford: Oxford University Press, 1991), 1–6, makes the point that most scholars in the last century had "a considerable degree of assurance what Jewish worship was like in the first century," but that this assurance had almost entirely evaporated by the turn of the century. To begin with, Bradshaw draws attention to the fact that no surviving synagogue prayer book goes back earlier than the ninth century. Moreover, instead of assuming that the rabbis shaped daily prayers, thereby insuring a degree of uniformity, Bradshaw demonstrates that recent scholars have concluded that "diversity and variety" characterized this development and that the rabbis, by the end of the second century, had only partially succeeded in bringing a degree of standardization to the prayer life of their followers. In brief, Bradshaw concludes that a survey of all the relevant documents leads to the conclusion that three regular prayers were used by many ordinary Jews during the first century: the *Shema,* the *Tefillah,* and grace at meals. The *Kaddish* only developed later; hence there is no certainty that the Lord's Prayer was shaped by first-century prayers used in the synagogue as scholars such as Jeremias and Dunn have supposed.

> Exalted and *hallowed be his* great *name*
> in the world which he created according to his will.
> May he *establish his kingdom* in your lifetime
> and in the lifetime of the whole household of Israel,
> speedily and at a near time.[10]

The entire prayer expresses the Jewish hope that God's kingdom will come and God will establish his kingdom "speedily." The italicized phrases in particular help show the remarkable affinity to the opening petitions of the Lord's Prayer. Thus when the Lord's Prayer is appreciated as an expression of the longstanding hope of Israel one can justifiably imagine that this prayer would have been easily understood and readily received even by Jewish fishermen.

I Believe with a Perfect Faith in the Coming of the Moshiach

Judaism lives primarily within orthopraxis (rightly serving God), while Christianity has placed its emphasis on orthodoxy (rightly believing God). Nonetheless, Jews do sometimes formulate what Christians understand as "creeds." One such important faith summary was prepared by Moses Maimonides (d. 1204) in his commentary to the Mishnah tract *Sanhedrin*. This is familiar to Jews as the *Shloshah-Asar Ikkarim* ("The Thirteen Articles of Faith") and is publicly recited in some congregations. Each of the thirteen articles begins with "I believe with a perfect faith . . . ." The first is as follows: "I believe with a perfect faith that God is the Creator and [he] guides all creation." The fifth affirms: "I believe with a perfect faith that God only and no one else is worthy of our prayers." For our discussion here, however, the twelfth proposition is of special importance: "I believe with a perfect faith in the coming of the *moshiach,* and though he may tarry, still I await him every day."

The Hebrew term *moshiach* in the above "creed" refers to what has come into the English language as "Messiah" or "Christ" (from the Greek word *christos* = "the anointed"). Jews, however, are often painfully aware that when Christians use such terms they mean very different things:

> The term *"moshiach"* or *"messiah"* literally means "the anointed one" and refers to the ancient practice of anointing kings with oil when they took the throne. The *moshiach* is the one who will be anointed as king in the End of Days. The word *"moshiach"* does not mean "savior." The notion of an innocent, divine or semi-divine being who will sacrifice himself to save mankind from the consequences

10. Dunn, *Partings of the Ways*, 38.

of their own sin is a purely Christian concept that has no basis in Jewish thought. Unfortunately, this Christian concept has become so deeply ingrained in the English word "messiah" that this English word can no longer be used to refer to the Jewish concept.[11]

Accordingly, in what follows I will do what we often do in dialogue— we use "*moshiach*" when emphasizing the Jewish understanding and "messiah" when emphasizing the Christian understanding.

Catholic Faith in the Coming of the Messiah

In order to understand what Jews may be reacting to, I decided to look at the description of the Messiah found in the official *Catechism of the Catholic Church*. The results confirmed the cautions voiced above. The *Catechism* declares that "Jesus . . . unveiled the authentic content of his messianic kingship . . . in his redemptive mission as the suffering Servant [on the cross]" (§440).[12] Here the messianic kingship is portrayed entirely as a past event with no bearing whatsoever on the future reign of God. This is disappointing, for it demonstrates that the traditional medieval christology with its focus on the atoning death has been retained, without giving due attention to a half-century of Catholic biblical studies regarding the reign of God and without making use of Vatican II statements that might easily have been introduced at this point. Consider the following: "We are taught that God is preparing a new dwelling and a new earth in which righteousness dwells, whose happiness will fill and surpass all the desires of peace arising in the hearts of man [and woman]. Then with death conquered, the sons [and daughters] of God will be raised in Christ . . ." (*Gaudium et Spes* 39). The bishops here use the phrase "new earth" because the language of the reign of God has

---

11. Tracy R. Rich, "*Moshiach*: The Messiah," http://www.jewfaq.org/*moshiach*.htm. The character and activities expected of the moshiach have changed in the course of history. See Jacob Neusner, *Messiah in Context*, or Gershom Scholem, *The Messianic Idea in Judaism*, for more details. For a contemporary view, see http://www.moshiach.com/questions/topten/what_is_moshiach.php.

12. *The Catechism of the Catholic Church* followed the schema used in the *Roman Catechism* produced after the Council of Trent. Thus the atoning death stands as the primary metaphor for understanding Jesus' mission and forms the horizon of understanding for making sense of how Jesus is the "Christ" (especially §440). All the biblical material cited above regarding the centrality of the reign of God in the mission of Jesus finds occasional references here and there. The citations from Vatican II offered above are grouped together under the heading "The Hope for the New Heaven and the New Earth" (§§1042–50) but show little evidence of having been integrated into Jesus' role as Messiah.

been so traditionally associated with "going to heaven." Notice that the future tense is used throughout and that the general resurrection is associated with the *moshiach*.

This being said, the bishops then caution those who get so fixated on God's future that they fail to fix their faucets, their families, and their failing world:

> Far from diminishing our concerns to develop this earth, the expectancy of the new earth should spur us on, for it is here that the body of a new human family grows, foreshadowing in some way the age which is to come. That is why . . . such progress [now] is of vital concern to the [future] kingdom of God. (*Gaudium et Spes* 39)

The progress named here is not principally in the areas of technological, agricultural, or industrial development, but specifically focused on "human dignity, brotherly communion, and freedom." These "fruits of our nature," the bishops assure us, will be "cleansed . . . from the stain of sin, illuminated and transfigured, when Christ presents to his Father an eternal and universal kingdom of truth and life, a kingdom of holiness and grace, a kingdom of justice, love, and peace" (*GS* 39). To this end the bishops further note that "Christ is now at work in the hearts of men by the power of his Spirit; not only does he arouse in them the desire for the world to come but he quickens, purifies and strengthens the generous aspirations of mankind to make life more humane . . ." (*GS* 38). What the bishops identify as the ongoing work of the *moshiach*, however, only comes to completion in the age to come: "Here [now] on earth the kingdom is mysteriously present; when the Lord comes it will enter into its perfection" (*GS* 39). In sum, the work of Jesus as Messiah does not come to completion with his death (as the *Catechism* implies); rather, the Spirit continues to work in the hearts of believers until, on the last day, Jesus returns to complete his mission. "Then comes the end," explains Paul, "when he [the *moshiach*] hands over the kingdom to God the Father . . . then the Son [the *moshiach*] himself will also be subjected to the one [the Father] who put all things in subjection under him, so that God [the Father] may be all in all" (1 Cor 15:24, 28).

Whether Jesus Fulfilled All the Jewish Prophecies

For nearly two thousand years Christians have rallied around Jesus and hailed him as the one whom God has sent as the *moshiach* of Israel. Immediately after the fall of Adam and Eve in the Garden, for example, Christians discover the first promise that God would send a redeemer in the words directed to the serpent: "I will put enmity between you [the serpent] and the woman, and between your offspring and hers; he [her offspring] will strike your head, and you [the serpent] will strike his heel" (Gen 3:15). On the face of it one might suspect that we have here some ancient Jewish folklore designed to explain why there is a mutual antagonism between people and snakes. The children of Eve fear snakebite, so they kill snakes by clubbing them on the head. Before she ate the fruit of the forbidden tree, it should be noted, Eve felt no fear or antagonism toward the serpent. On the contrary, she found the serpent to be an attractive dialogue partner prompting her to explore the hidden power of the forbidden fruit.

According to the *Catechism of the Catholic Church*, "this passage in Genesis is called the *Protoevangelium* ('first Gospel'), the first announcement of the Messiah and Redeemer, of a battle between the serpent and the Woman, and the final victory of a descendant of hers" (§410). The *Catechism* in this case has championed the allegorical reading of Irenaeus (130–200 C.E.) in which the woman = the Virgin Mary and her offspring = Jesus. Far from being an etiology for why humans kills snakes, therefore, this obscure Jewish text becomes, in Christian eyes, a revelation of how the future *moshiach* will strike out and destroy evil (serpent = Satan) from the face of the earth.[13]

Consider a second example. The early Church Fathers saw in the command of God and the willingness of Abraham to sacrifice his "only son" (Gen 22:16) a prefiguring of the future mystery of redemption wherein the Father of all would willingly sacrifice his only-begotten Son. The blessings follow: "Because you have done this, and have not withheld your son, your only son, I will indeed bless you, and I will make your offspring as numerous as the stars of heaven and . . . *by your offspring* shall all the nations of the earth gain blessing for themselves, because you have obeyed my voice" (Gen 22:16-18; emphasis added). According to Christian commentators, "your offspring" here refers primarily to the

---

13. One can see, from this first instance, that the hidden meanings found in Gen 3:15 go far beyond the literal meaning of the text within its original context. It is even a stretch of the imagination to regard Gen 3:15 as a messianic text. Donald Juel, in his excellent book *Messianic Exegesis* (Philadelphia: Fortress Press, 1988), notes that one finds in Christian exegesis of the Jewish Scriptures something akin to rabbinic midrash—it was a "highly artful, even fanciful, history of interpretation" (p. 13). Catholic biblical scholars such as Bruce Vawter point out serious problems in the continued use of Gen 3:15 as the "protoevangelium" of salvation (*On Genesis: A New Reading* [Garden City, NY: Doubleday, 1977] 83–84).

future Messiah who will not only redeem Israel but "all the nations of the earth" as well. Thus, Abraham's willingness to sacrifice his son has been used by Christians as prophetically prefiguring how God would in the future accomplish universal redemption through Jesus Christ.[14]

The early followers of Jesus clearly regarded their teacher as God's favored Son. Peter, as the tradition has it, was the first to believe that Jesus was also God's *moshiach.* He came to this although "flesh and blood has not revealed this to you, but my Father in heaven" (Matt 16:17). This makes clear that Jesus did not preach or teach anything about his messianic connection; Peter had this knowledge through divine inspiration. On the way to Jerusalem the disciples are obsessed with "who is the greatest" (Matt 18:1 par.), and the Zebedee sons want to be Jesus' first lieutenants when he arrives "in [his] kingdom" (Matt 20:21 par.). They clearly anticipate that Jesus would reveal himself as the *moshiach* in Jerusalem. What a brutal letdown, then, when Jesus is handed over to Pilate and crucified as an insurrectionist. "No one expected the Messiah to suffer. . . . No one expected the Messiah to rise from the dead, because he was not expected to die."[15] These events undoubtedly threw the disciples into despair and confusion. Gradually, over time, however, they discovered in their Jewish Scriptures (they had no other authoritative source) ways of squaring what actually had happened with their abiding hope that Jesus would be appointed as God's *moshiach.* Paul did this in his way. Each of the four evangelists did it in his own way. Everyone came to believe that Jesus' suffering, death, and resurrection were "according to [God's plan as revealed in] the [Hebrew] Scriptures."

Given this historical background, it is no surprise that Christians today are persuaded that the Hebrew Scriptures (especially Genesis 22, Psalm 22, and Isaiah 53) contain over a hundred texts that reveal both the promise and the character of the *moshiach.* We have examined two of these texts above. When one relies on this pattern of "prefiguring" and "fulfillment," the temptation is very strong for Christians to confront Jews with a list

---

14. Both the *Aqedah* (the binding of Isaac) and the atoning death of Jesus serve to transform events of horror into events of honor. Just as Jews could speak of the unfathomable blessings that emerged due to the "sacrifice" of Isaac, Christians on their part claimed that no sin is ever forgiven without the merits of Christ's Passion and death. These merits bedazzle the onlooker and cover over the implied cruelty of God. See, for example, Elie Wiesel, *Messengers of God: Biblical Portraits and Legends* (New York: Random House, 1976), and Philip Borenstein, "Sermon for Second Day of Rosh Hashannah 5757 (1996)," http://www.rjca.org/5759rh2akedah.html.

15. Juel, *Messianic Exegesis,* 13.

of "prefiguring" texts in their Scriptures with the expectation that they will (if their minds are opened) recognize in Jesus their "fulfillment."

In the Middle Ages, Christians forced Jews to enter into public debates whose purpose was to persuade Jews that Jesus was the *moshiach*. Fulfillment texts played a major role in these debates. When conversions did not materialize, Christians blamed and demeaned Jews in the following terms:

- Jews are stubborn or stupid (or some combination thereof).
- Jews have been spiritually blinded by God to the meaning of their own Scriptures.
- Jews are being prepared for eternal damnation (due to their blindness).

Compulsory sermons for Jews become normal after the sixth century.[16] When these sermons did not have the desired effect some Christians relieved their frustration by beating "stubborn Jews" as they had seen schoolmasters beat recalcitrant pupils. Happily, these times are nearly over. I say "nearly" because I am aware that, as you are reading this book, militant Evangelical circles continue to send out missionary teams (college students for the most part) to vacation in the state of Israel with the express intent of snaring unsuspecting Jews into recognizing Jesus as the moshiach.[17] One has only to surf the web to locate their sites.

A Rabbi Responds: Whether Jesus May Have Been the Messiah

Fundamentalist Christians have prepared pamphlets, comic books, and websites especially targeting Jews who, as they say, ". . . never have had the opportunity to explore the possibility that their Scriptures point to Jesus." The Christian who wrote the email below was undoubtedly persuaded that he might be able to offer Rabbi Richman such an "opportunity."

16. William Horbury, *Jews and Christians: In Contact and in Controversy* (Edinburgh: T & T Clark, 1998) 227.

17. This form of misguided proselytism seldom works, for various reasons: (a) because it operates in ignorance of the Jewish history of interpretation of the text, (b) because it arrogantly presupposes that the "Christian interpretation" represents the only true meaning that could possibly be found in the text, and (c) because it promotes an image of the Messiah that runs counter to the *moshiach* of every informed Jew. It was one thing for the early Christians to find in their Hebrew Scriptures allegorical interpretations that supported their continued adherence to Jesus and his Judaism; it is quite another thing for later Christians to use these same allegorical interpretations to uproot and destroy the foundations of Judaism.

To Rabbi Chaim Richman,

Greetings from a Christian living in Washington, D.C. Do you think that Jesus may have been the messiah? Why or why not . . . ? In the New Testament it is written that Jesus fulfilled all of the prophecies of the prophets and the law. . . .

I am including a list of biblical verses that I would like you to look at. . . . Also the Psalms speak of many prophecies fulfilled by Jesus. . . . Please take a look and see if Jesus was the *moshiach.*

Again I say that I hope that this letter did not offend you, however I must do what G-d requires of me.

Thank you very much.

(signed —)

Here is Rabbi Richman's response:

My dear friend,

Thank you very much for your sincere letter. . . .

The identity of the messiah is not up to you or me; it is up to his performance to prove. . . . Can a little booklet one receives in the mail prove that the messiah has come? Is that all it takes? The state of the world must prove that the messiah has come; not a tract. Don't you think that when the messiah arrives, it should not be necessary for his identity to be subject to debate—for the world should be so drastically changed for the better that it should be absolutely incontestable!

According to the prophets of the Bible, among the most basic missions of the messiah are:

- to cause all the world to return to G-d and His teachings,
- to restore the royal dynasty to the descendants of David,
- to oversee the rebuilding of Jerusalem, including the Temple, in the event that it has not yet been rebuilt;
- to gather the Jewish people from all over the world and bring them home to the Land of Israel,
- and to reestablish the Sanhedrin,
- restore the sacrificial system . . .

You have stated that in the New Testament it is written that Jesus fulfilled all of the prophecies. . . . But which of these above requirements did Jesus fulfill? And if he is going to fulfill them the second time [when he returns], why did he not attend to them the first time? This in itself is one concept which no amount of Biblical sleuthing can find a prophetic basis for—[namely] for the notion that the messiah does not accomplish these things upon his [first] appearance, and therefore must return a second time. . . .

Finally, there had to be an explanation for the first coming and its catastrophic end. The basic structure of this explanation was to shift the function of the messiah from a visible level (the only level emphasized by the Bible)—where it could be tested—to an invisible level—where it could not. The messiah's goal, at least the first time around, was now not said to be the redemption of Israel (which had clearly not taken place) but the atonement for original [and actual] sin[s]. . . .

But for Jews, if the Bible's description of the messiah has not been fulfilled, then for authentic Jews there can only be one explanation: he has not yet come. To Jews, who were often subjected to mockery and contempt when asked where their messiah was, this conclusion was painful. But an honest facing of the facts makes it inescapable. In adversity and joy, through holocaust and statehood, Jews who are truly faithful to the Torah and prophets can only repeat the words of their forefathers: "I believe with complete faith in the coming of the messiah; and though he may tarry I shall wait for him every day."

I have had no intention, Heaven forbid, to offend you. But just as you feel that you must do what G-d requires of you, so have I done as well. If you, or any of our readers, wish to correspond with me and truly establish a dialogue, I am at your service. . . .

(signed —)

When I was engaged in debating during my high school years we were trained to ferret out the best possible arguments of our opponents and to devise ways to turn them around to our own advantage. In the case of Rabbi Richman's letter, consequently, I am prompted to accept it and to weigh its true merits:

1. To begin with, I would have to agree with Rabbi Richman that the messianic expectations listed in his letter (plus many more unlisted) were not accomplished by Jesus and, if the truth be known, there is no way for either of us to know how many or how few will be accomplished when the Lord actually does come.

2. Going further, I would have to acknowledge as a believer and as a scholar that the Hebrew Scriptures contain such a diverse set of particulars regarding the end times that it is accurate to say that no single individual could ever fulfill *everything*. Within the collected apocalyptic poems of Isaiah, for instance, there are times when the Egyptians are slated for utter destruction (31:3) and other times when the Lord "will send them a savior and will defend and deliver"

(19:20) so that, in the end, they too will receive his favor: "Blessed be Egypt my people" (19:25). Similarly, there are times when the Lord, speaking through the prophet Isaiah, limits the final ingathering to "your offspring [Israel]" (43:5), while at other times, the prophet (or someone speaking in his name) says that "all nations and tongues" (66:18) will be gathered by the Lord.

3. Those churches and synagogues claiming that the Bible contains a single, unified scenario for the arrival of God's reign have not yet dealt squarely with the sheer diversity and incompatibility found within the prophetic and apocalyptic writings. Unless Christians and Jews get a measure of honesty on this issue, both sides will end up continually talking past each other.

Dialogue That Honors a Jewish Interpretation of Scripture

How, then, would one start a true dialogue? Well, to begin with it would be very helpful for each side to acknowledge that, by virtue of their belonging to one group or the other, they have been schooled to expect certain things from God in the future and to neglect other things. Next, each side might want to explore how their separate commitments lead them to use and reuse certain prophetic texts while turning a blind eye to other texts. In so doing, both sides might come to realize that their "opponents" are not just self-serving or idiosyncratic in their selection of texts, but rather that there is an authentic diversity of religious and intellectual passions operative when it comes to God's future. If these initial honest admissions go well, then participants from each side might more easily make sincere inquiries and learn to respect the diversity of viewpoints that will be expressed between and among those present. Furthermore, each side might discover that, at times, their use of a prophetic text is paper-thin and bound to carry little conviction, whereas in other cases the textual meaning seems rock solid. In the end all those involved might be willing to allow that they are poised before a future that is in God's hands and is bound to hold surprises for all concerned.

In 2001, official Vatican explorations of the Jewish interpretation of the Hebrew Scriptures opened up a new era of honesty. This began by posing to Catholics a potentially embarrassing question:

> The horror in the wake of the extermination of the Jews (the *Shoah*) during the Second World War has led all the Churches to rethink their relationship with Judaism and, as a result, to reconsider their

interpretation of the Jewish Bible, the Old Testament. It may be asked whether Christians should be blamed for having monopolised the Jewish Bible and reading there what no Jew has found.[18]

This admission is noteworthy. On the basis of the convictions described above, Christians have pushed forward "their interpretation" of "their messianic fulfillment texts" without any regard for the Jewish understandings of the texts in question. Jews were even sometimes beaten because they failed to find these "Christian interpretations" within their texts. The Vatican document honestly asks whether Christians "should be blamed for having monopolised the Jewish Bible and reading there what no Jew has found." The Vatican team responded as follows:

> Christians can and ought to admit that the Jewish reading of the Bible is a possible one, in continuity with the Jewish Sacred Scriptures from the Second Temple period, a reading analogous to the Christian reading which developed in parallel fashion. Both readings are bound up with the vision of their respective faiths, of which the readings are the result and expression. Consequently, both are irreducible.[19]

Here is a new attitude! No longer can it be said that Jews are hard-headed dunces unable to recognize the correct interpretation of their own Scriptures. Rather, the Vatican allows that the Jewish interpretations (devoid of any hidden references to Jesus) are "possible" (nay, even more, "valid") because they grew out of the Jewish history of interpretation and are responsive to the particular set of religious passions nurtured by that community. The same thing, of course, could be said of Christian exegesis—it also is "possible" (here again, I would say, "valid") for the very same reasons. The conclusions drawn are twofold: (1) "Both readings are bound up with the vision of their respective faiths," and (2) "Both are irreducible."

In brief, for eighteen hundred years Christians have interpreted the Jewish Scriptures in such a way as to undercut Jewish values and Jewish integrity. The presumption was that, in the face of two irreducibly different interpretations of any given text, only one could be right; hence, the Jews had to be wrong! Now, however, the Vatican has acknowledged that

18. Pontifical Biblical Commission, "The Jewish People and their Sacred Scriptures in the Christian Bible," published with a preface by Joseph Cardinal Ratzinger (Rome: Vatican Press, 2001), §22.
19. Ibid.

the Jewish reading of Abraham's sacrifice of Isaac is valid *for them,* while our finding of a hidden reference to the forthcoming sacrifice of Christ is valid *for us.* The Vatican then goes on to draw the practical conclusion that Catholics "can learn much from Jewish exegesis practiced for more than two thousand years." Reciprocally, Catholics, for their part, can hope that Jews "can derive profit from Christian exegetical research."[20]

Mutual Unwillingness to Sanction a Tyrannical Future

After having arrived at this mutual recognition of how and why our interpretations of messianic texts are irreducibly different, the dialogue partners might be able to move on to reflect honestly on the tyrannical power that would be necessary to implement certain prophetic anticipations. To take an example, consider a specific case from Rabbi Richman's list, namely the expectation that the messiah would "cause all the world to return to G-d and his teachings." Such a hope finds an honored place in the daily prayers of Jews and is widespread in the prophetic literature—"To me [the God of Israel] every knee shall bow, every tongue shall swear" (Isa 45:23). In like fashion, Christians generally expect that in the end times the teachings of Jesus will be universally accepted by all humanity "so that at the name of Jesus every knee should bend" (Phil 2:10).

For the sake of argument let us imagine that Phil 2:10 will be fully implemented by the Lord when he comes. In this new world order, are we to suppose that the teachings of the rabbis and the patterns of synagogue prayer will suddenly lose their legitimacy and deserve to be outlawed and stamped out? Are we to imagine that the Jewish way of life will have no sanction whatsoever in the eyes of Jesus and his twelve disciples (who would presumably be raised from the dead as believing Jews)? How could any *moshiach,* even one who had a divine charisma and worked repeated miracles, be expected to bring the entire Jewish world to turn itself inside out in order to welcome a Christian theology, a Christian liturgy, and Christian eschatology? A world tyrant (the anti-Christ or a neo-Nazi revival) might be able to coerce a measure of conformity in these matters, yet strong-arm measures would violate freedom of conscience and debase human rights. Must the Christian Messiah then become a ruthless tyrant in order that "at the name of Jesus every knee should bend" (Phil 2:10)?

20. Ibid.

As for myself, I say to you, the reader, that if this were to come to pass, Christians and Jews would have to band together in order to overthrow such a tyranny! No divine future can be tolerated that forces Jews to their knees by virtue of any coercive power whatsoever. Even if the Son of God would do it, it would still be "unworthy of God" and have to be overthrown. This, for me, is the breathtaking realization that grips my soul when I read triumphalistic texts such as Phil 2:10.[21]

Mutual Uncertainties Regarding God's Future

The renowned Catholic scholar Karl Rahner stated quite boldly his conclusion that "the imaginative portrayals of Scripture [regarding the last days] cannot be harmonized with one another."[22] According to Rahner, fantastic and impossible metaphors are deliberately used to remind readers that the future, as future, remains both known and unknowable: "Now we see in a mirror, dimly, but then we will see face to face" (1 Cor 13:12). Thus it would be a mistake to imagine that "the sheep will be [literally] turned into wolves" (*Did.* 16:3) or that the elect "will be caught up [literally] in the clouds" (2 Thess 4:17). If this were so, we would do well to study the behavior of wolves or take up skydiving in order to prepare ourselves for the last days. We would be likewise mistaken to join with Tim LaHaye[23] in his expectation that, when the rapture takes

21. Texts such as Phil 2:10 deserve a cautionary footnote in Catholic Bibles that might read something like this: "The Jews remain very dear to God . . . and should not be spoken of as rejected or accursed" (*Nostra Aetate* 4); hence we can be certain that God will respect their rightful beliefs and religious liberty in the world to come. Given the enormity of crimes inflicted on Jews in the name of Jesus, it remains doubtful whether, following the general resurrection, these same Jews will be inclined to bend their knees 'at the name of Jesus.' If God returns to 'wipe every tear from their eyes' (Rev 21:4), there might be some prospect that Jesus would eventually gain some recognition among the people of Israel. For the moment, however, Christians should recognize that it would be cruel and inhumane for God to impose Jesus on the Jews in any capacity whatsoever in the world to come. Texts such as Phil 2:10 must therefore be understood as representing a prophetic prospect that has been subverted by the conduct of Christians in the course of history."

22. Karl Rahner, "The Hermeneutics of Eschatological Assertions," *Theological Investigations IV* (Baltimore: Helicon Press, 1966) 335.

23. Launched in 1995, the *Left Behind* series authored by the retired fundamentalist pastor Tim LaHaye, in collaboration with the fiction writer Jerry B. Jenkins, has sold fifty million copies and spawned three New York Times best-sellers (as of late 2002). According to LaHaye "the enormous success of our books indicates that there are still millions of people in our country who believe that the Bible has the answer to the problems of life and Bible prophecy reveals what the future holds for our troubled world" (*Time*

place, vehicles will be running out of control and causing havoc everywhere because their drivers have been instantaneously caught up in the clouds. Accordingly, I would like to challenge the eschatological values of Tim LaHaye by asking him: "What kind of God would cause such senseless destruction when initiating his finest hour?"

Relative to the Hebrew Scriptures, humility and truth would seemingly enable us as Christians to adhere positively to the way of Jesus without imagining that all or most of the prophetic texts either directly or indirectly point to his life, death, and resurrection. The sheer complexity, incompatibility, and obscurity of the Jewish prophetic texts ensure that no Messiah or messianic series of events could possibly fulfill them all. When the disciples of Jesus found aspects of his life obscurely referred to in the Hebrew Scriptures, they were selectively reading back into their cherished Jewish sources key aspects of Jesus' life. Their faith in Jesus, it must be made clear, came from their intimate association with Jesus, and not the other way around. No one became a disciple of Jesus by virtue of drawing together a thousand prophetic texts and then scoring every living Jew for many generations to see whether someone comes up with a "perfect" match. This would be sheer lunacy.[24] Even more importantly, the early disciples of Jesus used their Scriptures to support their adherence both to Jesus and to Judaism. Most modern disciples, in contrast, are intent on using the Hebrew Scriptures to bring Jews to Jesus while entirely subverting or negating their adherence to Judaism. This in itself must serve as a "warning sign" and a "wake-up call" to both Christians and Jews as to how perfidious this enterprise is and how contrary to both the spirit and the letter of the early church traditions.

When it comes to the use of prophetic texts, Christians and Jews should be able to say to themselves and to each other that we cannot know when God will elect to establish his reign on earth, nor can we know the precise details of God's reign. Jews, naturally and legitimately, will want to in-

---

magazine). In the first volume of this ten-volume series flight attendants aboard a 747 bound for Heathrow suddenly find half the seats empty save for the clothes, rings, and dental fillings of believers who were suddenly raptured. Down on the ground, great numbers of cars and trucks on the highways suddenly go out of control because their drivers have been likewise raptured.

24. In 2001 the Vatican noted: "It would be wrong to consider the prophecies of the Old Testament as some kind of photographic anticipations of future events. All the texts, including those which later were read as messianic prophecies, already had an immediate import and meaning for their contemporaries before attaining a fuller meaning for future hearers" (Pontifical Biblical Commission, "The Jewish People," § 21).

clude the ingathering of all the dispersed Jews from all over the world into the land of Israel *(Eretz Yisrael)*. Might it not be possible, on the other hand, that many Diaspora Jews would elect to remain rooted within those regions they have come to know and love through long habituation? Furthermore, might it not be the case that there would be an ecological and sociological disaster should all Jews living in all times elect to return to the land of Israel? Going further, if the Lord awaited by Israel is just and favors the oppressed, would it not be expected that the needs and the purposes of the Palestinians would gain some permanent recognition and generous response on the part of the Lord in the world to come? Abraham opposed the Lord face to face when his plans included the destruction of the innocent with the guilty (Gen 18:23-25). Would not the sons and daughters of Abraham be expected to oppose any formation of God's future land of Israel that would be crassly insensitive to the legitimate needs and rights of their Palestinian neighbors?[25]

Whether Jesus Will Restore the Kingdom of Israel When He Returns

The Acts of the Apostles presents a dramatic summary of Jesus' last days on earth before he was taken up into heaven:

> After his suffering he presented himself alive to them by many convincing proofs, appearing to them during forty days and speaking

25. A few pages earlier I objected vehemently to the literal fulfillment of Phil 2:10 (see n. 18 above). Now I endeavor to examine the Jewish expectation of the ingathering of the exiles in the face of ecological, sociological, and political realities of which the Jewish prophets were ignorant. My hope is that modern Jews would continue to argue that the Lord's justice cannot be set aside by those who narrowly argue that the Hebrew Scriptures support the view that not an inch of land (conquered by recent wars) can legitimately be returned to the *goyim*. My hope earlier was to demonstrate that Christians can and must challenge those Bible thumpers who imagine that Phil 2:10 gives them the right to trample on the religious sensibilities and legitimate practices of the Jews (or the Muslims) here and now because God himself holds out a future in which he will trample any Jew who does not bend his knee at the name of Jesus. All in all, Christian-Jewish dialogue can (and sometimes does) empower believers to go home and clean up the mess made by their own coreligionists in their own houses. I, for one, have been empowered within this dialogue to prepare the topics in this book in such a way that I directly and immediately challenge cherished Catholic positions. I do this because most Catholics are blissfully ignorant of how deep the poison of anti-Judaism goes within the routine attitudes and sanctioned literature of their church. I will scandalize many in speaking as I do. On the other hand, those who continue to support a polite and inoffensive Catholic-Jewish dialogue also scandalize by what they are afraid to reconsider and to challenge in their own faith. The same thing, of course, can be said of Jewish participants.

about the kingdom of God. . . . So when they had come together, they asked him, "Lord, is this the time when you will restore the kingdom to Israel?" He replied, "It is not for you to know the times or periods that the Father has set by his own authority. . . ." (Acts 1:3-7)

Three things stand out: (1) According to Luke's text "the kingdom of God" was the principal theme of Jesus' discourses with his disciples after his resurrection, just as it had been during the entire time of his ministry in the synagogues of Galilee. (2) Next, it is the Jewish disciples of Jesus who ask, "Is this the time when you will restore the kingdom to Israel?" This question clearly indicates that Jesus' disciples expected him to wrest political sovereignty from the Romans and restore the Davidic kingdom. Christians have become so comfortable for so long with excluding Israel from the promises and blessings of God that I wager most Christians would be embarrassed to find the disciples of Jesus were concerned specifically about the future of God's people. (3) Finally, Jesus makes it clear that the Father (and not Jesus) has set the agenda for the future and that the disciples cannot know God's timetable. Despite this caution, nearly every generation has witnessed some Christians passionately persuaded that they have outwitted God and discovered a "hidden" timetable of signs in the prophetic texts that can be known only by the elect.[26]

Whether Christians Have Destroyed Jesus' Future

The Christian Scriptures give ample testimony to the supreme importance Jesus had for the lives of those Jews who had accepted him and

---

26. During the 1980s, Edgar C. Whisenant distributed 300,000 copies to ministers and sold 4.5 million copies in bookstores of his best-seller, *88 Reasons Why The Rapture Will Be in 1988*. He calculated the Rapture would occur between the 11th and the 13th of September (Rosh Hashanah). After his prediction failed, he rushed to amend his calculations, saying the Rapture would take place at 10:55 a.m. on September 15. Then he opted for October 3. Chastened by his three successive misses, he took time out to reconsider the whole question and published another book, *The Final Shout: Rapture Report of 1989*. His calculations now led him to identify Rosh Hashanah of 1989. Undefeated, he then went on to revise his calculations for 1993 and published *23 Reasons Why a Pre-Tribulation Rapture Looks Like It Will Occur on Rosh-Hashanah 1993*. Stumped again, he then went on to calculate the destruction of the earth in *And Now the Earth's Destruction by Fire, Nuclear Bomb Fire* (1994). None of his later books received any sustained attention. B. J. Oropeza, impressed by Whisenant's resilience, wrote a book entitled *99 Reasons Why No One Knows When Christ Will Return* (Downers Grove, IL: InterVarsity Press, 1994). For an overall survey of failed predictions see http://www.abhota.info/end3.htm.

walked in his ways. For modern Christians, however, a new situation has arisen that may nullify God's choice of Jesus as the *moshiach:*

1. Christians have shamed the God of Israel by painting him as locked in unforgiveness from the fall of Adam to the death of Jesus. Such a doctrine, even in its mitigated forms, has always stood in contradiction to the lavish experience of forgiveness described in both the Hebrew Scriptures and the parables of Jesus. Christians have, accordingly, proclaimed a false and misleading god to the Jews, and the Jews were right to reject it entirely. Since this falsehood is so intimately associated with the name of Jesus, it remains unclear whether God could endorse Jesus as the *moshiach* of Israel in the end times without giving a false witness and tacit approval of an abhorrent misrepresentation of God.

2. According to Matthew's gospel, Jesus anticipated that his disciples would some day "sit on twelve thrones, judging the twelve tribes of Israel" (Matt 19:27-28). How could the disciples of Jesus be expected to properly judge or guide Israel if they have been poisoned by a doctrine that "salvation is only found in the name of Jesus" and that "salvation consists in applying to Jews the merits Jesus earned by dying on the cross"? One could assume, of course, that the Twelve would openly challenge the catastrophic effects of the church's misguided claims. In so doing, however, the Twelve would be setting themselves over and against the long-standing beliefs of Christians and, accordingly, risk being rejected as not true "disciples of Jesus." Given this terrible ambiguity, it remains unclear whether God would grant Christians any significant role in relation to Israel in the world to come.

3. The church must also struggle with Elie Wiesel's charge that "any messiah in whose name men are tortured is a false messiah."[27] Thus, in humility and truth, Christians must wonder whether the long history of Christian harassment, intimidation, and torture of Jews does not entirely preclude God from giving anyone associated with these horrendous events any significant role in the future of Israel. One can speak glibly of Jesus as being Jewish and sinless; however, this does not remove the pain and horror of millions of Jews who were tormented in the name of Jesus Christ. Wiesel himself recounts his own story:

---

27. Elie Wiesel, *The Oath* (New York: Random House, 1973) 138.

> As a child I was afraid of the church . . . not only because of what I inherited—our collective memory—but also because of the simple fact that twice a year, at Easter and Christmas, Jewish school children would be beaten up by their Christian neighbors. A symbol of compassion and love to Christians, the cross has become an instrument of torment and terror to be used against the Jews.[28]

Just as it is impossible to contemplate that God would use former S.S. officers to keep order during the final judgment and usher Jews into the world to come, so too it remains unclear whether the God of Israel could be so crass and insensitive as to allow the crucified Savior to be the *moshiach* of Israel.

In humility and truth, consequently, we must admit that the false doctrines and horrendous deeds of Christians may have temporarily (and perhaps even permanently) ruined the chance that Jesus of Nazareth formerly had of playing some significant role in God's future for his beloved Israel. No appeal to the infallibility of the popes or the persistent faith of the church could possibly overturn this terrible conclusion. In fact, when understood correctly it is the very teaching and conduct of the popes and the persistent faith and conduct of the church that will be used by God to explain why the name of Jesus has been withdrawn as his choice for Israel's *moshiach*.

Can a Jew Be Certain that Jesus Was Not the Moshiach?

From what has already been said it is clear that Jews can take their stand within their religious tradition and say, with calm assurance, that Jesus was not the *moshiach*. This is true primarily because Jews cannot rightly imagine that God's *moshiach* was somehow sent into the world unequipped to effect even a small part of God's design for Israel in the end times. To this can be added the painful fact that the smoke of burning children at Auschwitz conclusively demonstrates that God's kingdom has not arrived. Just as there are false Messiahs, so too there are also false claims as to the presence of the kingdom (made by well-meaning Christians). The smell of the flesh of burning children keeps Jews honest on this point.

Rabbi Eugene B. Borowitz speaks forthrightly for hundreds of thousands of Jews when he says, quite categorically, that the name of Jesus

---

28. Elie Wiesel, "Art and Culture after the Holocaust," in Eva Fleischner, ed., *Auschwitz—Beginning of a New Era?* (New York: KTAV, 1977) 406.

of Nazareth has to be struck from the list of potential candidates for *moshiach*. His reasons are clear and uncompromising:

> This Jesus is the one who validated the hatred and oppression of his own people. He is the Jesus who stands for crusades, inquisitions, ritual murder charges, and forced conversions. He is the Jesus who did not protest the Holocaust. That Jesus may not hate his kinfolk in his heart, but he has stood idly by while his kinfolk bled.[29]

One can still hear the reverberations of anger between the lines. Jews like Rabbi Borowitz, consequently, can barely stomach the hypocrisy of pious Christians who naïvely applaud Jesus as the Messiah. Jews like Rabbi Borowitz shake their heads and tremble in rage whenever they encounter zealous Christians contorting the Hebrew Scriptures into saying that the *moshiach* had to undergo a barbaric death in order to coax God into forgiving sins. Such a scheme of things perverts the Jewish image of a just and merciful Father that is plainly written in their sacred texts. It also demonstrates how ignorant Christians can be of the Jewish experience of receiving God's love and forgiveness (as shown in chapter 2). The shame is not that Christians experience the loving forgiveness of the God of Israel through Jesus; the shame is that so many Christians believe that no one who does not praise Jesus can legitimately have such an experience.

On the brighter side, some Jews have explored the teachings and deeds of Jesus of Nazareth and come away with admiration in their hearts. At the turn of the twentieth century, for example, Max Nordau, the faithful collaborator of Theodor Herzl, founder of the Zionist movement, wrote, "Jesus is the soul of our soul, as he is flesh of our flesh."[30] Martin Buber, a little later, began describing Jesus as the "elder brother" to whom "belongs an important place in Israel's history of faith."[31] Since then a handful of Jewish scholars have made extensive studies of the person and the teachings of Jesus.[32] The study of Schalom Ben-Chorin, in particular, captures both the affinity and the strangeness that most Jews experience when making contact with Jesus through the Christian Scriptures:

29. Eugene B. Borowitz, "Jesus the Jew in the Light of the Jewish-Christian Dialogue," *Proceedings of the Center for Jewish-Christian Learning: 1987 Lecture Series* (St. Paul: College of St. Thomas, 1987) 17.

30. Cited in Hans Küng, *On Being a Christian* (Garden City, NY: Doubleday, 1976) 173.

31. Martin Buber, *Two Types of Faith* (New York: Harper & Row, 1975) 12–13.

32. Among the better known Jewish studies of Jesus that have appeared in English are the following: David Flusser, *Jesus* (New York: Herder & Herder, 1969); Joseph Klausner, *Jesus of Nazareth* (New York: Macmillan, 1925); Pinchas Lapide (with Jürgen Moltmann),

I feel his brotherly hand which grasps mine, so that I can follow him. . . . It is not the hand of the Messiah, this hand marked with scars. It is certainly not a divine, but a human hand, in the lines of which are engraved the most profound suffering. . . . The faith of Jesus unites us, but faith in Jesus divides us.[33]

Rabbi Pinchas Lapide met with Jürgen Moltmann in a small parish church in Germany and, quite unexpectedly, a very intense and open dialogue took place. During this exchange Lapide acknowledged some things that must have sent shudders of delight through the hearts of the Christians present. To begin with, he said, "I accept the resurrection of Easter Sunday not as an invention of the community of disciples, but as a historical event."[34] Next he explained that, for him, "Jesus is immortal."[35] Furthermore, Lapide allowed that Jesus is truly "son of God"[36] and that "the Christ event leads to a way of salvation which God has opened up to bring the Gentile world into the community of God's Israel."[37] Having come so far, Lapide then took the bold final step of characterizing the success of Christianity in converting the Gentile world as a "messianic event."[38] Having said all these heartwarming things about Jesus and the movement he left behind, Lapide then baffled his Christian hearers by admitting that he was, nevertheless, unable to say with certainty that Jesus is the *moshiach*. Why so? He explained:

No Jew knows who the coming *moshiach* is [with certainty], but you [Christians] believe to know his identity with certitude. I cannot contrapose your certainty with a no, but merely with a humble question mark. Thus I am happily prepared to wait until the Coming One comes, and if he should show himself to be Jesus of Naza-

---

Jewish Monotheism and Christian Trinitarian Doctrine (Philadelphia: Fortress Press, 1970); Claude G. Montefiore, *The Synoptic Gospels* (London: Macmillan, 1927); Samuel Sandmel, *We Jews and Jesus* (Oxford: Oxford University Press, 1965); Geza Vermes, *Jesus the Jew* (New York: Macmillan, 1973). For an excellent overview and analysis see Donald A. Hagner, *The Jewish Reclamation of Jesus* (Grand Rapids: Zondervan, 1984).

33. Schalom Ben-Chorin, *Bruder Jesus* (Munich: List Verlag, 1967) 14. See the English translation: *Brother Jesus: the Nazarene Through Jewish Eyes,* translated and edited by Jared S. Klein and Max Reinhart (Athens: University of Georgia Press, 2001).

34. Pinchas Lapide and Jürgen Moltmann, *Jewish Monotheism and Christian Trinitarian Doctrine* (Philadelphia: Fortress Press, 1981) 59.

35. Ibid., 60.

36. Ibid., 67.

37. Ibid., 69.

38. Ibid., 71.

reth, I cannot imagine that even a single Jew[39] who believes in God would have the least thing against that.[40]

This is baffling. Lapide clearly entertains a wait-and-see attitude. In so doing he graciously puts aside all his terrible memories of what has been done to Jews in the name of Jesus. One might think he is playing a game with his audience to sugarcoat his quiet "no" to Jesus. That is possible. From my reading of the entire dialogue, however, my hunch is that Lapide trusts God to make the right choice for Israel—even if it entails his choice for Jesus. In the end, consequently, Lapide humbly professes a messianic faith that allows God to be God! Would that Christians would do likewise.

Conclusion

At the end of this chapter many things come into focus: that the core of Jesus' ministry was his heralding of the coming of the kingdom/reign of God, that Jesus did not fulfill many of the Jewish expectations regarding the expected *moshiach,* and that Christians must ponder whether the long history of Christian harassment, intimidation, and torture of Jews combined with the church's persistent perjorative theology of God and of Judaism does not entirely preclude that God would assign Jesus any significant role when it comes to the future of Israel.

Given our differences on so many points, it seems important to close this chapter by remembering what unites us—that we all anticipate the coming of the kingdom, the resurrection of the dead, the final judgment, and life everlasting. A dialogue group composed of rabbis and priests in Los Angeles summarized their findings as follows:

> The concept of the Kingdom of God serves as a source of comfort and hope in both Judaism and Christianity. God is King, so good will ultimately prevail; thus the human struggle against evil is meaningful. Our roots give us security and strength, but it is our vision of the future promised by God that enlightens our minds and gladdens our hearts.[41]

---

39. At this moment Rabbi Lapide obviously wasn't thinking of those Jews who think like Rabbi Borowitz.

40. Lapide and Moltmann, *Jewish Monotheism,* 79.

41. The Los Angeles Priest-Rabbi Committee offers this conclusion to its dialogue on the importance, the nature, and the contemporary implications of the kingdom of God.

In effect, since the *moshiach* of Israel is not the Messiah of Christians, the anticipation of the kingdom of God has much to divide us. Yet, since the God of David is coming on behalf of Israel and those Gentiles who have been grafted onto the root of Israel thanks to Jesus, there is much to "enlighten our minds and gladden our hearts." This will become even clearer in the final chapter.[42]

Appendix: Reflections for Troubled Christians

As I gradually became aware of how the theology of the atoning death that I learned from the Ursuline Sisters was biblically, theologically, and pastorally defective, I was disorientated and confused. My beloved teachers had given me only one sure measuring stick for determining the greatness of Jesus—that he loved me enough to give up his life so that my sins would be forgiven and I would be forever happy with him in heaven. As Paul said, "Rarely will anyone die for a righteous person—though perhaps for a good person someone might actually dare to die. But God proves his love for us in that while we still were sinners Christ died for us" (Rom 5:7-8). Yet how could I glibly maintain the atonement theory of my youth when it so evidently clashed with the experience of God's forgiveness in the Hebrew Scriptures, with the content of Jesus' parables, with the faith and practice of the early church in Acts, with the symbolism of the darkness and tearing of the veil in the Passion narratives, and with the intent of Paul's theology? More especially, how could I continue to honor Jesus as savior of the world if indeed sins were being forgiven (both before and after Jesus) without any reference to his atoning death?

In what follows I offer three reflections on how Christianity borrowed from Israel its theology of suffering, sacrifice, and atonement. These three are not exhaustive, only illustrative. At the present time scholars and pastors are exploring such modalities, and I do not presume to know how any or all of these approaches will reassert themselves within the Christian tradition. Nonetheless, I include them here because they offer lines of consideration that might be helpful for those who are distressed to discover the shortcomings of Christian atonement theologies. These reflections may facilitate a deeper appreciation of how Jewish and Christian modes of thinking interacted in the past and offer topics for collaborative Jewish-Christian studies.

42. If you would like to share your reflections or see what others have produced, go to www.salvationisfromthejews.info.

1. *The Binding of Isaac as Atoning for Sins.* Abraham "bound his son Isaac, and laid him on the altar, on top of the wood" (Gen 22:9). The Jewish tradition refers to this event as the *Aqedah* ("binding"). With time the binding, even though it was not formally a sacrifice, did begin to appear equivalent to a sacrifice. "The rabbis argue that even if God had not provided a ram to be offered in his place, Isaac would gladly have given his life, so that the value and the merit [of a true sacrifice] belong to him."[43] Following the rule that the pouring out of blood was part of every atoning sacrifice, Geza Vermes explains that the tradition gradually evolved in the direction of supposing that the binding of Isaac was so tight that it cut into his wrists and at least some of his blood was shed. Some rabbis went to the extreme of supposing that a third of his blood was shed because of the tight binding.[44]

As the *Aqedah* was being reflexively elevated to the status of a sacrifice, the merits associated with this "sacrifice" were being expanded as well. In the rabbinic midrashic literature the following benefits were attributed directly to the *Aqedah:*

- The blood on the doorposts secured the preservation of the firstborn sons of the Israelites because "when I [the Lord] see the blood, I will pass over you (Exod 12:13) [for] I see the blood of the *Aqedah* of Isaac" (*Mekhilta* [4th century c.e.] 1.57).
- The Israelites were preserved when they entered the Red Sea because of the blood shed by Isaac (*Mekhilta* 1.222-223).
- God relented from destroying the people when they worshiped the golden calf because of the *Aqedah* (*Exodus Rabbah* [12th century c.e.] 44.5 on Exodus 32).
- God sent an angel to destroy Jerusalem following the sinful census of David (2 Samuel 24; 1 Chronicles 21) but then called the angel back when "he saw the blood of the *Aqedah* of Isaac" (*Mekhilta* 1.57, 88).
- The mountain on which the *Aqedah* took place was the mountain where the sanctuary of Solomon was later built. Furthermore, the offering of the morning and evening sacrifice (a lamb) had its efficacy because it was performed so that "the Holy One, blessed be he, may remember the *Aqedah* of Isaac" (*Leviticus Rabbah* [5th century c.e.] 2.11).

43. Geza Vermes, *Scripture and Tradition in Judaism* (Leiden: Brill, 1973) 205.
44. Ibid., 205.

- Blowing the ram's horn each Rosh Hashanah[45] is associated with recalling the *Aqedah* of Isaac; it is efficacious for the forgiveness of sins (*Leviticus Rabbah* 29.9; *b. Rosh Hashanah* 16a).
- At the end of time, "through the merits of Isaac who offered himself on the altar, the Holy One, blessed be he, shall raise the dead" (*Pesikta de-Rav Kahana* [5th century c.e.], *Piska* 32, f. 200b.) by sounding the ram's horn (Zech 9:14).

What one can notice here is how, the moment Isaac's submission to God became a pleasing "sacrifice," the *Aqedah* was increasingly accepted as a "precious moment" guiding the meditations and discussions of rabbinic Jews and entitling them to contemplate previously unrecognized consequences ("the merits of Isaac"). Here one has an illustration of how generations of Jews were nourished by a "precious moment" in their collective history. It was only natural, given their intimacy with God, that they would have done this with the conviction that God shares their admiration for the *Aqedah*. If anything, the expansion of the merits of the *Aqedah* illustrates how a single "precious moment" in the Jewish tradition can diffuse its efficacy into a hundred other unexpected moments.

Consider, for a moment, the fifth item in the list above. Nowhere in the Hebrew Scriptures does one find anything associating the morning and evening sacrifice of a lamb with the *Aqedah*. The only hint in this direction is Abraham's saying "God himself will provide the lamb for a burnt offering, my son" (Gen 22:8). If we go more deeply, however, we can see that only a tradition that prizes holiness of life and submission to God above all things could imagine that the *Aqedah* is what comes into God's mind when he smells the sweet aroma of the flesh burning on the altar of the temple. Thus God is well pleased and draws close to Israel (pardoning/forgetting their sins).

Philo (20 b.c.e.–50 c.e.), an Alexandrian Jew, a contemporary of both Jesus and Paul, writes at great length that "God looks upon even the smallest offering of frankincense by a holy man as more valuable than ten thousand beasts which may be sacrificed by one who is not thoroughly virtuous" (*Spec. Leg.* 1.51 [273]). In fact, Philo goes so far as to suggest that those who truly love God and neighbor can "bring nothing" save "themselves . . . the most excellent of all sacrifices" (*Spec. Leg.* 1.50 [272]). This consuming passion for holiness of life can be seen as also

45. The rabbis referred to Rosh Hashanah as *Yom HaDin*—the Day of Judgment. It is on Rosh Hashanah that each of us stands before God and appeals for forgiveness for our sins. http://www.kolel.org/pages/holidays/RoshHashanah_intro.html.

shaping the writer of Hebrews, who understood Jesus as having rejected animal sacrifices in favor of offering the best and most pleasing sacrifice, namely himself—"See, God, I have come to do your will, O God" (Ps 40:8; Heb 10:7, 8). R. Joshua ben Levi, in his turn, taught his disciples that "a person who is genuinely humble does Scripture [Ps 51:19] treat as if he had made offerings of all the sacrifices" (*b. Sotah* 5b).

It should not come as a surprise that, by the early second century, Christian writers were making explicit use of the *Aqedah* to explore the efficacy of Jesus' death. Some scholars would even see this influence as already evident in the formative period of the Christian Scriptures.[46] More important for our own times is the realization that the early church created its intellectual matrix and spirituality within (and later at the boundaries of) Judaism. The *Aqedah* must have appealed to Christians because it provided a metaphor not only for understanding Jesus' death,[47] but also for how their own "sufferings" and "sacrifices" would also be pleasing to God.

The notion of sacrifice in the letter to the Hebrews is made out of the same cloth as the *Aqedah*. In Hebrews 2, Jesus is presented as "trustworthy" (2:12, 17-18) to the readers precisely because he has shown himself to be "a merciful and faithful high priest in the service of God" by walking through the path of suffering and temptation. This prepares

---

46. Many scholars believe that the Christian Scriptures already provide clear evidence of use of the *Aqedah* (Heb 11:17-20, Rom 8:32, John 3:16). See Robert J. Daly, "The Soteriological Significance of the Sacrifice of Isaac," *CBQ* 39 (1977) 45–75; Hans Joachim Schoeps, "The Sacrifice of Isaac in Paul's Theology," *JBL* 65 (1946) 385–92; J. Edwin Wood, "Isaac Typology in the New Testament," *NTS* 14 (1968) 583–89. Others, however, have drawn a distinction between references to Genesis 22 in the Christian Scriptures and the *Aqedah*, where the focus is on the atoning sacrifice of Isaac. See Philip R. Davies and Bruce D. Chilton, "The Aqedah: A Revised Tradition History," *CBQ* 40 (1978) 514–46.

The dating of the origins of the *Aqedah* within Judaism is also debated. Firm evidence cannot be found before the late first century (Josephus, *Ant.* 1.222-236; 4 Macc 13:12; Pseudo-Philo, *Liber Antiquitatum Biblicarum* 18.5, 32.2-4, 40.2).

47. The Aqedah is frequently expanded upon and featured as a foreshadowing of Jesus. Consider, for example, this small section from a sermon by the Rev. Marek P. Zabriskie: "From the earliest times Christians saw Isaac as a Christ figure. The parallels are striking. Isaac, like Jesus, was miraculously conceived. Both Isaac and Jesus entrusted themselves to their fathers. Each carried the wood for his own sacrifice. The journey to Mount Moriah took three days. Jesus spent three days in the tomb before his resurrection. A ram was substituted for Isaac. Jesus was substituted for all humanity to atone for our sins" ("Sacrifice: A Sermon by the Rev. Marek P. Zabriskie Delivered at St. Thomas Episcopal Church in Fort Washington, Pennsylvania on Sunday, March 12, 2006" http://216.239.51.104/search?q=cache:eHxqrKn1w3wJ:www.stthomaswhitemarsh.org/docsPublic/LisaFiles/documents/SermonsArticles/Sacrifice.pdf+%22isaac+and+jesus&hl=en&gl=us&ct=clnk&cd=26).

the reader for Hebrews 11–12, where the sufferings of Abraham, Moses, and Jesus are appealed to as assurance to readers that their own sufferings are also "for our good, in order that we may share his [God's] holiness" (12:10). The same holds for sacrifice. First the letter to the Hebrews shows how Jesus' new and superior order of sacrifice—"See, God, I have come to do your will, O God" (Heb 10:7, 8)—has rendered obsolete the former animal sacrifices. Then, when it comes time for us to "offer to God an acceptable worship," this is spelled out in very practical modes of holiness: "Let mutual love continue. Do not neglect to show hospitality to strangers . . ." (13:1-6). These ordinary acts are specifically identified as "sacrifices . . . pleasing to God" (13:16). This would not be evident or acceptable without the earlier notion that Jesus' "sacrifice" consisted in his total and loving submission to God (as Philo describes above) and not in his being tortured to death by the Romans.

Where does the heresy of Anselm's vicarious atonement begin? It started at the moment when God's plan of salvation was reduced to the problem of making atonement for sins. As a result, the efficacy of Jesus' Passion and death took on such enormous importance that it completely obscured the efficacy of his Incarnation and public ministry,[48] it undercut the salvific contribution made by the holiness of life and the public ministry of the disciples of Jesus, and it denied me, as a Catholic, any significant role in my salvation and in the salvation of the world.[49] When it comes to Judaism, Christian vicarious atonement theories obscured the

48. Thomas Aquinas, in his *Summa Theologica,* teaches that Christ's life had to be in accord with the purposes of the Incarnation: "first, that he might publish the truth . . . secondly, he came in order to free men from sin [by his preaching] . . . thirdly, he came that by him we might have access to God . . ." (*S.T.* III 40, 1). Aquinas finds it entirely natural to speak of "the efficacy of his persuasion" and "the force of his righteousness" as the means used by God to achieve these three goals. Later, when considering Christ's Passion, however, Aquinas seemingly forgets that he had earlier declared (with the Church Fathers) that "from the beginning of his conception Christ merited our eternal salvation" (*S.T.* III, 48, 1, *ad* 2) because now he begins to focus entirely on the necessary and sufficient merits of Christ's atoning death. In my judgment Aquinas was never able to successfully integrate the juridical and pastoral dynamics of salvation; hence, with time, the efficacy of Jesus' death ran roughshod over his Incarnation and public life. For details see Milavec, "Is God Arbitrary?" 75–85, and idem, *To Empower,* 64–72.

49. When a religious metaphor is twisted so tightly that it breaks down the self-confidence and self-worth of the Christian or Jewish believer, clearly it becomes dangerous to the spiritual health of those who accept it. No competent father disciplines his children by saying, "You can do nothing good! You can contribute nothing! Only Jesus (or Isaac) is the least bit capable in my eyes. Let him do everything for you." Rather, our Father says "You are up to it, my daughter/son! Remember how my servants, Jesus and Isaac, were able to keep faith in the face of uncertainty, opposition, temptation, suffering, and even,

contribution that eighteen hundred years of Judaism made to salvation history, undercut the soteriological importance of Jesus' Judaism, and perniciously distorted the Jewish Scriptures by refusing to allow that the God of Israel offers a whole spectrum of solutions when dealing with sin and that vicarious atonement is, at best, a very minor and poorly attested band within this wider spectrum.

In Christian circles Isaiah 53 has become the favored text[50] for demonstrating that the Jewish prophets foretold Jesus' intention to bear the sins of the world. This trend, however, is out of step with first-century Christianity. Isaiah 53 is curiously absent from the apostolic preaching in Acts and from the Passion narratives of the Gospels. One might think that, in the eyes of these sacred writers, Isaiah 53 was understood as not applying to the *moshiach*. Of the seven instances of the use of Isaiah 53 in the Christian Scriptures (Rom 10:16; 15:21; Matt 8:17; John 12:38; Luke 22:37; Acts 8:35; 1 Pet 2:24), only the last three references link the "servant" to Jesus' death. In all of these instances, however, "nothing is intimated . . . about the meaning of Jesus' death, certainly not in terms of vicarious or expiatory sufferings."[51] Within the Jewish interpretative tradition, moreover, the "servant" who "was crushed because of our iniquities" was normally understood as "Israel." Only rarely was this servant thought of as the *moshiach*.[52]

In sum, the unfolding of interpretation of the *Aqedah* illustrates how a single "precious moment" in the Jewish tradition was nurtured in order to diffuse its efficacy into a hundred other unexpected moments. The tragedy of the atonement theory as developed by Anselm is that it

---

death. Follow in their footsteps. Learn from them." Thus what the letter to the Hebrews and the *Aqedah* teach is that Jesus and Isaac are "pioneer[s]" (Heb 2:10) who open a path we can follow. Keeping faith, even in the face of suffering, is what binds us to Jesus and Isaac—it does not separate us from them. Likewise, offering pleasing sacrifices to God is what binds us to Jesus and Isaac—not what separates us.

50. When Mel Gibson returned to his faith after abandoning it for a dozen years, the cross was still frozen as the symbol of God's gracious love for sinful humanity. Thus it is no accident that at the very opening of his film, *The Passion of the Christ*, Gibson presents the words of Isaiah 53:5 as encapsulating the whole subject of his film. For more details see http://ecumene.org/SHOAH/Mel_Gibson's_Passion_Milavec.html.

51. Sam K. Williams, *Jesus' Death as Saving Event: The Background and Origin of a Concept.* HDR 2 (Missoula: Scholars Press, 1975) 224.

52. The fourth-century *Targum of Johathan* does have "my servant the *moschiach*" (Isa 53:13). From this point onward, however, the canonical text is shifted away from vicarious suffering. Instead of the servant "bearing" the sins of the people, he prays for them and their sins are forgiven (53:4), or he instructs them and their sins are forgiven (53:5). Suffering is simply taken out of the equation. See Williams, *Jesus' Death as Saving Event*, 119–20.

nurtured a single moment in the life of Jesus and proceeded to overextend its efficacy so completely as to distort or obliterate the efficacy of every other moment in salvation history.

2. *Jewish Martyrdom as a Ransom Payment.*[53] In the year 166 B.C.E. the ninety-year-old Jewish priest and teacher Eleazar and an unnamed mother along with her seven sons were publicly and gruesomely tortured to death in Jerusalem on the orders of the Syrian king Antiochus IV Epiphanes because they refused to abandon their "religious principles" (4 Macc 5:38). Instead of terrorizing the populace into submission, however, the spectacle turned the crowds against the "tyrant" and stiffened their resolve to defy Antiochus in the future (4 Macc 5:33-36; 6:16-21; 7:9). Even Antiochus and his council "marveled at their endurance" (4 Macc 17:17). According to the chronicles of his martyrdom, Eleazar called out to God as parts of his body were "burned to his very bones" (4 Macc 6:26):

> You know, O God, that I might have saved myself [by capitulating to the king's commands]. I am dying in burning torments for the sake of the law [Torah]. Be merciful to your people [Israel], and let our punishment be a satisfaction on their behalf. Make my blood their purification and take my life as a ransom for theirs. (4 Macc 6:27-29, altered for improved clarity)

The language of this prayer implies that Eleazar willingly offered his own body as a burnt offering to make satisfaction for the sins (of Jewish defectors?). His blood, meanwhile, is given to purify the people,[54] and his death is offered as a ransom for their release. When "the tyrant" (as Antiochus is repeatedly called) later leaves Jerusalem, this is proof that "the blood

53. David Flusser, an Israeli scholar and rabbi, made it his life work to study the Christian Scriptures. In his judgment, "The idea that a martyr atones for the sins of Israel is Jewish. The atoning death of Jesus was later thought of as the exclusive act of salvation, as the main purpose of Jesus' coming" ("Theses on the Emergence of Christianity from Judaism," *Face to Face* [1983] #36).

54. In the case of Eleazar his blood purifies those suffering from the contamination (for example, eating pork and athletic contests in the nude) brought in by Antiochus and his allies. Today it is difficult for us to understand how blood can be a purifying agent. In the ancient world, however, it was different. The blood of sacrifices in the temple was regarded as a cleansing agent (Lev 16:18-19; Heb 9:13; Rev 5:9). Under other circumstances blood was regarded as defiling/contaminating (Lev 6:27; 17:10-12; Rev 16:6). When we read texts such as "the blood of Jesus . . . cleanses us from all sin" (1 John 1:7) or "they have washed their robes . . . in the blood of the Lamb [Jesus]" (Rev 7:14), this signifies the cleansing power attributed to the blood from a sacrificial animal. This blood was not so regarded because of the death of the animal; rather, it was thought that the life force somehow resided in the blood. Care must be taken, accordingly, that all references to the "blood of Christ" in the Christian Scriptures are not seen as oblique references to his death.

of those devout ones and their death" was acceptable to God as "an aton-ing sacrifice" (4 Macc 17:22).

In brief, the language of the text makes it clear that these terrible deaths were efficacious sacrifices as opposed to merely being "senseless acts of resistance." Since 4 Maccabees is generally agreed to have been written between 20 and 54 c.e., it evokes themes of heroic resistance in the face of tyrannical powers that might have formed the background for Paul's depiction of the death of Jesus.[55]

3. *The Precarious Mission of the Prophets.* The prophets God sent to Israel were not well received.[56] Rather, during their lifetimes they were de-spised and persecuted. Nehemiah, in his chronicle, ascribed a violent death to all the prophets during the Israelite monarchy: "They . . . killed your prophets who had warned them" (Neh 9:26). In contrast, Chroni-cles, speaking of this same period, provides a more moderate summary: "They [the people] kept mocking the messengers of God, despising his words, and scoffing at his prophets" (2 Chr 36:16).

Consider, for example, the specific difficulties that befell Jeremiah be-cause of his mission as God's spokesman: he received death threats (Jer 11:21), his friends abandoned him (20:10), the priest Pashhur had him beaten and put in stocks (20:2), the royal officials beat him and put him under house arrest (37:15), and he was thrown into a muddy well and left to die (38:9). In addition to this open hostility, Jeremiah also faced the interior anxiety of associating himself with the plight of his people (4:19-22; 8:18-22; 13:17-19). He even had bouts of self-doubt and depres-sion, feeling that his whole life has been a failure (20:18).

55. A new generation of scholars has raised the question whether Paul so sugarcoated Jesus' death as to remove the bitter truth that Jesus died as a Jewish victim of Roman oppression. When Pilate had "King of the Jews" posted on Jesus' cross, this was not an "article of faith" but a stern warning meant to intimidate and terrorize any would-be followers. In our modern world where systems of domination continue and the mecha-nisms of social repression are routinely approved and sanitized in the public media, this new generation of scholars is asking whether Paul advocates a capitulation to these pow-ers (as in Romans 13) or whether the death of Jesus stiffens their resistance (as in the case of Eleazar) against oppression. See Neil Elliott, *Liberating Paul: The Justice of God and the Politics of the Apostle* (Maryknoll: Orbis, 1994) 94–101 and John Dominic Crossan and Jonathan L. Reed, *In Search of Paul: How Jesus' Apostle Opposed Rome's Empire with God's Kingdom* (San Francisco: HarperSanFrancisco, 2004) 404–13. My own contribution to this issue can be found in *The Didache: Faith, Hope, and Life of the Earliest Christian Communities, 50–70 c.e.* (New York: Newman Press, 2003) 872–909.

56. One might be tempted to think of the prophet Jonah as an exception. In fact, how-ever, his successful mission was directed toward the pagans of Nineveh and not the house of Israel. See Matt 12:38 *parr.*, where Jesus alludes to Jonah and contrasts his own failing mission.

In the Synoptics, Jesus is repeatedly identified with one or more of the prophets (Mark 6:14-15 par.). Jesus was regarded as a prophet because of his experience of being sent by God (Mark 1:38; 2:17; 10:45 par.; Matt 5:17; 10:34-36; 11:19 par.; Luke 12:49), his heralding of the reign of God (Mark 1:14, 38-39; 3:14; 4:1-32; 5:20 par.), his judgment speeches (Matt 11:21-24; 21:23; 23:13-39; Luke 6:24-26; 10:13-15), and also his prophetic deeds (Mark 11:12-14, 15-17, 20-25 par.).[57] In Matthew's Gospel the sufferings of Jesus' disciples and, by implication, the sufferings of Jesus as well are clearly associated with the treatment traditionally afforded the prophets of Israel: "Blessed are you when people revile you and persecute you and utter all kinds of evil against you falsely on my account. Rejoice and be glad, for your reward is great in heaven, for in the same way they persecuted the prophets who were before you" (Matt 5:11-12).

When Jesus asked, "Who do people say that I am?" his disciples presented the views held by the crowds: "John the Baptist; and others, Elijah; and still others, one of the prophets" (Mark 8:28 par.)—a prophetic identity in every case. This same identity is used to account for Jesus' rejection in his hometown of Nazareth: "Prophets are not without honor except in their own country and in their own house" (Matt 13:57; Luke 4:24). According to Luke, Jesus compared his own unwillingness to work signs in Nazareth with Elijah's and Elisha's taking up residence with and healing outsiders (Luke 4:25-28). Closely associated with this are the occasions on which Jesus predicted that "we are going up to Jerusalem, and the Son of Man will be handed over to the chief priests and the scribes . . ." (Mark 8:31; 9:31; 10:33-34 par.). While scholars regard the placement and the details within these predictions as the literary creation of Mark, the distinct possibility remains that "Jesus' experience at Nazareth served as a dramatic anticipation of the final and decisive rejection of Jesus by the Jews at Jerusalem."[58]

It comes as no surprise, then, that when Jesus entered Jerusalem "the crowds were saying, 'This is the prophet Jesus from Nazareth in Galilee'" (Matt 21:11). In a more ominous tone, Luke has Jesus being warned by the Pharisees of a death threat from Herod, but he brushes it off, saying, "I must be on my way, because it is impossible for a prophet to be killed outside of Jerusalem" (Luke 13:33). In Jerusalem itself, when Jesus is in

---

57. See the exceptional analysis of these and other issues in David E. Aune, *Prophecy in Early Christianity and the Ancient Mediterranean World* (Grand Rapids: Eerdmans, 1983) 153–88.

58. Ibid., 159. Surely the treatment received by John the Baptizer was also a prefiguring of the hard times to come for Jesus.

the thick of controversy, the reader is told that "they [the temple priests] wanted to arrest him, but they feared the crowds, because they regarded him as a prophet" (Matt 21:46 par.). Jesus' reputation as a prophet, therefore, appears to have shielded him from being arrested openly during his days in Jerusalem. At night, on the other hand, the crowds were gone, and Jesus was quite vulnerable. He died as did the other prophets of Israel.[59]

For the Synoptics there is no presumption that Jesus had to die so that sins would be forgiven or the Gates of Heaven thrown open.[60] "According to early Christianity, the motif of the violent fate of the prophets was used to understand the significance of the death of Jesus, who was by implication the latest and greatest of the prophets."[61] Jesus' suffering, consequently, was principally accounted for by the precarious nature of his mission as a Jewish prophet whom God sent to Israel.

In sum, it is evident that Judaism offered many diverse ways for understanding Jesus' sufferings other than vicarious atonement. In each case what is evident is how holiness of life, societal transformation, and intimacy with God are interwoven into the fabric of the forgiveness of sins. The study of Judaism, consequently, can serve to enable Christians not only to recover their roots, but to recover those strands of piety that have been obscured by the triumph of vicarious atonement theories surrounding Jesus' death on the cross.

59. The Parable of the Wicked Tenants (Mark 12:1-12; Matt 21:33-46; Luke 20:9-19, and *GThom*, logia 65-66) illustrate how the early church identified the mission of Jesus in continuity with the prophets of Israel (see also Heb 1:1-2). Clearly Jesus was progressively honored as more than a prophet, yet his suffering and death were initially understood as woven out of the same fabric as the traditional non-reception of the prophets. According to the parable the father's will was to send his son to succeed in a mission when others had failed: "They will [surely] respect my son" (Mark 12:6). Nothing in the parable even comes close to suggesting that the father needs his son to die for some noble, mysterious purpose, nor can the death of the beloved son be construed as having anything to do with forgiving sins. The presenting dilemma in each case is whether the tenants set in charge will or will not respond to God's servants (i.e., the prophets) who are sent to them. For details see Milavec, "Mark's Parable of the Wicked Husbandmen as Reaffirming God's Predilection for Israel," *JES* 26, no. 2 (1989) 305–12, and idem, "A Fresh Analysis of the Parable of the Wicked Husbandmen in the Light of Jewish-Catholic Dialogue," in Clemens Thoma and Michael Wyschogrod, eds., *Parable and Story in Judaism and Christianity* (New York: Paulist Press, 1989) 81–117.

60. Edward Schillebeeckx, *Jesus: An Experiment in Christology* (New York: Seabury, 1979) 284: "There is no trace of a soteriological motivation for Jesus' suffering and death."

61. Aune, *Prophecy in Early Christianity*, 157. Nearly all scholars who allow that there was a development in the understanding of Jesus after his resurrection are persuaded that the disciples initially associated Jesus' suffering with his prophetic mission. According to Edward Schillebeeckx, "Jesus' death stands in a very broad tradition that opens up more far-reaching perspectives: the tradition of the martyrdom of the prophet sent by God and the rejection of his message" (*Jesus*, 275).

Six

The Unsavory Odor
of Christian Evangelization

> Missionaries with one purpose and plenty of money
> are destroying our people.
>
> —Rachelle[1]

Jews do not imagine that God is somehow hampered in his mysterious designs just because so few people in the world are practicing Judaism. Some converts do come, but, following the tradition of the rabbis, such would-be converts are initially discouraged and sent away three times. If they persist in returning, however, they are instructed in the rudiments of the Torah and then immersed in water (in the case of men, they are circumcised as well).

The Christian term "evangelism" and the church's aspiration "to preach to the whole world" have left a very bad taste in Jewish mouths. What Jews have known of "evangelism" began as pious exhortations given by holy men. Then, in the course of time, "evangelism" turned toward less worthy means, as when Jews were forced to assemble and listen to sermons directed against them. When Jews did not convert in sufficiently large numbers, the frustration of Christians knew no bounds; they resorted to burning Jewish books and synagogues, and finally to burning Jewish bodies.

---

1. Rachelle, the Jewish mother of three sons, tells her dramatic story of how she saved her youngest son, Ryan, from a false conversion to a brand of evangelical Christianity that belittled Judaism ("Rachelle's Story," http://www.jewsforjudaism.org/web/personalstories/rachelle.html).

All in all, modern-day Jews get uneasy when Christians become enthusiastic about evangelization. On the one hand, some Jews are flattered to think that Christians are concerned about their spiritual welfare. On the other hand, they soon become annoyed when they discover that Christians fail to recognize what Jews know about themselves, namely, that they are already called (beginning with Abraham), already confirmed in the ways of God (by virtue of doing Torah), and already assured of inclusion in God's final kingdom (by virtue of the grace of their chosenness). Pinchas Lapide, an Orthodox rabbi and Israeli scholar, responds to those Christians trying to convert him to Jesus in the following terms:

> Since Sinai we have known the way to the Father. You, on the other hand, were very much in need of it. Therefore, your becoming Christian is for me a portion of God's plan of salvation, and I do not find it difficult to accept the church as an instrument of salvation. But please, you do not need to sprinkle sugar on top of honey, as you do when you wish to baptize us. The sugar on top of honey is simply superfluous. We are already "with the Father" and we know the way. . . .[2]

This chapter has three goals: to recall the history of the evangelization of Jews with a special emphasis on the case of Edgardo Mortara; to examine the church's mission to evangelize from the vantage point of Jesus; and to explore Paul's declaration that Israel's "hardening" (Rom 11:11-12) was providential and that "all Israel will be saved" (Rom 11:26).

Pius IX and the Kidnapping of Edgardo Mortara[3]

The year was 1858. A young woman in Bologna confessed to her parish priest that six years earlier she had worked illegally as a maid for a Jewish family named Mortara. While she was serving in the household, the one-year-old son of the Mortaras fell ill. The pious teenage girl, thinking that the Jewish boy might die without baptism, took it upon herself to

2. Pinchas Lapide and Jürgen Moltmann, *Jewish Monotheism and Christian Trinitarian Doctrine* (Philadelphia: Fortress Press, 1981) 69–70.
3. Formerly the unsavory aspects of papal conduct were discreetly concealed from Catholic audiences. Today, however, a new openness is evident. See the following recent books that treat the Mortara case: Peter De Rosa, *Vicars of Christ* (New York: Crown Publishers, 1988) 195; David I. Kertzer, *The Popes Against the Jews* (New York: Alfred A. Knopf, 2001) 38–85; Garry Wills, *Papal Sin: The Structures of Deceit* (New York: Doubleday, 2000) 40–45.

secretly baptize him. Later, the boy recovered. On hearing this story from the woman in the confessional, her parish priest insisted that he had to inform the church authorities.

After considering all aspects of the case the clerical authorities concluded that little Mortara was effectively a Christian by virtue of his baptism. They further concluded that his parents, being Jews, were entirely unfit to foster his Christian identity. Accordingly the police, acting under clerical orders, seized the seven-year-old Edgardo from his home and sequestered him in the Vatican. He was placed under the care of a group of nuns. Pope Pius IX took a fond interest in the boy. In fact, he won him over with presents and gradually gained a place in his heart such that Edgardo began addressing him as "uncle." With time Edgardo even became a priest, and Pius IX assigned to him the special mission of reaching out to "the fallen race of Jews" so that they too, like him, might come to know the grace and mercy of Christ.

The pleas of the Mortaras for the return of their son fell on deaf ears. Those who supported the return of Edgardo to his parents argued that parents had the natural right to raise their own children in their own religion.[4] Pius IX, given his growing personal interest in this case, argued that spiritual rights took precedence over natural rights and that Edgardo's baptism effectively released him from the constraints of his Jewish parents. All over Europe, even some notable Catholics raised objections:

> But Pius was impervious to argument. When a Catholic wrote a respectful letter suggesting that Edgardo should be returned, the Pope scribbled on the bottom of the letter, "aberrations of a Catholic . . . [who] doesn't know his catechism." When his own Secretary of State, Cardinal Antonelli, suggested that Pius might be alienating other countries by such a high-handed use of power, the Pope answered that he did not care who was against him: "I have the blessed Virgin on my side."[5] He told the Catholic ambassador

4. Thomas Aquinas argued that children should not be baptized without their parents' consent, since they have immediate authority over them (*S.T.* III 68,10, *ad* 2).

5. Pius IX solemnly declared the Immaculate Conception as a belief to be held by all the faithful on December 8, 1854. Four years later an unexpected miracle was reported from Lourdes. Bernadette Soubirous, an uneducated French girl of fourteen, reported to her bishop that she had been visited by a "mysterious lady" in an apparition. The bishop wisely asked Bernadette to ask the lady who she was. When she did so, she received the reply, "I am the Immaculate Conception." This was popularly hailed as a firm confirmation, coming from Our Lady herself, that she agreed with the earlier papal initiative. Pius

from France that the Mortaras had brought their trouble on themselves by illegally employing a Christian as their servant.[6]

The Unsavory History of Forced Conversions

The actions of the parish priest, the police, and the pope in 1858 were not entirely unexpected. Catholics were always encouraged to perform emergency baptism in cases where unbaptized children were "in danger of death." Once baptized, however, the child was considered regenerated by Christ's Spirit, and when this fact was made known to the authorities the child was taken from his/her Jewish home and placed in a pious Christian home in order to ensure proper Catholic nurturing. This was common practice. In Rome itself during the years 1814–1818 scholars have discovered no fewer than sixty instances in which children were forcibly separated from their Jewish parents following such emergency baptisms.[7] Again, in 1864, six years after the uproar that accompanied the abduction of Edgardo, "a nine-year-old Jewish boy, Giuseppe Coen, was baptized without his parents' permission in Rome and sequestered from them."[8] The Mortara case, consequently, was just the tip of a giant iceberg.

In earlier centuries the records show that large numbers of Jewish adults were terrorized into accepting baptism. Father Edward H. Flannery, a pioneer in Jewish-Catholic dialogue, wrote *The Anguish of the Jews* to chronicle the relations between Christians and Jews in Europe during the course of two thousand years. Here is his account of the condition of the Jews in Spain in the late fourteenth century:

> Three months later [in 1391] the holocaust began. With renewed fury, the mob broke into the *Juderia* [the required Jewish ghetto] of Seville and left it in ruins. Four thousand Jews were killed, but the majority . . . escaped death by accepting baptism. From Seville, the carnage spread like a plague throughout all Spain . . . engulfing some seventy Jewish communities. In some *Juderias* not a single Jew was left, and many synagogues were turned into churches. Authorities were helpless before the onslaught.[9]

IX, consequently, felt that he had the blessed Virgin on his side not only in making his earlier dogmatic declaration but also in refusing to return Edgardo.

6. Wills, *Papal Sin,* 42.

7. Kertzer, *The Popes,* 42–59, where many cases are documented.

8. Wills, *Papal Sin,* 45.

9. Edward H. Flannery, *The Anguish of the Jews* (New York: Paulist, 1985) 132.

Even after these pogroms died down, Fr. Flannery notes that the remaining Jews in Spain "appeared to the Church as a scandal and a temptation to their converted brethren."[10] Thus Jews were forced to listen to pious sermons and to attend public debates orchestrated to persuade Jews of the manifest superiority of Christianity and the utter bankruptcy of Judaism. Even holy men who were later to be canonized as saints in the Catholic Church were caught up in the fervor of this unholy enterprise:

> St. Vincent Ferrer, Dominican, miracle-worker, an excellent preacher, [was] totally dedicated to the conversion of the Jews. Throughout Castile and Aragon, he passed from synagogue to synagogue, the Torah in one hand, the crucifix in the other and a band of the devout at his heels. . . . He is credited with 35,000 baptisms of Jews between 1411 and 1412. When he failed to persuade he was severe and is believed to have inspired the first compulsory Spanish ghettoes and the oppressive legislation of 1414 that narrowly circumscribed Jewish social activities.[11]

The combined effect of forced sermons, public debates, crowded ghettos, and intrusive legislation was that a steady stream of Jewish converts poured into the church. Each Sunday nearly a hundred thousand converts from Judaism crowded into the various Spanish churches for the Eucharist. The Catholic populace was aware that some of these Jews were not persuaded of the infinite merits of Christ but had entered into "baptisms of convenience" calculated to effect their escape from the diseased and crowded conditions of ghetto existence and from the severe curtailment of their legal rights. Thus converted Jews were mercilessly watched by their neighbors for any sign or indication that their conversion was not sincere or that they held on to any of their former Jewish customs. If so, the authorities were notified.

In time the number of suspected false conversions was so large that a special Inquisition was formed in 1480 to handle the problem. This Inquisition inspired elaborate regulations for detecting and uprooting incomplete conversions. When the Dominican priest Torquemada became the Inquisitor General in 1483, "the Inquisition attained an efficiency and ruthlessness that held not only *Marranos* but all Spanish Jewry in a state of terror."[12] Accusations multiplied. Confessions were extracted through

---

10. Ibid., 133.
11. Ibid., 134.
12. Ibid., 137.

the use of systematic and progressive tortures.[13] Those convicted of apostasy were burned at the stake. Public burnings reminded other converts, who were derisively called "pigs" *(marranos)* by the Catholic populace, that those who failed to keep their baptismal vows had to suffer dire consequences.

Every Jew remembers 1492. Christians know this date because it marks the sailing of Columbus who, in quest of a new route to China, discovered the "new world" of the Americas. Jews, however, remember the date because it was in that year that the pious Christian rulers of Spain, Ferdinand and Isabella, decreed that every Jew had three choices: convert to Christianity, forever leave their country, or be put to death. At the time this was regarded as a fair resolution to the Jewish question.

Needless to say, the brutality of these times has largely passed. For Christians, however, this short recital helps to explain why Jews shudder when Christians manifest any zeal for the conversion of the Jews. Even when conversions were used to rescue a Jew from mob violence, they must be lamented and their results must rend the heart of fathers and mothers who, of necessity, can imagine what they might feel if the tables were turned. Consider the following true story:

> The [Jewish] parents were fortunate in being able to place their son with a [Christian] friend who lived outside the [Warsaw] ghetto. . . . The parents were shipped off to Auschwitz, separated, and managed by hook and crook to survive the final solution. Neither was aware of the fate of the other or of the[ir] child. At the age of five, supplied with a new birth certificate by a Roman Catholic parish, the boy walked out of the ghetto holding the hand of the woman who saved his life. He was spirited away to a Roman Catholic orphanage in the countryside, where he went to church every Sunday, said his prayers twice a day, and learned the Our Father and Hail Mary. The nun who looked after the children converted the boy to Christianity. She taught him that he "would have

---

13. Elvira del Campo was brought before the Tribunal of Toledo because it was reported that she never ate pork and she changed her underclothes every Saturday. When it was discovered that her Catholic mother had Jewish ancestry, the Tribunal suspected that she might be a crypto-Jewess. Mercilessly tortured, the young woman asked repeatedly to be told what crime she must confess to in order to stop the administration of more pain. After such intense indignities (including being stripped of her clothes), she lapsed into incoherent speech. For details, see the four-volume work of Henry Charles Lea, *History of the Inquisition in Spain* (New York: Macmillan, 1922) III 6.7.24, http://libro.uca.edu/lea3/6lea7.htm.

to give up all Jewish things." He was baptized. He was taught the classic Christian attitude toward Jews. When he and his mother were reunited after the war, "he hated everything Jewish." "The Jews," he said, "killed the Lord Jesus."[14]

Anyone who repudiates Hitler's "final solution" must likewise repudiate everything in Christian theology and practice that systematically destroys the faith of Jews. The nun in this story was surely not an evil person; far from it. She accepted the boy into the orphanage at some risk to herself and others. One might even imagine that she regarded the boy's conversion as an act of necessity since children are unable to undertake a double-identity that requires systematic dissimulation. The boy's physical life was thus spared at the cost of obliterating his religious identity. One can only imagine the anguish of his mother and the disturbance within the boy himself at discovering that he himself and his parents were Jews. The poison of anti-Judaism within Christianity was thus calculated to turn his personal being against his own identity and his own family. The nun in this story was thus an unwitting contributor to Hitler's final solution.

The Beatification of Pius IX

In 1998 the Vatican announced that steps were being taken to examine whether Pius IX was deserving of beatification. Those who favored Pius IX regarded the act of beatification as the normal route whereby the church could officially celebrate the "heroic virtues" of Pius IX and confirm him as "a model of Christian life." In April of 2000, when his body was exhumed from the crypt of the Basilica of St. Lawrence, it was found to be dried out but almost perfectly preserved from decomposition. Some conservative prelates took this to mean that the Lord had "miraculously" preserved his body so that, following his beatification, "his preserved corpse" might become "an object of veneration."[15]

Monsignor Brunero Gherardini, the Vatican prelate charged with promoting the beatification, was surprised and disturbed that letters of protest filled his mailbox. Italian Catholics voiced their reservations regarding Pius IX. So did liberal Catholics elsewhere who feared that the

14. From Alexander Donat's personal memoir, *Holocaust Kingdom*, cited in Sidney G. Hall III, *Christian Anti-Semitism and Paul's Theology* (Minneapolis: Fortress Press, 1993) 12.

15. R. Jeffrey Smith, "Jewish Groups Object to the Beatification of Pius IX," *The Columbus Dispatch* (Columbus, Ohio) July 7, 2000.

beatification of Pius IX would endorse and promote the triumphalistic policies of Pius IX that led to the declaration of papal infallibility at Vatican I. Added to this were the objections of Jews. It so happened that a symposium of concerned Jews and their Catholic allies met in Rome on 21 June 2000 under the leadership of a member of the Mortara family. After reviewing the case of Edgardo Mortara they drafted a strong letter of sympathy with the Mortara family. In part this letter read: "While we do not wish to directly insert ourselves into the beatification decision, we feel a moral obligation to at least share our perspective that (the abduction) . . . not only caused unspeakable pain to the parents . . . but it demonstrated a fundamental disrespect and disdain for Jews, for Jewish feelings, and indeed for basic God-given human rights."[16] In responding to this letter a Vatican official tried to explain that "in the process of beatification, this [the abduction] wasn't taken into account because it was a habit of the times." Father Giacomo Martina, s.j., professor at the Pontifical Gregorian University in Rome, further argued that "the Mortara story demonstrates the profound zeal of Pius IX (and) his firmness in carrying out what he perceived to be his duty at the cost of losing personal popularity."[17]

On the negative side, Fr. John W. O'Malley, s.j., a professor at the Weston Jesuit School of Theology, wrote an article in *America* analyzing the series of offensive deeds that ought to be reconsidered relative to the impending beatification. He closed with a very pointed question: "Beatifications deal with the past, but are actions done in the present and for the present. Pius will on September 3rd [2001] officially become a model of sanctity. For whom is this model meaningful, for whom intended?"[18]

My own objections were much more direct. I addressed the issue in a letter to the editor published in the *National Catholic Reporter*:

> Pius IX does not deserve beatification. He deserves to be investigated for his crimes against humanity. John L. Allen (*NCR* 09/03/00) amply enumerates his crimes against the Jewish people but only partially portrays the measure of suffering inflicted upon the inhabitants of the Papal States. After a brief flirtation with democratic reforms (1848), Pius IX disbanded the parliament, nullified the constitution, and ruled the Papal States (1/3 of Italy) with

16. Ibid.
17. Ibid.
18. John W. O'Malley, "The Beatification of Pope Pius IX," *America* (February 11, 2000) 6.

an iron hand. He made it a crime to advocate democratic reform or Italian unification. His secret police *(Sanfedisti)* instituted a climate of terror. Enemies of the Papal States were convicted in hasty trials. Harsh sentences were imposed. Ringleaders were left hanging on the gallows as a warning to other would-be advocates of reform. In 1862, no less than 12,000 priests petitioned the pope to support Italian aspirations and say a few words in support of democracy. Pius IX disciplined every one of them.

While Pius IX had a momentary victory when he was granted nearly "absolute powers" in the church, this did nothing to shore up his "absolute powers" in civil matters. Vatican I was cut short in late 1870 when the French troops withdrew. The advancing troops of the unificationists were joyfully embraced as "liberators" from their oppressive, papal dictator. In the plebiscite that followed, the Romans voted overwhelmingly in favor of Italian unification. Pius IX sent out letters to the Catholic heads of state in Europe pleading for a military intervention to restore his "absolute civil powers." No one came. Humiliated, he refused to meet with elected officials of the Italian government. Then he abused his episcopal powers by excommunicating them.

Sure, the Vatican position is that Pius IX "sincerely believed" (p. 12) in what he did. But so did Hitler! As Catholics, we expect the Vatican to investigate Pius IX, to acknowledge the crimes he committed, and to atone for his sins (as the relatives of Edgardo Mortara have the right to expect). Anything less would be an affront to the Gospel of Jesus Christ.[19]

The Preaching Mission of the Church

The abuses of the past need not be repeated. In our own day we have every reason to expect that great care will be taken to ensure that evangelization addressed to Jews includes no offensive or coercive measures. One might even ask whether the church must engage in the evangelization of Jews if it is to be faithful to its divine founder. Essentially, the church is committed to the continuation of the mission given to it by Jesus. This mission has been aptly defined in the official document *Dominus Jesus* as follows:

> The Lord Jesus, before ascending into heaven, commanded his disciples to proclaim the Gospel to the whole world and to baptize all

19. Aaron Milavec, letter to the editor, *National Catholic Reporter,* February 29, 2000. Also http://vatican2.org/milavec.htm.

nations: "Go into the whole world and proclaim the Gospel to every creature. He who believes and is baptized will be saved; he who does not believe will be condemned" (Mark 16:15-16; Matt 28:18-20; cf. Luke 24:46-48; John 17:18, 20, 21; Acts 1:8). The Church's universal mission is born from the command of Jesus Christ. . . .

At the close of the second millennium, however, this mission is still far from complete. For that reason, Saint Paul's words are now more relevant than ever: "Preaching the Gospel is not a reason for me to boast; it is a necessity laid on me: woe to me if I do not preach the Gospel!" (1 Cor 9:16). This explains the Magisterium's particular attention to giving reasons for and supporting the evangelizing mission of the Church, above all in connection with the religious traditions of the world. (§§ 1, 3)

These statements aptly specify the source, the scope, and the urgency of the church's mission. So far, so good. There are some ambiguities, however:

1. The Gospel Jesus proclaimed was the nearness of the reign of God. In effecting his mission, Jesus moved from town to town. In any given town he was content to sow the seed of the Gospel and to let it germinate in the hearts and the minds of believers. At no time did he imagine that every believer would somehow leave home, family, and occupation and follow him, nor did he organize believers into some form of communities that would have regular rituals and prayers after he left them.

The final command Jesus gave to his disciples was to continue his mission, going into the towns and cities of the whole world so that, in the end, they would "proclaim the good news to the whole creation" (Mark 16:15). In fact, the urgency of this mission was precisely derived from the realization that the time was short. According to Matthew it was so short that the disciples might not even be able to circulate "through all the towns of Israel before the Son of Man comes [as in 25:31]" (10:23). Hence, in this view Jesus would in no way have envisioned a program of creating communities and building churches in every town and country throughout the entire world, and he certainly would never have imagined that somehow the salvation of the world required everyone, everywhere, to become a Christian.

2. Jesus appears to have limited the number of his closest disciples quite deliberately to twelve. This number may have been symbolic—one disciple for each of the twelve tribes of Israel.[20] In any case a disciple was expected

---

20. Francis Schüssler Fiorenza, *Foundational Theology: Jesus and the Church* (New York: Crossroad, 1984) 84–87, 135–37, 140.

to leave home, family, occupation in order to devote himself or herself full time to an intensive apprenticeship in order to be able to continue the ministry of Jesus. In the gospels, accordingly, Jesus is portrayed as sending his disciples out in pairs with instructions to proclaim the kingdom, to heal, and to exorcise just as he did (Matt 10:1-12). If this was in fact the case, only a small number of believers ever became disciples and, in point of fact, the number of disciples was always limited by restrictions on time, money, and need.[21] Even twenty-five disciples, for example, would have been so demanding on Jesus that they would have restricted his mobility and taxed his energies so much that his roving mission would have been neglected or entirely ground to a standstill.

This means that the mandate to "make disciples of all nations . . . teaching them to obey everything that I have commanded you" (Matt 28:19-20) could not and would not have envisioned fashioning communities, building churches, and erecting education complexes so that everyone in the world could be trained as a disciple. From what has already been noted above, Jesus knew that only a relatively few disciples were needed for what he had in mind. Twelve would be able to cover all the towns of Israel. For "the nations," however, additional disciples would be necessary. According to the Gospel of Luke, Jesus sent out seventy disciples (Luke 10:1-11) much as he had sent out the Twelve (Luke 6:13, 9:1-6). Within the Jewish framework it was normally supposed that there were seventy nations; hence the sending out of seventy disciples (again in pairs) might be a symbolic way of anticipating the evangelization of the whole world.[22]

---

21. The normal expectation in the centuries surrounding the turn of the era was that a master of Torah (a rabbi) would, during the time of his training, have sufficient resources to provide for the material well-being of his disciples. See, for example, Aaron Milavec, *To Empower as Jesus Did* (New York: Edwin Mellen, 1982) 114–20.

22. Joseph A. Fitzmyer, *The Gospel According to Luke. AB* 28, 28A (Garden City, NY: Doubleday, 1979, 1983). Some ancient manuscripts have Luke speaking of "seventy" while other manuscripts have "seventy-two." Fitzmyer explains: "It has often been thought to reflect the nations of the world in the table of Gen 10:2-31 and would symbolize the coming evangelization of the Gentiles and Diaspora Jews by the disciples, whereas the Twelve would have been sent to Israel itself. . . . In the Masoretic text of Genesis, the descendants of Japheth, Ham, and Shem number seventy, whereas in the Septuagint, they are seventy-two" (p. 846).

On the other hand, Fitzmyer notes that the seventy are sent "ahead of him in pairs to every town and place where he himself intended to go" (Luke 10:1) and the Twelve are later sent "to all nations" (Luke 24:47). Fitzmyer is mistaken in this latter comment. According to Luke the Twelve are "witnesses" that "repentance and forgiveness of sins is to be proclaimed in his name to all nations" (Luke 24:47). Nothing is specifically said to

In sum, no one in the early church would have imagined that the missionary objective was "to make every single person in the whole world a disciple," which would have amounted to a massive overkill. Likewise, Jesus' sending out disciples never carried with it any threat that those who rejected the Gospel were somehow destined for an eternity in hell. This threat was manufactured only later.

3. Even a program of baptizing does not imply that everyone is called to full-time discipleship. John the Baptizer, it must be remembered, used the rite of baptism by way of confirming the *teshuvah* of those who received the Gospel of the kingdom. When the baptism was completed, these people went home and lived out their lives at the threshold of the kingdom they now expected. Building programs and community organization were not part of this picture.

The same thing holds for the eucharistic meals celebrated by the early believers. These meals took place in their homes.[23] The presence of Jesus and the anticipation of the kingdom were always a part of these meals. No building programs were needed or anticipated. Even community organization was kept to a minimum. According to the record in Acts, when the Twelve discovered that their energies were being taxed by the daily distribution of bread to the widows, they had the community appoint seven men for this part-time task. Their logic was: "It is not right that we should neglect [heralding] the word of God in order to wait on tables" (Acts 6:2). The Twelve, in this instance, were clearly saying that nothing should hinder their mission to preach the coming kingdom to those who have not yet heard the Good News. Whatever came later in the form of building programs, founding schools, administering hospitals, and opening soup kitchens was not part of the mission assigned to the church by Jesus. All in all, there is a great difference between the missionary mandate as understood and practiced by Jesus and the "call to evangelize" practiced by the church in the course of its history.

---

the effect that the Twelve themselves would personally undertake such a mission. In fact, since Luke also wrote Acts, he nowhere suggests that the Twelve had any special mission to the Gentiles. Peter did baptize some Gentiles in Caesarea (Acts 10–11), yet it was the likes of Paul and Barnabas who directly evangelized the nations.

23. Archaeological studies show that what later became known as "churches" or "houses of the Lord," i.e., buildings set aside for Christian use, did not exist before the late third century. The Christian Scriptures make clear that the disciples of Jesus met in the temple courtyards (Acts 5:12) and in private homes (Acts 12:12; 16:40; 20:20; Rom 16:5; 1 Cor 16:19; Col 4:15).

The Limits of Jesus' Mission to Israel

As for the mission to the Jews, weight must be given to the fact that Jesus reckoned twelve disciples as adequate. Moreover, it must be allowed that Jesus thought the original Twelve were able to complete the task. In Jesus' mind there was no plan to return repeatedly to those towns that had not welcomed the Good News. Rather, "if anyone will not welcome you" in a particular place, then the disciple was told to "shake off the dust from your feet as you leave that house or town" (Matt 10:14). Likewise, there was no expressed intention on the part of Jesus for the Twelve to ordain successors so that the mission to Israel would continue without interruption to the end of time. What the Twelve did not accomplish was to be left in God's hands. From these considerations it follows that Jesus would never have imagined that the mission to Israel must somehow continue in every time and every place until every living Jew became a disciple, abandoned his or her local synagogue, and joined a Christian church.

Our understanding of Jesus is so jaundiced today by recent practice that it is sometimes presumed that any Jew receiving the Gospel must somehow effectively step outside of Judaism and be baptized as a "Christian." To correct this gross misunderstanding it is important to frame the mission of Jesus correctly. Those who believed the Good News that Jesus preached along the shores of the Lake of Galilee and those who heard his teaching of the ways of God in their synagogues never for one moment imagined that the anticipation of the kingdom somehow meant leaving the synagogue and going to the church of their choice. Jesus may have had his differences with the synagogue leaders of his day, yet he never supposed that those Jews who welcomed his Good News would somehow separate themselves from the prayers and study going on in their local synagogues. When Christians reflect on these things, it must appear that the poison of conflict that has been historically created between the church and the synagogue has, in fact, resulted in an either-or program of evangelization. *One thing, however, has to be made absolutely clear: The abandonment of Judaism was never a goal of Jesus' mission to Israel.*[24]

Matthew 10 provides a sort of manual to guide the conduct of disciples on mission. What one learns from this manual is that disciples travel light and depend on local hospitality for the duration of their stay. The pair of disciples brings "peace" *(shalom)* to the household of their hosts

---

24. Readers may want to revisit ch. 3, which affirms the centrality of Israel in the mind and heart of Jesus and the early church.

once a "worthy"[25] household was found. There is no mention of setting up household churches. Believers already had a synagogue where they could meet, discuss, and live out the message of the kingdom. No one imagined that those who anticipated the coming of the reign of God preached by Jesus were somehow abandoning Judaism; to the contrary, the kingdom message was delivered by Jews and for Jews. The message itself had to do with the fulfillment of God's promises to Israel. Being Jewish was the *sine qua non* of receiving and understanding the kingdom message. Only much later (as shown in chapter 4 above) did Gentile Christians (wrongly) insist that embracing Jesus' message and being Jewish were incompatible.

If disciples were not welcomed, they were required to leave (Matt 10:14) and never return. The gospel never suggests that one returns a second time in order to give the members of the household another chance. It never implies that one builds a missionary compound so that a steady stream of evangelization can soften local resistance, nor are traveling missionaries advised to return seven times or seventy times in cases in which the seeds of the kingdom did not at first take root. Even Jesus appears to have given up on his hometown the first time it rejected him (Luke 4:16-30). There were simply too many people ready to receive the Good News to linger or to lament individual failures (see Matt 9:35-36).

Paul and Barnabas followed roughly the same practice on their journeys. The case of Antioch is typical. Like Jesus, they immediately went to the synagogue, for they knew that the Jews of the city would be gathering there. They delivered their message. Here is the result:

> As Paul and Barnabas were going out, the people urged them to speak about these things again the next sabbath. When the meeting of the synagogue broke up, many Jews and devout converts to Judaism followed Paul and Barnabas, who spoke to them and urged them to continue in the grace of God.
>
> The next sabbath almost the whole city gathered to hear the word of the Lord. But when the Jews saw the crowds, they were filled with jealousy; and blaspheming, they contradicted what was spoken by Paul. Then both Paul and Barnabas spoke out boldly, saying, "It was necessary that the word of God should be spoken

---

25. The judgment that a household is "worthy" has nothing to do with the wealth or poverty, the size, or the merits of a particular householder. Rather, the worthy household is one that extends hospitality to strangers and, as a result, receives God's blessing, the Good News of the kingdom. In this connection see Matt 10:40-43.

first to you. Since you reject it and judge yourselves to be unworthy of eternal life, we are now turning to the Gentiles. For so the Lord has commanded us, saying, 'I have set you to be a light for the Gentiles, so that you may bring salvation to the ends of the earth.'" (Acts 13:42-47)

Here, as elsewhere, Paul and Barnabas maintain the rule that the Jews have a priority in receiving the Good News. They receive it initially, but when they are invited back for the following Sabbath, the consensus goes against them. One can presume that the pair stayed in a worthy household during the week between Sabbaths. Once rejected, Paul and Barnabas wasted no time. They did not pass out tracts in the hope that some Jews would read them at home and seek them out later. They did not even suppose that they should have another go at it on the following Sabbath before throwing in the towel. No, they left the synagogue immediately and turned their attention to the Gentiles in the city. The narrative implies that the pair found some sympathetic Gentiles during their one-week stay. Now that the Jews of the city had shown themselves uninterested, their attention was turned to other people and other towns.

Note also that the missionary pair use the words of Isaiah to establish their mission to the Gentiles. Paul at no time appears to be aware of the missionary injunction found at the end of Matthew's gospel. Thus when the local Jews block their ears the Jewish mandate to be light to Gentiles is invoked: "I [the Lord] will give you as a light to the nations" (Isa 49:6). The implied message is clear: If you Jews refuse to receive the Good News and become the light-bearers for the local Gentiles, then we (Paul and Barnabas) must do what the Lord God expects of us under these circumstances. The Gentile mission, consequently, is never understood as having been started once and for all. In every place where the pair travels, the first to receive the message of the kingdom will *always* be the Jews (Acts 13:5, 14; 14:1; 16:13; 17:1, 10, 17; 18:4, 19; 19:8; 28:17, 26-28). If they open their hearts, the pair stay with them and leave it to them to share their blessings with the Gentiles. When resistance is encountered, however, the Jewish pair must respond to the mandate of the Lord God as spoken to Isaiah, even though the local Jews fail to do so. If one looks at Acts closely one will find this pattern repeated in all the places where Paul and Barnabas go.

Since it is not self-evident, one must also note what is never said: namely, that those who accept the prophetic message of Jesus must somehow leave their local synagogues and form "churches" apart from the Jews. Even in the letters of Paul, where it is evident that mixed assemblies of Jews and Gentiles are coming together for prayer, guidance, and to celebrate the Eucharist, one hears absolutely nothing about Jews separating themselves from their local synagogues. Such an initiative would be pure nonsense. The message of the Good News, after all, is intended for God's beloved people. The kingdom is, first and foremost, God's gift to the Jews. They are the children of the promise. Remember again all the passages cited in chapter 3 that make clear that redemption is centered in Israel. Gentile inclusion simply means that, since the kingdom is close at hand, those non-Jews who put aside their idols and accept the hope of Israel will be included in the ingathering of Israel on the last day. Like Jesus, Paul never understands either himself or any other Jew's reception of the Gospel as a separation from Judaism. Near the end of Acts, Luke presents Paul as declaring in Greek before the Roman tribune and again in Hebrew before the Jewish crowd, "I am a Jew" (21:39; 22:3). From this one can understand that Luke-Acts sees no incongruity in being a "Christian" and a "Jew" at the same time.

The Final Inclusion of Israel

Now it is possible to consider the meaning of Paul's assurance that, at some point, "all Israel will be saved" (Rom 11:26). François Refoulé has written a book-length examination of this text and endeavored to recover Paul's original intention.[26] For our purposes here it suffices to note how Refoulé dismisses three misrepresentations frequently read into Paul's text:

- Paul never hints that he is offering a divine revelation that some future generation of Jews will accept the Gospel and become Christians. The very notion that Jews who are disobedient now will, in the end times, "be grafted back *into their own* olive tree" (Rom 11:24, emphasis added) would preclude the notion that Jews will somehow cease being Jews and be cut off from their ancestral traditions.
- Paul never hints that the Gentile church displaces Israel as the sole recipient of divine election. Paul's metaphors demonstrate that salvation comes to the Gentiles because they are cut off from their wild stock (paganism) in order to be grafted onto the root of Israel. "Remember that it is not you that support the root, but the root that supports you" (Rom 11:18). According to Paul, therefore, Israel is the "universal

26. François Refoulé, "*Et ainsi tout Israël sera sauvé*" (Paris: Cerf, 1984).

sacrament of salvation." The church, consequently, can only lay claim to participate in this function if and when it acknowledges having been grafted onto the root God planted, namely Israel.

- Finally, Paul never hints that only a remnant of faithful Jews serves God's purposes while the unfaithful majority hinders it: quite the opposite. Just as Paul argues in Romans 4 that Abraham is father of both the circumcised and the uncircumcised, in Romans 11 he contends that God deliberately made use of the disobedience of the many in order to make possible the harvesting of the Gentiles. The section above made this clear.

How, then, does Paul envision that "all Israel will be saved" (Rom 11:26)? Given everything that has already been said about the centrality of the reign of God in the message of Jesus and in Paul, the answer must now be evident. When God comes at the end of this age to gather the exiles and to shelter Israel in the kingdom established for it, then all Israel will be saved. Consider this in the context of Paul's letter:

> I want you to understand this mystery: a hardening has come upon part of Israel, until the full number of the Gentiles has come in. And so all Israel will be saved; as it is written, "Out of Zion will come the Deliverer; he will banish ungodliness from Jacob." "And this is my covenant with them, when I take away their sins." As regards the gospel they are enemies of God for your sake; but as regards election they are beloved, for the sake of their ancestors; for the gifts and the calling of God are irrevocable. (Rom 11:25-29)

Initially Paul refers to the hardening as limited in duration, for God's plan is to allow a period of time for "the full number of the Gentiles" to receive the Good News of the kingdom. Once this takes place, "all Israel will be saved," according to the prophecy written in Isa 59:20—The Lord God comes as the Deliverer of Israel, and he will purify Israel at his coming.

How so?

According to Isaiah 33 the Lord God comes first to bring the fire of destruction upon the Gentiles bent on destroying Israel: "And the peoples [Gentiles] will be as if burned to lime" (Isa 33:12; see also 59:18). At the same time the Lord God comes to bring purification and salvation for Israel (Isa 33:13-22; 59:20-21). Paul paraphrases Isaiah from memory in order better to capture his meaning thus: "Out of Zion will come the Deliverer; he will banish ungodliness from Jacob. And this is my covenant with them, when I take away their sins" (Rom 11:26-27). Isaiah's theme is that God and God alone is the redeemer of Israel: *"I am the* LORD, *and besides me there is no savior"* (Isa 43:11, emphasis added; see also 29:22; 33:22; 37:20; 43:1-3; 44:6, 23; 47:4; 48:17, 20; 49:3, 7, 26; 54:5; 59:20; 60:16; 62:12; 63:16). And the Lord God comes, in the last days, to purify Israel, to "banish ungodliness," to "take away their sins." Each of these phrases is roughly equivalent. The hardening that has come over Israel, which is the Lord's doing (Rom 11:7-8), will then be removed by the Lord on the last day. Thus "all Israel will be saved" (Rom 11:26) by the Lord himself when he comes.

This means that, in Paul's mind, *the church was never meant to bring salvation to Israel! God alone will save Israel.* In Romans, Paul only assigns one purpose to the church: "to make Israel jealous!" (Rom 11:11). Nothing else. No tracts. No preaching. No berating. No punishing. No converting Israel. Just as God "hardened" Israel originally, he will come to purify it on the last day, "for God has the power to graft them in again" (Rom 11:23). Paul's warning to the Gentiles is "do not become proud, but stand in awe" (Rom 11:20).

Evangelism That Does No Harm

Christians have experienced the grace of God at various times and in various places. For this we are thankful. It is not surprising, therefore, that Christians would feel compelled to praise God and invite others to do likewise. Evangelization, consequently, is a natural extension of a heartfelt Christianity. From this point of view, not to share the gifts and blessings of God would be a reprehensible act mired in stinginess and/or fear.

When it comes to the evangelization of the Jews, however, great care must be taken to ensure that the act of sharing the Good News with Jews does not feed on images of Israel that are false or demeaning. On the basis of what has been said above, consider the following:

1. Frequently Christians evangelize Jews because they are persuaded that Jews have no access to the mercy and forgiveness of God apart from Jesus. These Christians are unable to see that they have a notion that God was somehow locked in unforgiveness from the sin of Adam to the death of Jesus (as discussed in chapter 3), an idea that has no secure place either in the revelation to Israel or in the teachings of Jesus. Furthermore, such Christians must turn a blind eye to the testimony offered in favor of the mercy and forgiveness of God within the Hebrew Scriptures, within the teaching and deeds of Jesus, and within the living experience of Israel down to our present day.[27]

27. Compare John Paul II, "Address to Jewish Leaders in Miami," September 11, 1987.

2. Frequently Christians evangelize Jews precisely because they imagine that the church and only the church offers the divinely sanctioned means of salvation. These Christians are unable to take into account the priority of Israel in God's plan of salvation (as explained in chapter 3). Furthermore, they generally shore up triumphalistic notions of the church's superiority by downplaying or entirely ignoring the importance of Israel in salvation history.

3. Frequently Christians evangelize Jews because they imagine they are fulfilling a mandate of Jesus to which they are solemnly bound. These Christians are unable to take into account that Jesus never had any intention to bring his people closer to God by drawing them away from the faith of their ancestors and from participation in the life of their synagogues. Moreover, these Christians ignore the testimony of God, who called Jews as Jews to a universal mission: "I [the Lord] will give you as a light to the nations" (Isa 49:6). Any form of evangelization that distorts the very image of God and denies the graced abundance of God's forgiveness to Israel, that demeans Israel in order to exalt the church, or that downplays the Jewishness of Jesus and of the early church—while refusing to acknowledge Israel as having a divine mission to the nations entirely prior to and independent of Jesus—can never be blessed by the Lord and can never be sanctioned by Catholics who are persuaded that Jews are "partners in a covenant of eternal love which was never revoked" (*Nostra Aetate* 4).

In brief, the danger is that most of what Christians have hitherto known as evangelization has been based on seriously defective notions of the faith, the experience, and the role of Israel in God's plan of redemption. Should Christians, for example, rediscover that the mercy and forgiveness of God existed prior to and independent of the death of Jesus, Christians might be compelled to rejoice with Jews regarding what they have come to discover about the Lord (albeit from different sources). Instead of cultivating a triumphalistic spirit that rushes to exalt what is mine and denigrate what belongs to the other, the new Christian evangelization might approach Jews with a humble spirit that is ready to share God's gift to the Gentiles at the same time that it is ready to hear from Jews what they have experienced of the Lord's parental care. If Jews were the first to abandon their idols and to affirm the living and true God, it must be allowed that they are "our elder brothers [and sisters]" who already know something of God and adhere to God's ways. This is the position effectively adopted by Cardinal Walter Kasper, who heads the Pontifical Commission for Religious Relations with the Jews:

> The term mission, in its proper sense, refers to conversion from false gods and idols to the true and one God, who revealed himself in the salvation history with His elected people. Thus mission, in this strict sense, cannot be used with regard to Jews, who believe in the true and one God. Therefore, and this is characteristic, there exists dialogue but there does not exist any Catholic missionary organization for Jews.[28]

In the course of time some few Jews will ask for admission to the family of Jesus and Mary. Likewise, some Christians will ask for admission to the family of Abraham and Sarah. Such conversions are bound to come. What remains abhorrent, however, is the determination on the part of some Christian churches to convert every Jew as though God somehow intends to obliterate Judaism and exalt the church in its place. Even when churches are bent on using kinder and gentler means, the objective of spiritual genocide of the Jews can never be promoted or imagined as the design of God. More to the point, if we were to rediscover the mission of the Jews to the nations, which existed before and independently of Jesus, it must be supposed that Christians would be naturally hesitant to advocate any campaign for the evangelization of Jews that would invariably hinder this divine mission assigned to Israel.[29] In the end, consequently, evangelization can indeed be a sincere sharing of the Good News of God delivered through Jesus, and Jews might be the recipients of such sharing, yet no church today can imagine itself to be a divine vehicle for disseminating the Good News without having first undertaken to examine itself and to confess all the forms of triumphalism and anti-Judaism that have formerly rendered its mission to Israel theologically flawed, pastorally dangerous, and offensive to God.

Conclusion

This chapter has explored the mission of the church. What has come to the fore is that the mission of Jesus to Israel came to completion during the time of Jesus' twelve closest disciples. What was especially highlighted was the fact that none of the Christian prophets to Israel in any way intended for any Jew to leave the synagogue and be baptized as a way of gaining entrance to a "new religion." Baptism was the rite adopted by

---

28. These words of Cardinal Kasper have been officially endorsed by their acceptance into the document *Reflections on Covenant and Mission,* which is presented in the final chapter below.

29. The final chapter will take up this argument in detail.

Jewish Christians intent on preparing for the Lord's coming at the end of time. Jews who were baptized always continued being Jews—before, during, and after the rite. That is why Paul and Barnabas openly identified themselves as Jews (e.g., Acts 21:39; 22:3) and never as former Jews. During their missionary journeys they likewise continually honored God's preference for Israel and gave the people of Israel priority when preaching the Good News of the kingdom (Acts 13:5, 14; 14:1; 16:13; 17:1, 10, 17; 18:4, 19; 19:8; 28:17, 26-28). Only in the case of Gentiles did baptism mark a conversion from one faith (idolatry) to another (the faith of Israel).

After the first few centuries the church got sidetracked into glorifying Jesus and inventing ever-new ways to honor his name. Preaching Jesus thus gradually subverted the original mandate of heralding the coming kingdom. "Faith in Jesus" came to entirely replace the "faith of Jesus." Increasingly, therefore, the church's message about the Messiah and the work of salvation took directions that eventually made little sense within the context of the original Jewish expectations of Jesus and his early disciples. Thus, with the passage of time, Jews found the Gospel preached by the church antagonistic to their faith and to the people of Israel. Jesus increasingly appeared to Jews as a false prophet intent on leading people astray. Had Jesus returned, he himself would have been unable to recognize the message of the church bearing his name as having anything to do with his own faith and mission to Israel.

Paul, in his own day, was seemingly aware that some Gentile converts were falling into an arrogant attitude toward Israel. The subsequent history of the Christian church illustrates how accurately Paul perceived this danger. Some Christians today have found in Paul the possibility of again giving thanks to God for the overwhelming Jewish rejection of the message of Jesus and honoring this rejection as the *felix culpa* made possible by God's initiative. Just as we received the light and mercy of the Lord of Israel thanks to Jewish disciples like Paul and Barnabas who came to our pagan ancestors after Jews in the local synagogue had turned a deaf ear, so, too, Christians need to allow that God, with no help on their part, will, in the end, revive and purify those beloved sons and daughters of Abraham whom he loved long before we were even in the picture. For this final act of mercy the church has no mission and no mandate. God, and God alone, will be the final Savior of Israel. To him be the glory forever![30]

30. If you would like to share your reflections or see what others have produced, go to www.salvationisfromthejews.info.

Seven

Reflections on Covenant and Mission

> The Church believes that Judaism . . . is salvific for them,
> because God is faithful to his promises.
>
> —Cardinal Walter Kasper

In August of 2002 a groundbreaking study document, *Reflections on Covenant and Mission,* was released by the Bishops' Committee on Ecumenical and Interreligious Affairs (BCEIA) of the United States Conference of Catholic Bishops in collaboration with delegates from the National Council of Synagogues (NCS).[1] From the Catholic side, members of the BCEIA came to the conclusion that "campaigns that target Jews for conversion to Christianity are no longer theologically acceptable in the Catholic Church."

1. For more than twenty years leaders of the Jewish and Roman Catholic communities in the United States have met semiannually to discuss a wide range of topics affecting Catholic-Jewish relations. Currently participants are drawn from the Bishops' Committee on Ecumenical and Interreligious Affairs (BCEIA) of the United States Conference of Catholic Bishops and from the National Council of Synagogues (NCS). The NCS represents the Central Conference of American Rabbis, the Rabbinical Assembly of Conservative Judaism, the Union of American Hebrew Congregations, and the United Synagogue of Conservative Judaism. The Consultation is cochaired by William Cardinal Keeler, the U.S. bishops' moderator for Catholic-Jewish relations, and Rabbi Joel Zaiman of the Rabbinical Assembly of Conservative Judaism and Rabbi Michael Signer of the Union of American Hebrew Congregations. The dialogues have previously produced public statements on such issues as "Children and the Environment" and "Acts of Religious Hatred."

At its meeting held on March 13, 2002, in New York City the BCEIA–NCS Consultation examined how the Jewish and Roman Catholic traditions currently understand the subjects of covenant and mission. Each delegation prepared reflections that were discussed and clarified by the Consultation as statements of the current state of the question in each community. The separate Roman Catholic and Jewish reflections on the subjects of Covenant and Mission presented below are the result of refinements of the initial statements.

Cardinal William H. Keeler of Baltimore, the U.S. bishops' Moderator for Catholic-Jewish Relations, explained that the document made public on August 12 represents the state of thought among the participants in a dialogue that has been going on for a number of years between the U.S. Catholic Church and the Jewish community in the United States. Cardinal Keeler further explained that while the document does not represent a formal position taken by the United States Conference of Catholic Bishops (USCCB) or the Bishops' Committee for Ecumenical and Interreligious Affairs (BCEIA), the release of the document was prompted by the desire to encourage serious reflection on these matters by both Jews and Catholics.

Landmark Features of the Reflections

While the document repeats and amplifies earlier Catholic statements respecting the eternal covenant of love that God has made with the Jewish people, new ground was also explored. Three aspects are of special significance:

1. *Judaism is a religion founded on authentic revelation, grace, and the promise of salvation independent of Christianity.*

> Judaism is a religion that springs from divine revelation. As Cardinal Kasper noted, "God's grace, which is the grace of Jesus Christ according to our faith, is available to all. Therefore, the Church believes that Judaism, i.e. the faithful response of the Jewish people to God's irrevocable covenant, is salvific for them, because God is faithful to his promises."[2]

2. *Jews, by virtue of their covenant with God, have a mission apart from Christianity.*

> [The Catholic Church] now recognizes that Jews are also called by God to prepare the world for God's kingdom. Their witness to the kingdom, which did not originate with the church's experience of

2. National Council of Synagogues and the Bishops' Committee for Ecumenical and Interreligious Affairs, *Reflections on Covenant and Mission* [hereafter abbreviated as *Reflections*] (12 August 2002), http://www.philosophy-religion.com/thought/reflections.htm, or http://www.bc.edu/research/cjl/meta-elements/texts/cjrelations/resources/documents/interreligious/ncs_usccb120802.htm. The text has not yet been divided into sections; hence, no section numbers can be indicated. Interested persons, however, can easily search the electronic text. All quotations, unless otherwise noted, are from the text of *Reflections*.

Christ crucified and raised, must not be curtailed by seeking the conversion of the Jewish people to Christianity.

3. *Jews have the right to articulate their own divine mission apart from Christianity.*

> The Church believes that the mission of the Jewish people is not restricted to their historical role as the people of whom Jesus was born "according to the flesh" (Rom 9:5) and from whom the church's apostles came. As Cardinal Joseph Ratzinger recently wrote, "God's providence . . . has obviously given Israel a particular mission in this 'time of the Gentiles.'" However, only the Jewish people themselves can articulate their mission "in the light of their own religious experience."

This last statement is of particular importance. The prevailing Christian notion that the Jewish people existed solely in order to bring forth Jesus Christ, the Redeemer, is expressly repudiated. The mission of the Jewish people (as explained in earlier chapters) is nothing less than to be "light to the nations" (Isa 49:6). The Catholic commission wisely and respectfully left it to the Jewish people to respond to God and to articulate their mission out of their own resources.

The second half of the document is a statement drafted by the Jewish delegates of the NCS, delineating the main lines of their covenantal calling today. The Good News for Jews is that God has been and continues to be the Redeemer of Israel. For Gentiles, Israel knows itself called by God to be "light" in the activity of collaborating with human beings everywhere "by setting up the structures of society that maximize the practice of justice and mercy and by engaging unendingly in the religious quest to bring healing to the broken world." The mission of Israel to the nations, consequently, is to act as God's messenger by inviting all persons of good will to undertake *tikkun ha-olam* ("repairing of the world"): *"Tikkun ha-olam*, perfection or repairing of the world, is a joint task of the Jews and all humanity. Though Jews see themselves as living in a world that is as yet unredeemed, God wills His creatures to participate in the world's repair."

The Catholic statement takes some bold steps forward, yet it will be evident to readers of this volume that many things are passed over in silence. For example, the document makes no reference to the biblical testimony that Israel is the first to be called and that the mission of the church is derived from and dependent on the prior mission of Israel (chapter 3 above). The document also makes no reference to the Jewish

experience of the fatherly love of God (chapter 2 above) or to the forgiveness of sins prior to and entirely independent of the preaching and atoning death of Jesus (chapter 5 above). By its nature the document represents
a compromise that balances conservative and prophetic elements within
the Catholic community. Nonetheless, for my part I am proud of what
has been accomplished even while I am aware (as are my readers) of
how the theological, liturgical, and pastoral distortions distilled from
drinking the poison of anti-Judaism go much deeper into the body of
Catholic existence than this document allows. Hence, for all its merits,
this document is only another small step on the way toward correctly
presenting Jews and Judaism within the Catholic tradition.

Critical Responses

After the document was released, strong voices of support and of
condemnation were heard. Robert A. Sungenis, for example, prepared
fifty-eight detailed pages of critical commentary that he then published
on the website of Catholic Apologetics International. At each point Sungenis uses the Catholic tradition *as it has been* to argue against the framers
of the document, who are appealing to the Catholic tradition *as it should
be*. Some of Sungenis' criticisms have merit and members of the BCEIA
would do well to discuss them and revise their document accordingly.
Overall, however, Sungenis strenuously resists the notion that "salvation" could exist for Jews outside of the church:

> The Old Covenant cannot save anyone. It never had the power to
> do so, even before Christ. The Old Covenant, as St. Paul argues in
> Romans 7:8-13, Galatians 3:10-12 and other places is the convictor
> of sin and the covenant that condemns in sin. Its failure to save was
> the whole reason that Christ had to come. This has been taught in
> Catholic theology since time immemorial.[3]

Dr. Sungenis and I, it must be remembered, both share a traditional
Catholic upbringing. I must allow, consequently, that he is on solid
ground respecting what "has been taught in Catholic theology." When
I was a young child the story of salvation offered to me by the Ursuline

3. Robert A. Sungenis, "Conversion of the Jews Not Necessary," *Catholic Apologetics
International*, 29. This article was published electronically in 2002, revised in response
to criticism, and then entirely removed in mid-2006. For the entire story see Christo-
pher Blosser, "Robert Sungenis and the Jews," *Fringe Watch*, 9 September 2006, http://
fringewatcher.blogspot.com/2006/09/on-robert-sungenis-and-jews.html.

nuns at Holy Cross Grade School in Euclid, Ohio, was something simple, compelling, and wonderful. Adam sinned and we inherited the consequences: God's grace dried up and the gates of heaven were sealed shut. For thousands of years people were dying, but no one was able to get into heaven. Everyone was waiting for God to send a redeemer. Then Jesus finally arrived and died for our sins on the cross. And, as my *Baltimore Catechism* so clearly demonstrated, at the moment when Jesus died on the cross, there, way up in the clouds, the gates of heaven were again being opened. Finally the souls of all the good people who had died could enter into heaven and be with God for all eternity. Dr. Sungenis undoubtedly identifies these same threads within his own formative years. True to his tradition, therefore, he cannot allow that Jews find salvation (as he understands it) within a "covenant" apart from and independent of Jesus.

What Dr. Sungenis fails to notice is that the story of salvation that he and I received was seriously distorted by the poison of anti-Judaism. When the history of salvation jumps from the tree in the Garden to the tree on Calvary it reduces to insignificance eighteen hundred years of God's dealings with his chosen people. More importantly, the story delivered to me disguised the fact that the long Jewish experience had very much to say about the mercy and forgiveness of God. Had I known how to receive the revelation in the Hebrew Scriptures (without being predisposed by the model of salvation given to me by my teachers), I would have found the image of a God hardened in stoic unforgiveness immediately after the first sin in the Garden to be a serious distortion that has no place in the faith and experience of Israel. I might even have noticed that Jesus was in no doubt regarding this point either (as shown in chapter 3). Should Dr. Sungenis begin to find some flaws within the Catholic tradition *as it has been* handed down to him, he would have good reason to embrace someone who was presenting the tradition *as it should be*. But this is seemingly not the case. He argues accordingly that the Catholic tradition *as it has been* is *as it should be*. Thus he names as "apostasy" the "novel doctrines" that have gripped the central organs of the Catholic Church "going as far back as the pontificate of John XXIII."[4]

Evangelical Protestants have also expressed their sense of the offensiveness of the document. Jim Sibley, coordinator of Jewish ministries for the

4. Ibid., 1.

Southern Baptist Convention, interprets the document's rejection of "campaigns that target Jews for conversion" as being tantamount to having "targeted Jews for exclusion from Gospel proclamation."[5] Sibley concludes that "there can be no more extreme form of anti-Semitism"[6] than for Jews thus to be denied the chance to hear the saving word of God. Father John Echert, in his discussions on the ETWN website, shows himself entirely in sympathy with Pastor Sibley: "Precisely because Jews share an expectation of the coming of the Messiah, they should be targeted and [are] the primary focus of our efforts for converts to Christ."[7]

Neither Pastor Sibley nor Father Echert would understand himself to be in the least degree anti-Jewish. Quite the contrary: both would be quick to declare that they have a true love for Jews when they endeavor to bring them out of the darkness of Judaism into the light of Christ. For the readers of this book, however, this is the sign of how deep and pervasive the poison of anti-Judaism has been within the long Christian tradition. According to Paul, Gentile converts were obliged to acknowledge that they were the wild branches that had the good fortune to be grafted onto the root of Israel. Over the centuries, however, Paul was quietly set aside in favor of the doctrine that Israel had been entirely rejected and God himself had embraced Christians as his new chosen people and the recipients of his salvation. Within this framework it was only natural that Christians would see the stiff-necked Jews as adhering to empty promises and performing meaningless rites. The solution, of course, was to remove Jews from their Judaism in order to bring them to the font of salvation. Thus, in the end, everything was reversed. Now the Jews were the wild branches who had no chance of salvation unless they were cut off from the synagogue and grafted onto Christ and his church. Following on this distortion, Christians were free to invent the notion of blood guilt to explain how not only a few Jews but all Jews were to be regarded as enemies of God because of their crime of crucifying Jesus. Christians were likewise free to invent schemes of salvation history that neglected or passed over in silence the place of Israel in God's plan of salvation. In the end even Jesus' proclamation of the reign of God was twisted to imply that he himself rejected his own Judaism in favor of founding the new and true

---

5. Jim Sibley, cited in Jerry Filteau, "New Catholic-Jewish Statement on Conversion Draws Controversy," *Catholic News Service*, August 26, 2002, http://www.catholicnews.com/data/stories/cns/200220826.htm.

6. Ibid.

7. John Eckert, cited in Filteau, "New Catholic-Jewish Statement," 2.

religion, namely, Christianity. The string of distortions was thus complete—each reinforcing all the others.

Purging the Poison of Anti-Judaism

When did the great reversal begin? Perhaps the first step was taken when the new pope, John XXIII, interrupted the liturgy of Good Friday and decreed that the prayer demeaning Jews was never again to be used in his cathedral church. Soon a Vatican commission was formed; then a Council was called. The bishops of Vatican II took bold steps in 1965 (against the tradition *as it had been*) when they declared that the Jewish people have been and continue to be "very dear to God . . . since God does not take back the gifts he bestowed or the choice he made" (*Nostra Aetate* 4). The attribution of blood guilt was declared off-limits. From that point onward a major step forward took place roughly every ten years. In 1974 Catholics were invited "to learn by what essential traits Jews define themselves in the light of their own religious experience." For over a thousand years the church had gotten into the habit of defining (or better, ill-defining) Jews and talking down to them. Now Catholics were to enter into a respectful dialogue and allow Jews to define themselves. In 1985 Catholics were told, point-blank, that "Jesus was and always remained a Jew" (*Notes* § 12), thereby putting an end to the imagined claim that Jesus himself rejected Judaism as a defective religion. In the same document Catholics were also made familiar with the ways in which Jesus shared common ground with the Pharisees of his day and were warned that "an exclusively negative picture of the Pharisees is likely to be inaccurate and unjust" (*Notes* § 19). In 1998 Catholics were told that "no one can remain indifferent [to the *Shoah*], least of all the Church, by reason of her very close bonds of spiritual kinship with the Jewish people" (*We Remember* § 1). Finally, in 2002, by virtue of *Reflections on Covenant and Mission*, Catholics are being asked to consider Judaism as "the faithful response of the Jewish people to God's irrevocable covenant" and, as such, "salvific" for Jews quite apart from any reference to or relationship with Jesus. Furthermore, Catholics are being invited to regard Jews as "also called by God to prepare the world for God's kingdom." Up to this point the church represented itself as alone mandated to play a role in God's plan for the salvation of the world. Now that monopoly is denied. In fact, this is the opening to understanding Israel as having a divinely authorized mission in the world that is prior to and independent of "the Church's experience of Christ crucified and raised." Accordingly, from this it follows that "their witness to the kingdom . . . must not be curtailed by seeking the conversion of the Jewish people to Christianity." In brief, conversion of the Jews hinders God's plan for salvation, which requires the witness of Jews "as Jews" and not as "Jews for Jesus."

Some Catholics and most fundamentalist Protestants have greeted these ongoing Catholic "changes" as marking the slow, progressive steps whereby the truth of Christ is being abandoned. Some Catholics would even see here "one of the signs of the end times, namely, 'apostasy.'"[8] For myself and many others, however, these very same steps mark our retreat from the poison of anti-Judaism that has distorted and blocked our image of Judaism and prevented us from discovering the faith and hope of Israel that characterized Jesus and his early disciples.

Change leaves many people unsettled and uncomfortable. For some, the changes seem arbitrary—"What will they want to change next?" For others, they seem unnecessary—"If it ain't broke, don't try to fix it." For still others, anti-Judaism will go away all by itself—"Drawing attention to it only makes it worse." For everyone involved, however, change is sometimes painful. *Reflections on Covenant and Mission* might even be viewed as the bitter medicine prescribed by our pastors to break down the toxins ingested while we eagerly fed on the nourishing aspects of our Catholic tradition. These *Reflections* might also be God's way of breaking our longstanding Catholic addiction to theological arrogance. The apostle Paul was the first pastor known to us who detected strains of arrogance circulating among the Gentile believers in Rome. He challenged them with the caution: "Remember that it is not you that support the root, but the root that supports you" (Rom 11:18).

John Paul II, in his "Address on the Fiftieth Anniversary of the Warsaw Ghetto Uprising," offered us something of his geopolitical wisdom when he boldly stated the following:

> As Christians and Jews, following the example of the faith of Abraham, we are called to be a blessing for the world [cf. Gen. 12:2ff.]. This is the common task awaiting us. It is therefore necessary for us, Christians and Jews, to be first a blessing to one another.[9]

---

8. Father John Echert of Saint Thomas University, St. Paul, MN, cited in Sungenis, "Conversion of the Jews," 58. See also in opposition to the document, and citing Echert, Cardinal Avery Dulles, s.j., "Covenant and Mission," *America* (October 14, 2002), available at http://www.sfarchdiocese.org/dulles.html.

9. John Paul II, "Address on the Fiftieth Anniversary of the Warsaw Ghetto Uprising," April 6, 1993, http://bc.edu/bc_org/research/cjl/Documents/John_Paul_II/warsawghetto6april1993.htm.

The objectives of those drafting the "Reflections on Covenant and Mission" might indeed be summarized in these terms—that Jews and Christians recaptured their respective traditions in order to cultivate a frame of mind whereby they could "first be a blessing for each other." In so doing, they redirected their steps toward serving the common task that both communities undertake "in order to be a blessing for the world."

May the Spirit of God bring our joint efforts to a speedy realization!

On the First Sunday of Lent during the Great Jubilee Year of 2000, an unprecedented "Mass of Pardon" was offered at St. Peter's Basilica. The highest officials of the Roman Catholic Church joined with the pope in asking God's forgiveness for the sins of Christians during the previous millennium. Among the sins confessed was the teaching of contempt and Christianity's treatment of "the People of Israel." More emphatic was Pope John Paul II's prayer at the Western Wall on March 26, 2000. Following the Jewish custom of praying at the Wall and then wedging written prayers into the thin spaces between the foundation stones of the Second Temple, John Paul II deposited these words: "God of our fathers, you chose Abraham and his descendants to bring your Name to the Nations: we are deeply saddened by the behavior of those who in the course of history have caused these children of yours to suffer, and asking your forgiveness we wish to commit ourselves to genuine brotherhood with the people of the Covenant." This prayer was signed by the pope personally and stamped with the official papal seal, as if to establish without question the seriousness and permanence of the Catholic Church's ongoing commitment to spiritual reform and to reestablish fellowship with the Jewish people.

Bibliography

Aquinas, Thomas. *Summa Theologica.* Translated by the Dominican Fathers from the Latin orig. of 1274. Two volumes. London: Burns & Oates, 1947.

Anselm of Canterbury. *Cur Deus Homo—Why God Became Man.* Edited and translated by Jasper Hopkins and Herbert Richardson. New York: Edwin Mellen, 1974.

Armstrong, Karen. *A History of God.* New York: Ballantine Books, 1993.

Aune, David E. *Prophecy in Early Christianity and the Ancient Mediterranean World.* Grand Rapids: Eerdmans, 1983.

Baeck, Leo. *Judaism and Christianity: Essays.* Translated with an introduction by Walter Kaufmann. Philadelphia: Jewish Publication Society, 1958.

Baltimore Catechism No. 3, Confraternity Edition. Explanatory material by Francis J. Connell. New York: Benzinger Brothers, 1949.

Bemporad, Jack, and Michael Shevack. *Our Age: The Historic New Era of Christian-Jewish Understanding.* Hyde Park, NY: New City Press, 1996.

Ben-Chorin, Schalom. *Bruder Jesus. Der Nazarener in jüdischer Sicht.* Munich: List Verlag, 1967. English: *Brother Jesus: The Nazarene through Jewish Eyes.* Translated and edited by Jared S. Klein and Max Reinhart. Athens: University of Georgia Press, 2001.

Bernardin, Joseph. *A Blessing to Each Other: Cardinal Joseph Bernardin and Jewish Catholic Dialogue.* Chicago: Liturgy Training Publications, 1996.

Bernstein, Alan E. *The Formation of Hell: Death and Retribution in the Ancient and Early Christian Worlds.* Ithaca: Cornell University Press, 1993.

Bialik, Hayim Nahman, and Yehoshua Hana Ravnitzky, eds. *The Book of Legends: Sefer Ha-Aggadah.* Translated by William G. Braude. New York: Schocken, 1992.

Borowitz, Eugene B. *How Can a Jew Speak of Faith Today?* Philadelphia: Westminster, 1969.

———. "Jesus the Jew in the Light of the Jewish-Christian Dialogue." *Proceedings of the Center for Jewish-Christian Learning: 1987 Lecture Series.* St. Paul, MN: College of St. Thomas, 1987.

Bradshaw, Paul F. *The Search for the Origins of Christian Worship: Sources and Methods for the Study of Early Liturgy.* Oxford: Oxford University Press, 1991.

———, and Lawrence Hoffman, eds. *Passover and Easter: Origin and History to Modern Times.* Two Liturgical Traditions, vol. 5. Notre Dame, IN: University of Notre Dame Press, 1999.

————. *Passover and Easter: The Symbolic Structuring of Sacred Seasons.* Two Liturgical Traditions, vol. 6. Notre Dame, IN: University of Notre Dame Press, 1999.

Brock, Rita Nakashima. "And a Little Child Will Lead Us: Christology and Child Abuse," in *Christianity, Patriarchy, and Abuse: A Feminist Critique,* Joanne Carlson Brown and Carol R. Bohn, eds. New York: Pilgrim Press, 1989.

Brown, Raymond E. "The *Pater Noster* as an Eschatological Prayer." *TS* 22 (1961): 175–208.

————. *The Gospel According to John.* AB 29, 29A. Garden City, NY: Doubleday, 1966.

Buber, Martin. *Two Types of Faith.* Translated by Norman P. Goldhawk. New York: Macmillan, 1951.

Burtchaell, James Tunstead. *From Synagogue to Church: Public Services and Offices in the Earliest Christian Communities.* Cambridge: Cambridge University Press, 1992.

Cargas, Harry James. *Shadows of Auschwitz: A Christian Response to the Holocaust.* New York: Crossroad, 1990.

Carter, Jimmy. *Palestine Peace not Apartheid.* New York: Simon & Schuster, 2006.

Catechism of the Catholic Church. Translated from the Latin original. Mahwah, NJ: Paulist Press, 1994.

Catechism of the Council of Trent. Translated by Rev. J. Donovan from the Latin original. Dublin: James Duffy Sons, 1829.

Carroll, James. *Constantine's Sword: The Church and the Jews: A History.* New York: Houghton Mifflin, 2001.

Carroll, John T., and Joel B. Green, eds. *The Death of Jesus in Early Christianity.* Peabody, MA: Hendrickson, 1993.

Cernera, Anthony J., ed. *Toward Greater Understanding: Essays in Honor of John Cardinal O'Connor.* Fairfield, CT: Sacred Heart University, 1995.

Charlesworth, James H., with Francis X. Blisard and Jerry L. Gorham, eds. *Overcoming Fear Between Jews and Christians.* New York: Crossroad, 1992.

Chilton, Bruce. *Pure Kingdom: Jesus' Vision of God.* Grand Rapids: Eerdmans, 1996.

Cohen, Jeremy, ed. *Essential Papers on Judaism and Christianity in Conflict: From Late Antiquity to the Reformation.* New York: New York University Press, 1991.

Cohen, Naomi W., ed. *Essential Papers on Jewish-Christian Relations in the United States: Imagery and Reality.* New York: New York University Press, 1991.

Cohen, Shaye J. D. "The Significance of Yavneh: Pharisees, Rabbis, and the End of Jewish Sectarianism." *HUCA* 55 (1984): 27–53.

Cohn-Sherbok, Dan. *The Crucified Jew: Twenty Centuries of Christian Anti-Semitism.* Grand Rapids: Eerdmans, 1997.

Commission for Religious Relations with the Jews. *Guidelines and Suggestions for Implementing the Conciliar Declaration Nostra Aetate (n. 4),* December 1, 1974, http://www.vatican.va/roman_curia/pontifical_councils/chrstuni/relations-jews-docs/rc_pc_chrstuni_doc_19741201_nostra-aetate_en.html.

Commission of the Holy See for Religious Relations with Jews. *Notes on the Correct Way to Present Jews and Judaism in Preaching and Catechesis in the Roman Catholic Church,* 1985, http://www.vatican.va/roman_curia/pontifical_councils/chrstuni/relations-jews-docs/rc_pc_chrstuni_doc_19820306_jews-judaism_en.html.

Commission of the Holy See for Religious Relations with Jews. *We Remember: A Reflection on the Shoah,* January 25, 1998, http://www.vatican.va/roman_curia/pontifical_councils/chrstuni/documents/rc_pc_chrstuni_doc_16031998_shoah_en.html.

Congregation for the Doctrine of the Faith. *Dominus Jesus—Declaration on the unicity and salvific universality of Jesus Christ and the Church,* August 6, 2000, http://www.vatican.va/roman_curia/congregations/cfaith/documents/rc_con_cfaith_doc_20000806_dominus-iesus_en.html.

Consultation of The National Council of Synagogues and The Bishops Committee for Ecumenical and Interreligious Affairs, USCCB, *Reflections on Covenant and Mission,* August 12, 2002, http://www.philosophy-religion.com/thought/reflections.htm.

Cook, Michael J. "Jesus and the Pharisees—The Problem as it Stands Today." *JES* 15 (1978): 441–60.

Crossan, John Dominic. *Four Other Gospels.* New York: Winston Press, 1985.

———. *Who Killed Jesus?* San Francisco: HarperSanFrancisco, 1995.

———. *The Birth of Christianity: Discovering What Happened in the Years Immediately After the Execution of Jesus.* San Francisco: HarperSanFrancisco, 1998.

———, and Jonathan L. Reed. *In Search of Paul: How Jesus' Apostle Opposed Rome's Empire with God's Kingdom.* San Francisco: HarperSanFrancisco, 2004.

Daly, Robert J. "The Soteriological Significance of the Sacrifice of Isaac." *CBQ* 39 (1977): 45–75.

———. *The Origin of the Christian Doctrine of Sacrifice.* Philadelphia: Fortress Press, 1978.

D'Angelo, Mary Rose. "*Abba* and 'Father': Imperial Theology and the Jewish Tradition." *JBL* 111 (1992): 611–30.

Danielou, Jean. *Gospel Message and Hellenistic Culture.* Translated, edited, and with a postscript by John Austin Baker. Vol. 2 of Jean Danielou, *History of Early Christian Doctrine Before the Council of Nicaea.* London: Darton, Longman & Todd, 1961.

Davies, Philip R., and Bruce D. Chilton. "The Aqedah: A Revised Tradition History." *CBQ* 40 (1978): 514–46.

Davies, W. D. *The Setting of the Sermon on the Mount.* Cambridge: Cambridge University Press, 1966.

De Rosa, Peter. *Vicars of Christ: The Dark Side of the Papacy.* New York: Crown Publishers, 1988.

Derrett, John Duncan Martin. *Studies in the New Testament.* Vol. 2. Leiden: Brill, 1978.

Doerr, Karin. "Memories of History: Women and the Holocaust in Autobiographical and Fictional Memoirs." *Shofar: An Interdisciplinary Journal of Jewish Studies* 18/3 (2000): 71–90.

Dunn, James D. G. *Jesus and the Spirit. A Study of the Religious and Charismatic Experience of Jesus and the First Christians as Reflected in the New Testament.* London: SCM Press, 1975.

———. *The Partings of the Ways: Between Christianity and Judaism and their Significance for the Character of Christianity.* London: SCM Press; Philadelphia: Trinity Press International, 1991.

Eakin, Frank E. *What Price Prejudice? Christian Antisemitism in America.* Mahwah, NJ: Paulist Press, 1998.

Efroymson, David, Eugene J. Fisher, and Leon Klenicki, eds. *Within Context: Essays on Jews and Judaism in the New Testament.* Collegeville, MN: Liturgical Press, 1993.

Eliach, Yaffa. *Hasidic Tales of the Holocaust.* New York: Oxford University Press, 1982.

Elliott, Neil. *Liberating Paul: The Justice of God and the Politics of the Apostle.* Maryknoll, NY: Orbis, 1994.

Ellis, Mark H. "At the End of an Era: A Meditation on Ecumenism, Exile and Gratitude." *Cross Currents* 53/1 (Spring 2003), http://www.crosscurrents.org/Ellisspring2003.htm.

Erst, Anna Marie. *Discovering Our Jewish Roots: A Simple Guide to Judaism.* Mahwah, NJ: Paulist Press, 1996.

Evans, Craig A., and Donald A. Hagner, eds. *Anti-Semitism and Early Christianity: Issues of Polemic and Faith.* Minneapolis: Fortress Press, 1993.

Fackenheim, Emil L. *The Jewish Bible after the Holocaust: A Re-Reading.* Bloomington: Indiana University Press, 1991.

Falk, Randall M., and Walter J. Harrelson. *Jews and Christians in Pursuit of Social Justice.* Nashville: Abingdon, 1996.

Finlan, Stephen. *Problems with Atonement: The Origins of, and Controversy About, the Atonement Doctrine.* Collegeville, MN: Liturgical Press, 2005.

Fisher, Eugene J. "Historical Developments in the Theology of Christian Mission," in *Christian Mission—Jewish Mission,* Martin A. Cohen and Helga Croner, eds. New York: Paulist Press, 1982, 4–45.

———. *Faith Without Prejudice: Rebuilding Christian Attitudes Toward Judaism.* New York: Crossroad, 1993.

———. *Interwoven Destinies: Jews and Christians Through the Ages.* New York: Paulist Press, 1993.

———. *Visions of the Other: Jewish and Christian Theologians Assess the Dialogue.* New York: Paulist Press, 1994.

———, and Leon Klenicki. *Spiritual Pilgrimage: Pope John Paul II, Texts on Jews and Judaism, 1979–1995.* New York: Crossroad, 1995.

Fitzmyer, Joseph A. *The Gospel According to Luke*. AB 28, 28A. Garden City, NY: Doubleday, 1979, 1983.

———. "Abba and Jesus' Relation to God," in *À Cause de L'Évangile: études sur les synoptiques et les Actes offertes au P. Jacques Dupont, O.S.B., à l'occasion de son 70e anniversaire*. LD 123. Paris: Cerf, 1987, 15–38.

Flannery, Edward H. *The Anguish of the Jews. Twenty-Three Centuries of Anti-Semitism*. New York: Macmillan, 1965.

Flusser, David. *Jesus*. New York: Herder & Herder, 1969.

———. "Theses on the Emergence of Christianity from Judaism." *Face to Face: An Interreligious Bulletin* (New York: Anti-Defamation League of B'nai B'rith) 9 (1983).

Fredriksen, Paula. "Judaism, the Circumcision of Gentiles, and Apocalyptic Hope." *JTS* n.s. 42 (1991): 532–64.

Friedlander, Albert H. *The Holocaust and Rabbinic Thought*. The Doefler Memorial Lecture. London: Council of Christians and Jews, 1979.

Gager, John G. *The Origins of Anti-Semitism*. Oxford: Oxford University Press, 1986.

———. "Paul's Contradictions—Can They Be Resolved?" *BRev* 14 (2000): 32–39.

Garber, Zev, and Richard Libowitz, eds. *Peace, In Deed: Essays in Honor of Harry James Cargas*. Atlanta: Scholars Press, 1998.

Gates of Prayer: The New Union Prayerbook. New York: Central Conference of American Rabbis, 1975.

Gaudium et Spes. Pastoral Constitution on the Church in the Modern World. In Austin Flannery, ed., *Documents of Vatican II*. Dublin: Dominican Publications, 1975. http://www.vatican.va/archive/hist_councils/ii_vatican_council/documents/vat-ii_cons_19651207_gaudium-et-spes_en.html.

Glock, Charles Y., and Rodney Stark. *Christian Beliefs and Anti-Semitism*. New York: Harper & Row, 1966.

Goodblatt, David. "The Place of the Pharisees in First Century Judaism: The State of the Debate." *JSJ* 20/1 (1989): 12–30.

Goodman, Martin. *Mission and Conversion: Proselytizing in the Religious History of the Roman Empire*. Oxford: Clarendon Press, 1994.

Goshen-Gottstein, Alon. "God the Father in Rabbinic Judaism and Christianity." *JES* 38/4 (2001): 470–504.

Greeley, Andrew M., and Jacob Neusner. *Common Ground: A Priest and a Rabbi Read Scripture Together*. Cleveland: Pilgrim Press, 1996.

Green, Joel B., and Mark D. Baker. *Recovering the Scandal of the Cross: Atonement in New Testament and Contemporary Contexts*. Downers Grove, IL: InterVarsity Press, 2000.

Greenberg, Irving. *For the Sake of Heaven and Earth: The New Encounter Between Judaism and Christianity*. Electronic resource. Philadelphia: Jewish Publication Society, 2004.

Gundry, Robert H. *Mark: A Commentary on His Apology for the Cross.* Grand Rapids: Eerdmans, 1993.

———. *Matthew. A Commentary on his Handbook for a Mixed Church Under Persecution.* Grand Rapids: Eerdmans, 1994.

Haag, Herbert. *Is Original Sin in Scripture?* New York: Sheed & Ward, 1969.

Haenchen, Ernst. *The Acts of the Apostles: A Commentary.* Translated by Bernard Noble and Gerald Shinn, under the supervision of Hugh Anderson; revised by R. McLean Wilson. Oxford: Blackwell, 1973.

Hagner, Donald A. *The Jewish Reclamation of Jesus: An Analysis and Critique of Modern Jewish Study of Jesus.* Grand Rapids: Zondervan, 1984.

Hall, Sidney G., III. *Christian Anti-Semitism and Paul's Theology.* Minneapolis: Fortress Press, 1993.

Hanson, Paul D. *The Dawn of Apocalyptic: The Historical and Sociological Roots of Jewish Apocalyptic Eschatology.* Philadelphia: Fortress Press, 1979.

Harnack, Adolph. *What is Christianity?* Translated by Thomas Bailey Saunders. New York: Harper & Row, 1957.

Heinemann, Marlene E. *Gender and Destiny: Women Writers and the Holocaust.* Westport, CT: Greenwood Press, 1986.

Hennecke, Edgar. *New Testament Apocrypha.* Edited by Wilhelm Schneemelcher. Translated by A. J. B. Higgins, et al.; edited by R. McLean Wilson. Vol. 2: *Writings Relating to the Apostles, Apocalypses, and Related Subjects.* London: Lutterworth; Philadelphia: Westminster, 1965.

Heyward, Carter. "Suffering, Redemption, and Christ: Shifting the Grounds of Feminist Christology." *Christianity and Crisis* 49 (1989): 381–86.

Hillesum, Etty. *An Interrupted Life: The Diaries, 1941–1943.* New York: Henry Holt, 1996.

Horbury, William. *Jews and Christians in Contact and Controversy.* Edinburgh: T&T Clark, 1998.

Hubaut, Michel. *La Parabole des Vignerons Homicides.* CahRB 16. Paris: Gabalda, 1976.

International Council of Christians and Jews. *Re-Reading Paul: A Fresh Look at his Attitude to Torah and to Judaism.* Victoria, Australia: jcrelations, 1995, http://www.jcrelations.net/en/?id=789.

Jacobs, Steven L., ed. *Contemporary Christian Religious Responses to the Shoah.* Lanham, MD: University Press of America, 1993.

———, ed. *Contemporary Jewish Religious Responses to the Shoah.* Lanham, MD: University Press of America, 1993.

Jeremias, Joachim. *The Prayers of Jesus.* London: SCM Press, 1967; Philadelphia: Fortress Press, 1968.

———. *New Testament Theology: The Proclamation of Jesus.* Translated by John Bowden. New York: Charles Scribner's Sons, 1971.

———. *Jesus' Promise to the Nations.* Translated by S. H. Hooke. Philadelphia: Fortress Press, 1982.

Jones, Alexander, general ed. *The Jerusalem Bible.* London: Darton, Longman, & Todd, 1966.

Juel, Donald. *Messianic Exegesis: Christological Interpretation of the Old Testament in Early Christianity.* Philadelphia: Fortress Press, 1988.

Katz, Steven T. "Issues in the Separation of Judaism and Christianity After 70 C.E.: A Reconsideration." *JBL* 103 (1984): 43–76.

Kee, Howard Clark, and Irvin J. Borowsky, eds. *Removing the Anti-Judaism from the New Testament.* Philadelphia: American Interfaith Institute/World Alliance, 1998.

Kertzer, David I. *The Popes Against the Jews: The Vatican's Role in the Rise of Modern Anti-Semitism.* New York: Alfred A. Knopf, 2001.

Kertzer, Morris N. *What Is a Jew?* New York: Macmillan, 1993.

Kessler, Edward, ed. *A Dictionary of Jewish–Christian Relations.* Cambridge: Cambridge University Press, 2005.

Kimelman, Reuven. "Birkat Ha-Minim and the Lack of Evidence for an Anti-Christian Jewish Prayer in Late Antiquity," in *Jewish and Christian Self-Definition,* E. P. Sanders, ed. 2 vols. London: SCM Press; Philadelphia: Fortress Press, 1981, 2:226–44.

Klausner, Joseph. *Jesus of Nazareth: His Life, Times, and Teaching.* Translated by Herbert Danby. New York: Macmillan, 1925.

———. *The Messianic Idea in Israel from its Beginning to the Completion of the Mishnah.* Translated from the 3rd Hebrew edition by W. F. Stinespring. London: George Allen and Unwin, 1956.

Koester, Helmut. *Introduction to the New Testament.* Vol. 1 *History, Culture, and Religion of the Hellenistic Age.* 2nd ed. Berlin: Walter de Gruyter, 1995.

Küng, Hans. *On Being a Christian.* Translated by Edward Quinn. Garden City, NY: Doubleday, 1976.

LaHaye, Tim F., and Jerry B. Jenkins. *Left Behind: A Novel of the Earth's Last Days.* Wheaton, IL: Tyndale House Publishers, 1995.

Lapide, Pinchas, and Jürgen Moltmann. *Jewish Monotheism and Christian Trinitarian Doctrine: A Dialogue.* Translated by Leonard Swidler. Philadelphia: Fortress Press, 1981.

Lea, Henry Charles. *A History of the Inquisition of Spain.* 4 vols. New York: Macmillan, 1922.

Le Goff, Jacques. *The Birth of Purgatory.* Translated by Arthur Goldhammer. Chicago: University of Chicago Press, 1981.

Lenowitz, Harris. *The Jewish Messiahs: From the Galilee to Crown Heights.* New York: Oxford University Press, 1988.

Lerner, Michael. *Jewish Renewal: A Path to Healing and Transformation.* New York: G. P. Putnam's Sons, 1994.

Levenson, Jon D. *The Death and Resurrection of the Beloved Son: The Transformation of Sacrifice in Judaism and Christianity.* New Haven: Yale University Press, 1993.

Levine, Amy-Jill. *The Misunderstood Jew: The Church and the Scandal of the Jewish Jesus.* San Francisco: HarperSanFrancisco, 2006.

Lindblom, Johannes. *Prophecy in Ancient Israel.* Philadelphia: Fortress Press, 1962.

Littell, Marcia Sachs, ed. *Liturgies on the Holocaust: An Interfaith Anthology.* Philadelphia: Anne Frank Institute of Philadelphia; Lewiston, NY: Edwin Mellen, 1986.

Loshitzky, Yosefa, ed. *Spielberg's Holocaust: Critical Perspectives on Schindler's List.* Bloomington: Indiana University Press, 1997.

Marchione, Margherita. *Yours is a Precious Witness: Memoirs of Jews and Catholics in Wartime Italy.* New York: Paulist Press, 1997.

McArthur, Harvey K., and Robert M. Johnston. *They Also Taught in Parables: Rabbinic Parables from the First Centuries of the Christian Era.* Grand Rapids: Zondervan, 1990.

Meier, John P. *A Marginal Jew: Rethinking the Historical Jesus.* Vol. 3. ABRL. New York: Doubleday, 1991.

Milavec, Aaron. *To Empower as Jesus Did: Acquiring Spiritual Power Through Apprenticeship.* Lewiston, NY: Edwin Mellen, 1982.

———. *A Pilgrim Experiences the World's Religions: Discovering the Human Faces of the Hidden God.* Lewiston, NY: Edwin Mellen, 1983.

———. "Mark's Parable of the Wicked Husbandman as Reaffirming God's Predilection for Israel." *JES* 26, no. 2 (1989): 305–12.

———. "A Fresh Analysis of the Parable of the Wicked Husbandmen in the Light of Jewish-Catholic Dialogue," in *Parable and Story in Judaism and Christianity,* ed. Clemens Thoma and Michael Wyschogrod. New York: Paulist Press, 1989, 81–117.

———. "The Heuristic Circularity of Commitment and the Experience of Discovery: A Polanyian Critique of Thomas Kuhn's Structure of Scientific Revolutions." *Tradition and Discovery* 16, no. 2 (1989): 4–19.

———. "Disappearance of Jewish Blood Guilt." *Cincinnati Judaica Review* 2 (1991): 66–75.

———. "The Birth of Purgatory: Evidence of the *Didachē.*" *Proceedings of the Eastern Great Lakes Biblical Society* 12 (1992): 91–104.

———. *Exploring Scriptural Sources: Rediscovering Discipleship.* Lanham, MD: Sheed & Ward, 1994/Rowman & Littlefield, 2004.

———. "The Saving Efficacy of the Burning Process," in *The Didachē in Context: Essays on its Text, History, and Transmission,* ed. Clayton N. Jefford. Leiden: Brill, 1995, 131–55.

———. "How the *Didachē* Attracted, Cooled Down, and Quenched Prophetic Fire." *Proceedings of the Eastern Great Lakes and Midwest Biblical Society* 19 (1999): 103–17.

———. "Religious Pedagogy from Tender to Twilight Years: Parenting, Mentoring, and Pioneering Discoveries by Religious Masters as Viewed from within Polanyi's Sociology and Epistemology of Science." *Tradition and Discovery* 23, no. 2 (1997): 15–36.

———. "Further Reflections on the Torn Veil." *Sophia* 8, no. 2 (2002): 216–19.

———. *The Didachē: Faith, Hope, and Life of the Earliest Christian Communities, 50–70 C.E.* New York: Newman Press, 2003.

———. "The Purifying Confession of Failings Required by the *Didachē*'s Eucharistic Sacrifice." *BTB* 33, no. 3 (2003): 64–76.

———. *The Didachē: Text, Translation, Analysis, and Commentary.* Collegeville, MN: Liturgical Press, 2003.

———. "Gibson's Passion as a Flawed Profession of Faith." *A Path for Jews and Christians,* February 22, 2004, http://ecumene.org/SHOAH/Mel_Gibson's_Passion_Milavec.html.

———. "Gentile Identity in the *Didachē* Communities as Early Signs of the Parting of the Ways." *Theological Review of The Episcopal Academy,* Spring 2006, http://www.ea1785.org/drum/trea/TREA5-06/milavectrea06a.pdf.

———. "How Acts of Discovery Transform our Tacit Knowing Powers in both Scientific and Religious Inquiry." *Zygon* 41, no. 2 (2006): 465–85.

Montefiore, Claude G. *The Synoptic Gospels,* edited with an introduction and commentary. London: Macmillan, 1927.

Mowinkel, Sigmund. *He That Cometh: The Messiah Concept in the Old Testament and Later Judaism.* Translated by G. W. Anderson. New York: Abingdon, 1951.

Neusner, Jacob. *The Rabbinic Traditions about the Pharisees before 70 A.D.* 3 vols. Leiden: Brill, 1971.

———. *From Politics to Piety: The Emergence of Pharisaic Judaism.* Englewood Cliffs, NJ: Prentice-Hall, 1973.

———. *Judaism: The Evidence of the Mishnah.* Chicago: University of Chicago Press, 1981.

———. *Messiah in Context: Israel's History and Destiny in Formative Judaism.* Philadelphia: Fortress Press, 1984.

———, and Ernest S. Frerichs, eds. *"To See Ourselves as Others See Us." Christians, Jews, "Others" in Late Antiquity.* Caroline McCracken-Flesher, literary editor. Chico, CA: Scholars Press, 1985.

———. "The Jewish–Christian Argument in the First Century: Different People Talking About Different Things to Different People." *Religious Studies and Theology* 6, nos. 1–2 (1986): 8–19.

———, William Scott Green, and Ernest S. Frerichs, eds. *Judaisms and Their Messiahs at the Turn of the Christian Era.* Cambridge and New York: Cambridge University Press, 1987.

———. *The Incarnation of God: The Character of Divinity in Formative Judaism.* Philadelphia: Fortress Press, 1988.

———. *Jews and Christians. The Myth of a Common Tradition.* Philadelphia: Trinity Press International; London: SCM Press, 1991.

────────. *Rabbinic Literature and the New Testament: What We Cannot Show, We Do Not Know*. Valley Forge and Philadelphia: Trinity Press International, 1994.

Nickelsburg, G. W. E. *Resurrection, Immortality, and Eternal Life in Intertestamental Judaism*. HTS 26 Cambridge, MA: Harvard University Press, 1972.

Nostra Aetate—Declaration on the Relation of the Church to Non-Christian Religions, October 28, 1965. http://www.vatican.va/archive/hist_councils/ii_vatican_council/documents/vat-ii_decl_19651028_nostra-aetate_en.html.

Notes on the Correct Way to Present the Jews and Judaism in Preaching and Catechesis in the Roman Catholic Church, 1985. http://www.vatican.va/roman_curia/pontifical_councils/chrstuni/relations-jews-docs/rc_pc_chrstuni_doc_19820306_jews-judaism_en.html.

Novak, David. *Jewish-Christian Dialogue: A Jewish Justification*. New York: Oxford University Press, 1992.

Oropeza, B. J. *99 Reasons Why No One Knows When Christ Will Return*. Downers Grove, IL: InterVarsity Press, 1994.

Osten-Sachen, Peter von der. *Christian–Jewish Dialogue: Theological Foundations*. Translated by Margaret Kohl. Philadelphia: Fortress Press, 1986.

Pannenberg, Wolfhart. *Jesus–God and Man*. Translated by Lewis L. Wilkins and Duane A. Priebe. Philadelphia: Westminster, 1968.

Patterson, Stephen J. *Beyond the Passion: Rethinking the Death and Life of Jesus*. Minneapolis: Fortress Press, 2004.

Pawlikowski, John T. *What Are They Saying About Christian-Jewish Relations?* New York: Paulist Press, 1980.

────────. *Christ in the Light of the Christian–Jewish Dialogue*. New York: Paulist Press, 1982.

────────, and Eugene B. Borowitz. *1987 Lecture Series: Proceedings of the Center for Jewish-Christian Learning*. St. Paul: College of St. Thomas, 1987.

Perelmuter, Hayim Goren. *Siblings: Rabbinic Judaism and Early Christianity at Their Beginnings*. New York: Paulist Press, 1989.

Perrin, Norman. *Rediscovering the Teaching of Jesus*. New York: Harper & Row, 1967.

Petuchowski, Jakob J. *Understanding Jewish Prayer*. New York: Ktav, 1972.

Pobee, John S. *Persecution and Martyrdom in the Theology of Paul*. JSOTSup 6. Sheffield: JSOT Press, 1985.

Pontifical Biblical Commission. *The Jewish People and Their Sacred Scriptures in the Christian Bible*, May 24, 2001. Vatican City: Libreria Editrice Vaticana, 2002. http://www.vatican.va/roman_curia/congregations/cfaith/pcb_documents/rc_con_cfaith_doc_20020212_popolo-ebraico_en.html.

Radcliffe, Albert. "How Dialogue with Jews Has Transformed the [Anglican] Holy Week Liturgy." *Jewish–Christian Relations*. http://www.jcrelations.net/en/?item=952.

Rahner, Karl. "The Hermeneutics of Eschatological Assertions," in idem, *Theological Investigations IV*. Translated with an introduction by Cornelius Ernst. Baltimore: Helicon Press, 1966.

Ratzinger, Joseph. *Eschatology, Death and Eternal Life.* Dogmatic Theology 9. Series edited by Johann Auer and Joseph Ratzinger. Translated by Michael Waldstein. Translation edited by Aidan Nichols. Washington, DC: The Catholic University of America, 1988.

Refoulé, François. *"Et ainsi tout Israël sera sauvé: Romains 11, 25-32"* LD 117. Paris: Cerf, 1984.

The Rites of the Catholic Church as Revised by Decree of the Second Vatican Ecumenical Council. New York: Pueblo, 1976.

Rivkin, Ellis. *The Shaping of Jewish History; A Radical New Interpretation.* New York: Scribner, 1971.

———. "Paul's Jewish Odyssey." *Judaism* 38 (1989): 225–34.

———. *What Crucified Jesus? Messianism, Pharisaism and the Development of Christianity.* New York: UAHC Press, 1997.

Robinson, James M., and Helmut Koester. *Trajectories through Early Christianity.* Philadelphia: Fortress Press, 1971.

Robinson, John A. T. *Jesus and His Coming.* 2nd ed. Philadelphia: Westminster, 1979.

Rordorf, Willy. *Sunday: The History of the Day of Rest and Worship in the Earliest Centuries of the Christian Church.* Translated by A. A. K. Graham. Philadelphia: Westminster, 1968.

Rubenstein, Richard L. *After Auschwitz: History, Theology, and Contemporary Judaism.* 2nd ed. Baltimore: Johns Hopkins University Press, 1992.

Ruether, Rosemary Radford. *Faith and Fratricide: The Theological Roots of Anti-Semitism.* New York: Seabury Press, 1974.

Russell, David S. *The Method and Message of Jewish Apocalyptic: 200 BC–AD 100.* Philadelphia: Westminster, 1964.

Saldarini, Anthony J. *Matthew's Christian–Jewish Community.* Chicago: University of Chicago Press, 1994.

Sanders, E. P. *Paul and Palestinian Judaism: A Comparison of Patterns of Religion.* Philadelphia: Fortress Press, 1977.

———. *Jesus and Judaism.* Philadelphia: Fortress Press, 1985.

———. *Jewish Law from Jesus to the Mishnah: Five Studies.* London: SCM Press; Philadelphia: Trinity Press International, 1990.

Sandmel, Samuel. *We Jews and Jesus.* New York: Oxford University Press, 1965.

———. *Judaism and Christian Beginnings.* New York: Oxford University Press, 1978.

Schillebeeckx, Edward. *Jesus: An Experiment in Christology.* New York: Seabury Press, 1979.

———. *Christ: The Experience of Jesus as Lord.* New York: Seabury Press, 1980.

Schnackenburg, Rudolf. *God's Rule and Kingdom.* Translated by John Murray. New York: Herder and Herder, 1963.

Schoeps, Hans Joachim. "The Sacrifice of Isaac in Paul's Theology." *JBL* 65 (1946): 385–92.

Scholem, Gershom. *The Messianic Idea in Judaism.* New York: Schockon Books, 1971.

Schüssler Fiorenza, Francis. *Foundational Theology: Jesus and the Church.* New York: Crossroad, 1984.

Schuster, Ekkehard, and Reinhold Boschert-Kimmig. *Hope Against Hope: Johann Baptist Metz and Elie Wiesel Speak Out on the Holocaust.* Translated by J. Matthew Ashley. Mahwah, NJ: Paulist Press, 1999.

Schwartz, Daniel R."Two Pauline Allusions to the Redemptive Mechanism of the Crucifixion." *JBL* 102 (1983): 259–79.

Shafiroff, Ira L. *Every Christian's Book on Judaism: Exploring Jewish Faith and Law for a Richer Understanding of Christianity.* California: Noga Press, 1998.

Shermis, Michael, and Arthur Zannoni. *Introduction to Jewish-Christian Relations.* New York: Paulist Press, 1991.

Sigal, Gerald. *The Jew and the Christian Missionary: A Jewish Response to Missionary Christianity.* New York: Ktav, 1981.

Skarsaune, Oskar. *The Proof from Prophecy: A Study in Justin Martyr's Proof-text Tradition: Text-type, Provenance, Theological Profile.* NovTSup 56. Leiden: Brill, 1987.

Smiga, George M. *Pain and Polemic: Anti-Judaism in the Gospels.* New York: Paulist Press, 1992.

Sparks, H. F. D., ed. *The Apocryphal Old Testament.* Oxford: Clarendon Press, 1984.

Stark, Rodney. "Jewish Conversion and the Rise of Christianity: Rethinking the Received Wisdom." *SBL 1986 Seminar Papers.* Edited by Kent H. Richards. Atlanta: Scholars Press, 1986, 214–29.

Stevenson, Kenneth. *Eucharist and Offering.* New York: Pueblo, 1986.

Stott, John R. W. *The Cross of Christ.* Leicester, England/Downers Grove, IL: InterVarsity Press, 1986.

TANAKH: The Holy Scriptures: The New JPS Translation According to the Traditional Hebrew Text. Philadelphia: Jewish Publication Society, 1985.

Taylor, Nicholas H. "The Social Nature of Conversion in the Early Christian World," in *Modelling Early Christianity: Social-Scientific Studies of the New Testament in its Context,* edited by Philip F. Esler. London: Routledge, 1995.

Theissen, Gerd, and Annette Merz. *The Historical Jesus: A Comprehensive Guide.* Translated by John Bowden. Minneapolis: Fortress Press, 1998.

Thoma, Clemens, et al., eds. *Parable and Story in Judaism and Christianity.* New York: Paulist Press, 1989.

Vawter, Bruce. *On Genesis: A New Reading.* Garden City, NY: Doubleday, 1977.

Vermes, Geza. *Jesus the Jew: A Historian's Reading of the Gospels.* New York: Macmillan, 1973.

———. *Scripture and Tradition in Judaism.* Leiden: Brill, 1973.

Wiesel, Elie. *The Oath.* Translated by Marion Wiesel. New York: Random House, 1973.

————. *Messengers of God: Biblical Portraits and Legends.* Translated by Marion Wiesel. New York: Random House, 1976.

————. "Art and Culture after the Holocaust," in *Auschwitz—Beginning of a New Era?* Edited by Eva Fleischner. New York: Ktav, 1977.

Wilken, Robert L. *The Myth of Christian Beginnings.* Notre Dame, IN: Notre Dame University Press, 1971.

Willebrands, Johannes. *Church and Jewish People: New Considerations.* New York: Paulist Press, 1994.

Williams, Sam K. *Jesus' Death as Saving Event: The Background and Origin of a Concept.* Harvard Dissertations in Religion 2. Missoula: Scholars Press, 1975.

Wills, Garry. *Papal Sin: The Structures of Deceit.* New York: Doubleday, 2000.

Wilson, Stephen G. *Related Strangers: Jews and Christians, 70–170 C.E.* Minneapolis: Fortress Press, 1995.

Wollaston, Isabel. "'What Can—And Cannot—Be Said': Religious Language After The Holocaust." *Literature and Theology* 6 (1992): 47–56.

Wood, J. Edwin. "Isaac Typology in the New Testament." *NTS* 14 (1968): 583–89.

Young, Brad H. *The Jewish Background to the Lord's Prayer.* Austin, TX: Center for Jewish–Christian Studies, 1984.

————. *Jesus and His Jewish Parables: Rediscovering the Roots of Jesus' Teaching.* New York: Paulist Press, 1989.

Young, James E. *The Changing Shape of Holocaust Memory.* New York: American Jewish Committee, 1995.

Zannoni, Arthur E., ed. *Jews & Christians Speak of Jesus.* Minneapolis: Fortress Press, 1994.

Zohar: The Book of Enlightenment. Translation and introduction by Daniel C. Matt. Ramsey, NJ: Paulist Press, 1983.

Index

Abraham, 7, 11, 12, 15, 18, 19, 22, 23, 36, 43, 46, 50, 59, 60, 61, 62, 68, 79, 82, 88, 102, 104, 126, 127, 133, 136, 144, 145, 147, 154, 169, 172, 173, 181

Acts of Apostles, 6, 9, 13, 17, 65, 67, 72, 79, 80–81, 90, 92–95, 98, 101–103, 116, 119, 121, 136–37, 143, 148, 162, 164, 167–68, 173

Adam, 3, 16, 22, 48, 58, 65–67, 70–71, 74, 76, 125, 138, 170, 178

Anselm of Canterbury, 62–64, 67, 72 n.25, 74, 148

Armstrong, Karen, 61 n.10

atonement, 64, 67, 69, 70–71, 75–76, 130, 143, 147–49, 152; theology of Jewish martyrdom, 148–49; theology of the binding of Isaac, 143–48; theology of the cross, 72–75, 142, 146–47

Augustine, 63

Auschwitz. See Shoah.

baptism, 15, 69, 88, 91–92, 102, 154, 155–56, 164, 172, 182

Baltimore Cathechism, 2 n.1, 57–58, 70, 82, 84

Bar Kochba, 96

Ben-Chorin, Schalom, 140 n.33

Benedict XVI, 6. See Ratzinger, Joseph Cardinal.

biblical interpretation: traditional, 124–26; current position, 130–32

blood guilt, 3–4, 23–25, 178

Borowitz, Eugene B., 30 n.7, 138–39

Brock, Rita Nakashima, 73 n.32

Bradshaw, Paul F., 121 n.9

Brown, Raymond E., 16 n.19, 17, 187

Buber, Martin, 73, 139 n.31

Bultmann, Rudolph, 17

catechisms, 2 n.1

church: her evangelizing mission to the Jews, 14–15, 152–53, 160–63, 169–71, 174–81; her origins, 87–113

Church of England, 19 n.23

circumcision, 101–103; why controversy regarding circumcision arose, 111–12

conversion of life, 69, 76, 164

Cook, Michael J., 109 n.41

covenant with Jews never abrogated, 4, 16, 45–51, 78–83; new covenant, 12, 16, 58; whether one or two, 12 n.15

Crossan, John Dominic, 100, 149 n.55

Daly, Robert J., 145 n.46

D'Angelo, Mary Rose, 30–31

Daube, David, 71

Deuteronomy, 18, 19, 27, 37, 43, 46, 50, 82, 104–105

dialogue. *See* interfaith dialogue.
Dominus Jesus, xiii–xiv, 9, 17 n.20, 21, 76 n.41
Dulles, Avery Cardinal, 180 n.8.
Dunn, James D.G., 30 n.7, 99–102

Echert, John, 177–78
Elliott, Neil, 149 n.55
Ellis, Mark H., xviii n.5
end times. *See* last days.
Epistle of Barnabas, 86–87
eschatology. *See* last days.
Eucharist, 88, 93, 105, 157, 168
evangelizing. *See* church.
Eve, 3, 71, 72 n.27, 125–26
Exodus, 18, 43, 45–47, 53, 104–105, 144

Fachenheim, Emil, 3
felix culpa, Jewish rejection of Jesus as, 21
feminist theologians, 73
Fiddler on the Roof, 29
Fiorenza, Francis Schüssler, 88–89, 161 n.20
Fiorenza, Joseph A., 9 n.11
Finlan, Stephen, 73
Fisher, Eugene, 3, 6–7, 13 n.16, 182
Fitzmyer, Joseph A., 31 n.10, 162 n.22
Flannery, Edward H., 155 nn.9–12, 156 nn.10–12, 181
Flusser, David, 148 n.53
forgiveness of sins: due to almsgiving, 69; due to baptism, 68; due to *teshuvah*, 68–69; due to the confession of failings, 67–68; due to the covenant, 45–51; due to Jesus' atoning death, 62–63, 66–67; due to Jesus' prayer on the cross, 4; only one means given for the, 66–67
Fredriksen, Paula, 77–78, 111–12, 210

Gager, John G., 10 n.14, 108 n.38

gates of Hades, 64–65, 67; not medieval hell, 63
gates of heaven, 58–60, 67, 71, 83, 178
Gates of Prayer, 26, 47 n.30
Gentiles: abandoning idolatry, 77; justified by faith, 111; mission to the, 14–15, 21, 76–78, 80, 93, 113, 166, 231; whether retribution or forgiveness awaits the Gentiles, 76–78, 81–82
God: as coming in the last days, 119–20; as consulting experts in Torah, 40–41; as "Father" within Judaism, 25–30; as lamenting the death of his Son, 70–72; as "Mother," 29; as praying, 46–47; as "Protector," 28; as punishing, 47; as redeeming Israel, 47–48; his universal plan of salvation, 13; as tearing his garments at the death of Jesus, 71; God of Israel, 28, 49, 78, 79, 133, 138, 139, 140, 148
Golden Rule, 110
Good Friday. *See* Holy Week liturgy.
Goshen-Gottstein, Alon, 31 n.10
Gospel of Bartholomew, 64–65
grace within the election of Israel, 41–42; outside the boundaries of the church, 8
gratitude, 35
Greek terms: *christos*, 122; *oikonomia*, 60; *Logos*, 60; *pater*, 31; *pistis*, 12
Green, Joel B., 74
Gundry, Robert, 70–71, 79 n.47

Haag, Herbert, 58, 72
Harnack, Adolph von, 88–89
heaven, going to, 2, 23, 119, 123
Hebrew/Aramaic terms: *Amidah*, 97, 115; *Diaspora*, 91, 101, 107, 116, 136; *Gehenna*, 70; *Kaddish*, 122; *kosher*, 56, 113; *messiah/moshiach*, 117, 123, 124, 129, 130, 133, 138; *minim*, 97,

98; *Mishnah,* 38, 39, 40, 99, 123; Shekhinah, 44; *Shema,* 115; *synagogue,* 7, 16, 17, 18, 19, 21, 22, 29, 34, 39, 45, 56, 61, 62, 80, 85, 86, 95, 97, 98, 99, 105, 107, 113, 114, 115, 119, 122, 133, 157, 165, 166, 167, 172, 173, 179; *teshuvah,* 69, 76, 164; *Torah,* 6, 12, 22, 37, 38, 39, 40, 41, 42, 43, 44, 45, 46, 48, 53, 56, 57, 61, 86, 94, 110, 111, 112, 114, 116, 130, 149, 153, 154, 157
Hebrews, Letter to the, 45, 71, 145–47, 222, 225–26
hellfire & Jews, xiv–xv, 1, 2, 7
Hillesum, Etty, 29–30
Hitler, Adolph, 158, 160
Holocaust. *See* Shoah.
Holy Spirit, 4, 8–9, 14, 79, 92, 93
Holy Week liturgy, 19–20
Hosea, 46–47

Ignatius of Antioch, 86–88
Incarnation, 36
inequality: social and economic, 178
interfaith dialogue, 13
Irenaeus, 60–61, 126
Isaiah, 17, 27, 47, 54, 76, 78–79, 81, 96, 105, 112, 127, 133, 167, 169–71, 176
Islam, 24, 75 n.38, 135 n.25
Israel, defined, xvi–xvii, 59 n.5
"Israel will be saved" (Rom 11:26), 13–15, 167–69
Israel: as first to hear the Word of God, 20; as God's elect, 41–42, 45–51; as saved by the Lord alone, 168; God's universal sacrament of salvation, 14, 174–75; mission to the Gentiles, 16, 174–75; people of, 14, 27, 28, 46, 48, 65, 87, 173; remnant of, 14

Jeremiah, 27, 96, 104, 150
Jeremias, Joachim, 30–32, 76, 81 n.50
Jerome, 38, 98

Jesus: always remained a Jew, 5, 68–70, 76–78, 83–85, 109, 179; as exemplifying the grace and richness already present in Judaism, 35; as expecting the inbreaking of the Kingdom of God, 119–22; as founding the church, 87-90; as fulfilling prophecies, 124–32; as gaining universal adoration, 133 n.21, 35 n.25; as handing over the kingdom to God the Father, 124; as restoring the kingdom to Israel, 78, 135–36; as a suffering prophet, 150–51; as the eschatological prophet-like-Moses, 18; as the eternal Son of God, 33, 36; as the exclusive means of salvation, 7, 16–18, 61–70; as the Messiah, 18, 78–82, 94–96, 136–38; as the stone rejected, 94; as the suffering redeemer, 61–63, 70–75; as rejected by Israel, 21, 23–24; as training disciples, 33–35
Jewish (rabbinic) tradition: regarding almsgiving, 69; regarding sacrifices, 49, 74, 75 n.39, 77, 98–99, 144–46, 149; regarding spontaneous prayers, 34 n.16, 114; regarding Torah study, 37–40, 115; regarding who is the Messiah, 95–96
Jews: as cursed by God, 5; as superior, 51–53; remain very dear to God, 4, 7, 21–22, 45–48, 78–83. *See also* covenant with Jews never abrogated and blood guilt.
John, 6, 17–19, 21–22, 25, 34–35, 59, 62, 64, 69, 74–75, 79, 88–89, 92–93, 95, 100–101, 120, 122, 148, 151, 160, 162, 164, 178–81
John Paul II, 20, 61, 169 n.27, 180–81
John XXIII, 24, 177, 179
Jonah, 149 n.56

Joseph and Aseneth, 27–29
Josephus, Flavius, 103–104, 106–108
Judaism: as a divinely authorized
    path of salvation, 4–11, 22, 45–51,
    78–82, 174; as a missionary enter-
    prise, 113 n.46, 174–75; as having a
    "common spiritual heritage" with
    Christianity, 25, 113–15, 119–22;
    as "our elder brothers," 20; as re-
    jected by God, 12; as mistakingly
    understood, 39, 54, 58–59; Reform,
    Orthodox, and Conservative,
    55–56. *See also* covenants.
judgment, final, 65–66, 76–78, 81–82,
    138, 141, 168–69. *See also* last days.
Justin Martyr, 59–60, 64–65

Kaddish, 121–22
Kasper, Walter Cardinal, 10 n.13,
    170–73
Keeler, William H. Cardinal, 174
Kertzer, David J., 153 n.3
Kertzer, Morris, 42–44
Kimelman, Rueven, 97
Kingdom of God explained, 76; by
    Jesus, 119–22; by Maimonides,
    122–23; in *Gaudium et Spes,* 123–24;
    in the Catholic Catechism, 123
    n.12. *See also* God: coming in the
    last days.
Kogan, Michael S., 61 n.9

LaHaye, Tim, 133–34
Lapide, Pinchas, 15, 140–41, 153 n.2
last days: 13, 66, 76–77, 91–92, 97, 111,
    120–21, 129, 132–33, 135, 137–38,
    167, 169, 180; Jesus' role, 136–38;
    Gentile inclusion with Israel, 127;
    Gentiles spared, 126; not know the
    hour, 136; tyranny of God, 133–35
Latin terms: *gratia,* 41; *felix culpa,* 21;
    Nostra Aetate, 24
Lerner, Michael, 44, 48–50

Levine, Amy-Jill, xviii
Leviticus, 104–105, 111
Leviticus Rabbah, 144–45
limbo, 2
Lord's Prayer: addressing God as
    "father," 30; linguistic analysis
    of the Lord's Prayer, 34–35; soft
    spots in Jeremias' interpretation
    of "Father," 30–32; whether the
    kingdom was expected as a future
    event, 77, 120–22
Luke, Gospel of, 5, 6, 29, 35–36, 54,
    69–70, 79–80, 92–94, 98–100, 106,
    119, 120–21, 137, 148, 151–52,
    162–63, 166, 168

Maccabees, Fourth Book of, 148–49
Maimonides, Moses, 122–23
Marian piety, 116
Mark, Gospel of , 19, 34, 58, 71, 85,
    100, 105–106, 110, 122, 151, 162
martyrdom, 148–49
Matthew, Gospel of, 17, 29, 34, 36, 71,
    80, 86, 89, 91, 94–95, 100, 110–11,
    118–19, 122, 127, 138, 148, 151–52,
    162–63, 165–66
McLaren, James, 107 n.37
Meier, John P., 30 n.8, 119
messianic expectation, 117–24
Midrash Rabbah, 143–44, 192
Milavec, Aaron, 33 n.14, 71 n.24, 72
    n.25, 120 n.6, 147 n.50, 149 n.55,
    151 n.59, 160 n.19, 162 n.21
mission to the Gentiles, 14–15, 152–
    53, 160–63, 169–71, 174–81
Moltmann, Jürgen, 15, 140–41
Mortara, Edgardo, 153–58
Moses, 18, 19, 22, 24, 25, 27, 36, 38, 39,
    40, 43, 44, 46, 47, 50, 53, 54, 61, 103,
    104, 105, 110, 111, 123, 147

Nazarenes, 96–97
Neusner, Jacob, xii, 29 n.3, 45 n.29, 50,
    84–85, 113

Nostra Aetate, xiii, 4–9, 13, 20, 22, 25–26, 36, 60, 62, 84, 171, 180

Notes on the Correct Way to Present Jews and Judaism, xiii, 5–6, 8–9, 21–22, 180

O'Malley, John W., 159 n.18

orality: relation to memorized prayers, 34–35

original sin, 57, 72 n.27

Osten-Sacken, Peter von der, 5

Pannenberg, Wolfhart, 73

parables: of Jesus, 69; of rabbis, 69 n.16

parousia, 210

Pauline theology: of church, 90; of Gentiles, 102; of Judaism, 10–15, 77–82, 110–11, 167–69; of Jesus' death, 74; of the Sabbath, 105–106

Pawlikowski, John T., 30 n.7

Pentecost, 90–93

Perrin, Norman, 117 n.2

Peter, 65, 67, 88, 92–95, 101–102, 121, 127

Peter, First Letter of, 65, 67

Petuchowski, Jakob, 34 n.16

Pharisees/Pharisaic revolution, 25, 37–40, 114–15

Phil 2:10 "every knee shall bend," 133 n.21, 35 n.25

Philo of Alexandria, 93 n.10, 104–105, 111, 145, 147

Pius IX, 153–60

Pius X, 89

Pontifical Biblical Commission, 131 n.18, 134 n.24

prayers, Jewish: *Amidah,* 97, 115; *Kaddish,* 122; *Shema,* 115; *Shemoneh Esreh,* 115

praying: impact of the Pharisaic revolution on, 34

prophets, 17–18, 35, 45–46, 49, 60, 64, 68, 70, 77–78, 80–82, 85–86, 99–100, 114, 116, 119–21, 126, 128–29, 130, 132, 134–36, 147, 149–51, 166, 168, 171–72, 176

rabbi, 43–44, 47, 48, 50, 52, 75, 86, 128–29, 139–40

Rahner, Karl, 133

rapture, 136 n.26

Ratzinger, Joseph Cardinal, 6–10, 131 n.18, 175

Reflections on Covenant and Mission, xiii, 174, 180, 181, 182

Refoulé, François, 14–15, 167 n.26

Rendtorff, Rolf, 58

repentance, 69, 76, 164

Revelations, 33

reward expected in last days, 150

Rivkin, Ellis, 114–15

Roman calendar, 104

Romans, Letter to the, 5, 11–15, 22–23, 58, 60, 76, 81–83, 88, 103–104, 106, 112, 143, 148, 154, 168–70, 176, 181

Rordorf, Willy, 105 n.35

rule of praying as the rule of believing, 19–20, 25–30

Ruther, Rosemary Radford, 32 n.13

Sabbath: as sign of covenant, 104; prayers, 25–27; rest, 103–106

sacrament, 2, 8, 15, 169

salvation, church as universal sacrament of, 7. *See* Judaism as a divinely authorized path of salvation and Israel as God's universal sacrament of salvation.

salvation history, 58–61

"Salvation is from the Jews" (John 4:22), 16–18

Sanders, E. P., 42, 69, 97 n.13, 100

Sarah, 12, 18, 28, 59, 62, 172

Satan, 63, 66, 126

Schillebeeckx, Edward, 18 n.22, 30 n.7, 73, 151 n.60

Shepherd of Hermas, 41
Shoah, 48–51, 53, 131, 140, 180
Sigal, Gerald, 75
Signer, Michael, 173 n.1
Singer, Tovia, 74
soteriology, defined, 61 n.10
Spanish Inquisition, 156–57
State of Israel, xvi–xviii, 51 n.36
Stott, John R.W., 70 n.20
Sungenis, Robert A., 176–77
synagogue, 7, 16, 17–19, 21–22, 29, 34,
    39, 45, 56, 61–62, 80, 85–86, 95, 97,
    98–99, 105, 107, 113–15, 119, 122,
    133, 157, 165–67, 172–73, 179

Talmud, 40, 42–43, 46–48, 50, 72, 96,
    98, 111, 145, 146; *Pesahim*, 47; *San-
    hedrin*, 96; *Shabbat*, 111; *Taanit*, 98
temple: destruction, 108–109; veil,
    70–71

Testaments of the Twelve Patriarchs, 111
Theissen, Gerd, 99
Thoma, Clemens, 69 n.16, 151 n.59
Thomas Aquinas, 63–64, 66–67, 154
    n.4
torture, 63, 116, 137, 141, 146, 148,
    156–57

Vatican II, 2, 4, 7–8, 20, 25–26, 36, 60,
    64, 84, 124, 180

way of life, 55, 112, 115, 132
We Remember, xiii, 180
Weisel, Elie, 137–38
Williams, Sam K., 147 nn.51–52
Wills, Gary, 153 n.3, 155 n.6, n.8
www.salvationisfromthejews.info, 53,
    83 n.51, 113 n.48, 142 n.42, 172 n.30

Zechariah, 79, 121

For those who have enjoyed reading this book,
please consider sharing your thoughts, feelings, and personal stories
at www.salvationisfromthejews.info.
Persons distressed by what they have read
are especially welcome.
The website features open discussion, published reviews,
insightful commentary, and spiritual nurture.
Be my guest!